SAVING LIVES IN SCILLY

Also by Vyvyen Brendon

Children of the Raj
Prep. School Children
Children at Sea

Saving Lives in Scilly

The Doctor, the Lighthouse Keeper and their Families

Vyvyen Brendon

*To Pam and Vic,
with thanks for your help
and encouragement,
and love from Vyvyen
April 2025*

UNITED WRITERS
Cornwall

UNITED WRITERS PUBLICATIONS LTD
Ailsa, Castle Gate, Penzance, Cornwall.
www.unitedwriters.co.uk

All Rights Reserved. No part of this publication may be reproduced, stored in a retrieval system, or transmitted, in any form or by any means, electronic, mechanical, photocopying, recording or otherwise, without the prior permission of the Copyright owner.

British Library Cataloguing in Publication Data:
A catalogue record for this book is
available from the British Library.

ISBN 9781852002176

Copyright © 2025 Vyvyen Brandon.

Printed and bound in Great Britain by
United Writers Publications Ltd.,
Cornwall.

To the memory of Emma Moyle (1858-1930)
Gladys Davis (1890-1980)
and Aline Davis (1921-2020)

Contents

Acknowledgements	9
Introduction	11
Chapters	
1 The Islands to Which They Came: 1812-1850	19
2 The Moyles of Penzance: 1810-1855	38
3 A Penzance Diaspora: 1855-1914	61
4 'The Reverend Delinquent': 1868-1908	85
5 Island Duties and Delights: 1840s and 1850s	108
6 Disasters and Misdemeanours: 1860s and 1870s	130
7 Leaving the Islands: 1880-1911	149
8 Lighthouse Keepers and their Families	172
9 Davis Wives, Widows and Daughters	185
10 Moyle Wives and Daughters	206
Epilogue: The Davis Family at War	237
Notes	259

Acknowledgements

Many people have accompanied me on my Cornish quest. Expert staff and volunteers at libraries and archive centres found ways to help me amid the difficulties resulting from closures and lockdowns. I'd like to thank in particular Kate Hale, Lucy Dean, Alison Clough and Rachael Utting at the Isles of Scilly Museum as well as its former curator Amanda Martin and trustee Richard McCarthy; Katie Herbert and Sally Francis at Penlee House Museum and Gallery, Penzance; Kim Piper at Kresen Kernow, Truro; Peter Judge at Praeds & Company Archive; Dr Nicholas Melia, Lydia Dean and Neil Adams at the Borthwick Institute, York; Natalie Toy and Steven Newman at York Minster Archives; Neil Jones and Nicole Ash at Trinity House Archives; Angela Broome at the Courtney Library, Truro; Maria Brownsea at Brookwood Cemetery; Matthew Piggott and Julian Pooley at the Surrey History Centre, Woking; Allen Packwood and Katharine Thompson at Churchill Archive in Cambridge.

I am also grateful to friends who have joined the search in other ways. My old school chums Judith Cooper and Phoebe Wyss helped me to revisit Reigate, where some of my forebears lived and died. Jean Glasberg discussed with me the experiences of her father who, like mine, served in the dangerous convoys to Murmansk and Archangel during the Second World War. The Cornish Bard, Richard Larn of Scilly and his wife Bridget gave me the benefit of their research into maritime matters. Fellow Bard, Jonathan Ball, has also shared his intimate knowledge of Scilly with me, to say nothing of his and his wife Victoria's generous Scillonian hospitality, complete with tattie cake. Laura Morris and Vic Gatrell have read the book and given generous advice and encouragement.

One of the joys of writing this family history is that I have made contact with several distant cousins, fellow-descendants of Doctor Moyle or Keeper Davis. Zelonie Moyle has shared much of her own meticulous family research; Judy DeCourcey of Canada and Sabrina Bettridge of Australia have made photographs of their emigrant forebears available on the Ancestry website; Peter Malec and Alfie Treneer, who still live in Scilly, opened up their collections of Moyle paintings and documents; Terry Lewis and his daughter Sophie May contributed poems written by one of the doctor's daughters as well as valuable information and photographs; and the late Francis Hicks gave me a rare treat, leading me up to the top of St Agnes lighthouse, in which he still lived.

Thanks are also due to closer relations for important contributions. I very much miss the vivid memory and technological expertise of my late brother, Rodney Davis, who sent helpful suggestions from his home in Spain. My cousins Chris Davis, Duncan Davis and Diana Page searched their virtual attics for mementoes while Ruth and Graham Vickery lent me the family material amassed by Ruth's mother Aline, reconstructed her father's experiences in a German prisoner-of-war camp and acted as excellent guides and photographers on the Isles of Scilly. My most constant travelling companion on this, as on so many other literal and literary journeys, has been my husband Piers, whose guidance has been invaluable.

Finally, I am delighted that this book will be published in Penzance, its natural home, and it has been a pleasure to work with Malcolm Sheppard, director of United Writers Publications. Every effort has been made to trace copyright holders for images and text used in the book and the publishers welcome information on any attributions which have been omitted. Acknowledgements are made in the appropriate endnotes.

Introduction

Moyle/Davis Family Tree

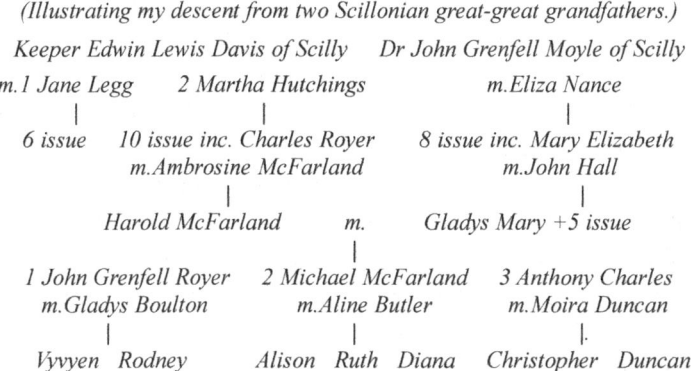

(Illustrating my descent from two Scillonian great-great grandfathers.)

Keeper Edwin Lewis Davis of Scilly   Dr John Grenfell Moyle of Scilly
m.1 Jane Legg   2 Martha Hutchings   m.Eliza Nance

6 issue   10 issue inc. Charles Royer   8 issue inc. Mary Elizabeth
         m.Ambrosine McFarland   m.John Hall

Harold McFarland   m.   Gladys Mary +5 issue

1 John Grenfell Royer   2 Michael McFarland   3 Anthony Charles
   m.Gladys Boulton   m.Aline Butler   m.Moira Duncan

Vyvyen   Rodney   Alison Ruth Diana   Christopher Duncan

This story centres on my two paternal great-great-grandfathers, both of whom spent over forty years engaged in saving lives on the Isles of Scilly. From 1839 to 1888 Edwin Lewis Davis was Keeper of St Agnes Lighthouse, perched on the westernmost point of Britain. The beacon he lit and watched every night warned approaching vessels of the islands' many outlying rocks and crags. And when high seas or fog defeated these efforts and ships were wrecked, he helped to look after victims washed up on the beaches below his lofty post. My other great-great-grandfather, John Grenfell Moyle MRCS, the islands' only doctor from 1849 to 1890, would soon arrive on the accident scene from his surgery on St Mary's. His usual daily routine involved journeys between the islands in a small gig-boat to set broken bones, perform operations, deliver babies, administer medicines and soothe the dying.

In their teenage years both men had sailed the oceans, Edwin as a merchant seaman progressing to master mariner, and John as a ship's surgeon on several voyages to India. Neither could have expected to settle for so long in Scilly after returning to dry land. The Elder Brethren of Trinity House did not usually leave a keeper in the same lighthouse for more than a few years, especially in Scilly where they feared that a local man like Edwin might fall in with the islands' legendary 'wreckers'. When John sailed the twenty-eight miles to St Mary's from his native Penzance, it was as a locum to cover for the incumbent doctor, who then died unexpectedly while on holiday, leaving the post vacant. In the event both my forebears married in Scilly, raised large families there and laboured on into their seventies, only quitting the islands on their retirement. Both endured hard times and personal tragedy but there is every sign that they appreciated their location. The St Agnes keeper was sometimes to be found showing visitors the prehistoric sights of neighbouring Gugh while the doctor found time to portray the islands' unique scenery in many fine oil-paintings.

Yet in due course my chapters depart from these picturesque shores. They follow the trail of the Davises and Moyles who joined the great Cornish diaspora, leaving their homeland to seek better prospects than it could offer. The males, preserving the family name, are easiest to trace. All John Moyle's eight brothers left Penzance for good, two as London bank clerks, one as a Yorkshire vicar, one as a Royal Navy lieutenant defending British interests in South America and the Crimea before settling in Canada, one as a sailor who drowned on his first voyage and four as gold rush emigrants to Australia and New Zealand. One of the brothers merited a chapter all to himself when I found that the respectable clergyman mentioned in family records became a serial fraudster, ending his extraordinary career in various British

Introduction

gaols and London workhouses. Of John's own two sons one died as a boy and the other was the only Moyle to stay on in Scilly, where his descendants still live. Meanwhile Edwin married young, became a widower and married again, fathering sixteen children in all, seven of whom were sons. Five of those sailed off as merchant sailors on Scillonian ships, a fatal course as it turned out. The other two were persuaded to follow their father's safer career as lighthouse keepers. A chapter traces their progress around the rocks, islands and coastlines to which they were dispatched, their wives following with children, goods and chattels.

Such valiant wives, as well as the sisters and daughters of both families, merit chapters of their own. Among them were women of remarkable independence: the itinerant Bible Christian preacher, Martha Hutchings from Somerset, who became Edwin's second wife; two Davis daughters who accompanied husbands to the Antipodes to face motherhood and widowhood in a strange land; the unmarried Jemima Davis who set up a successful dressmaking business in Scilly before her early death from tuberculosis; the oldest Moyle daughter, Emma, a spinster headmistress who made a home in Surrey for her retired father and three youngest sisters; her sister Mary who took her offspring to find employment in the Bradford mills after the death of her Cornish husband. Such autonomy was more difficult for others: the four pensionless widows of Davis master mariners reliant on the support of sons or daughters; John's mentally handicapped daughter Jessie; her illegitimate daughter Margaretta whose destination was a Surrey lunatic asylum. So often hidden from history, such retrieved lives illuminate both the subjection of Victorian women and their occasional triumphs.

As well as mapping spatial journeys I travel through time, into the vanished world of far Cornwall before the First World War. It was an age when doctors visited their patients in a pony and trap or a small boat, when there were no analgesics or antibiotics, when seafarers were at constant risk of shipwreck, when lighthouse lamps were lit by hand and watched all night, when needlewomen worked by candlelight, when family prayers took place three times a day, when to be born out of wedlock was a disgrace, when poverty could lead to the workhouse and when families had to cling together for mutual support. At the same time Augustus Smith became Lord Proprietor of the Isles of Scilly and made huge improvements to life there; Darwin's theory of evolution prompted Dr Moyle to question the literal truth of the Bible; and Brunel extended the Great Western Railway all the way to Penzance. Thus *Rambles Beyond Railways* quickly became a less appropriate title for a journey in which the writer Wilkie Collins encountered not only 'strong superstitious feelings of the ancient days of Cornwall' but also such signs of progress as a 'great public meeting of all the babies in Lizard Town' at which they were to be vaccinated against smallpox 'in one fell swoop'.[1] My Victorian forebears inhabited both these worlds. Their twentieth-century descendants had equally mixed experiences. Benefiting from such social improvements as Lloyd George's old age pensions and the young Winston Churchill's prison reforms, they were plunged into the savagery of two world wars, which claimed their lives or ruined their constitutions.[2]

The quest for my ancestors has been quite a journey in itself, starting as it did during the first covid lockdown of March 2020. Fortunately, I always had the internet at my disposal, leading me into the past through its store of treasures: handwritten census records, birth and death certificates, electoral rolls, marriage banns, shipboard logs and passenger lists, newspapers from all over the world, war records and early eye-witness accounts of life in Scilly. I was even able to track down the prison file of my namesake great-uncle, Vyvyan Moyle, the fraudulent vicar, complete with the compulsory mugshot. I discovered also that two Moyle descendants had compiled websites, which display more homely family photographs as well as artworks by their talented forebears.

It was some time before I was allowed access to tangible

Introduction

archive collections, such as the scorched Trinity House minute books which survived Second World War bombing, court records in temporary storage in a Scillonian warehouse or the daily headmistress's logs hand-written by Emma Moyle and housed in Surrey's excellent History Centre. I was sometimes frustrated in my search. The records which might explain Margaretta Moyle's admission to Netherne Lunatic Asylum were scattered when the institution was closed in the 1990s and the best efforts of dedicated archivists have not been able to retrieve them. For different reasons the papers of Scilly's Lord Proprietor, Augustus Smith, the doctor's friend and fellow magistrate, are inaccessible and will remain closed for another twelve years. When I decided to append an epilogue recounting the Second World War experiences of my father (another John Grenfell) and his brother Michael I found even more obstacles in my path. The horrors of Arctic convoys or of German POW camps had not been the stuff of family conversation, though Michael opened up more to his sons-in-law. I have found the Ministry of Defence equally unforthcoming, rigid in its insistence that a death certificate is the only proof of a former serviceman's demise. But with cousinly help, family mementoes and the work of military historians, I have been able to reconstruct the brothers' war stories.

The easing of covid restrictions eventually enabled me to travel to many of the places with which my relations were associated. I have entered the room which acted as the doctor's surgery in St Mary's; I have seen the tiny schools attended by Davis and Moyle offspring; I have photographed the simple Bible Christian chapel on St Agnes which Edwin and Martha Davis helped to build; I have viewed the harbours from which their sons sailed; I have met Scillonian relations who proudly showed me paintings by John Grenfell Moyle and his son Edwards; and I have found family gravestones in peaceful cemeteries overlooking the sea. The most evocative visit was facilitated by a distant cousin, who led me up a very steep ladder to the lamp room of St Agnes lighthouse from which our mutual great-great-grandfather kept watch. Other searches have proved unavailing. To finance the treatment of poor patients the doctor sold many of his paintings, which cannot now be traced or are jealously guarded by their private owners. His grave is similarly hidden from view, buried in the undergrowth of Reigate cemetery. The remains of his disgraced brother, Vyvyan, are even more elusive for they lie in an unmarked mass grave in Brookwood Cemetery, the largest burial place in the country built as an overflow for London's dead.

My greatest lack was a cache of written records to help me delve into the inner lives of my ancestors. If any of them committed their thoughts to private diaries there is little trace of them now. I did, however, possess a scrapbook kept by John Grenfell Moyle towards the end of his career. It looked unpromising but among the discoloured newspaper cuttings are jottings in his own hand, which on close inspection reveal a man of science questioning some of the received religious beliefs of his day.[3] I have also seen poignant poems written by my great-grandmother, Mary Hall, but it was only when I had done some research that I realised their significance – she had lost two sons in the First World War. Another poem came to light among the papers of my late uncle, Anthony Davis: a long piece of blank verse by his father Harold evokes the many moods of the 'rock-encircled isles' he knew so well. There must also have been personal letters exchanged among family members but neither I nor my cousins have found any such items in our attics. Just one eventually came to light: the Wellcome Institute has a letter in the doctor's hand which not only explains a patient's treatment but also records a few memories of his life in Scilly.

I missed, too, having the chance to talk to anyone who remembered the people I was writing about. I greatly regretted that, as a careless and self-obsessed youngster, I hadn't asked more questions of my grandparents, Harold and Gladys Davis, whose marriage linked the two Scillonian families. All I had was the echo in my head of Grandpa's voice. He used to talk to me, when I went to stay with them in Bournemouth, about his grandfather, the lighthouse keeper, and his master mariner father

Introduction

who died on board ship when Harold was only a few months old. He would also recite poetry he had learnt as a schoolboy in Scilly – and I can hear him still.

As well as that memory, I possessed a few mementoes passed on to me by my Granny: two inscribed leather volumes of a distinguished literary forebear Walter Moyle; a pocket-book in which John Grenfell Moyle's father (a Penzance doctor) recorded the births of his twelve children and of eight grandchildren; a passport issued in 1864 to one of his sons; and a prize medal awarded by a Penzance school to the same son, together with a programme of recitations. They had all been shut away for years in my cupboards but, once I started writing, I understood how they could help to tell the story. The same is true of two large Dutch plaques entrusted to my late brother; he understood that they had been given in lieu of payment for treatment by a sea captain to 'a doctor in our family who lived on the Isles of Scilly' – whom I now recognise as Dr John Moyle. There were also faded sepia photographs, some of which I was gradually able to identify with the help of my cousins. One of the most useful items was an ordinary school exercise book in which the doctor's oldest daughter, the schoolteacher Emma Moyle, had recorded what she knew about the family. Most important of all were the handwritten genealogies painstakingly compiled years before there was any internet access by my aunt Aline, who gave me copies in the hope that I would put them to use. In belated gratitude for these excellent study aids I have dedicated this book to the memory of these women from three generations: my great-great-aunt Emma Moyle, my granny Gladys Davis and my aunt Aline Davis, an early care-home victim of the covid pandemic.

As the oldest member of the next generation, I have done my best to flesh out the story of our forebears. I know that it must contain errors, omissions and bias but I felt compelled to make the attempt. A few 'famous men', as *Ecclesiasticus* says, have left a name behind them; but most people have no memorial and 'are perished, as though they had never been'.[4] Like other family historians, I have used as much material as I could find to commemorate my ancestors, to resurrect their hard remote lives and to write their story. As with an old quilt or scrapbook, there are mismatched fragments and missing portions. Nevertheless, this memoir pieces together the fabric of their existence and reveals the texture of the times they spent in Scilly, far Cornwall and distant destinations. It means that they will not be forgotten in their land and that their names will endure in history.

Chapter 1

The Islands to Which They Came
1812-1850

The family story goes that William Slater Davis sailed into Scilly's main harbour from the Atlantic during the later stages of the Napoleonic Wars on a ship which needed makeshift repairs to its damaged mast – which is odd since London records show him as a Bermondsey tinsmith.[5] My explanation of this typical family history conundrum is that Willam had entered naval service at the hands of the press-gang. It was a common fate for men working in dockland areas to be seized to join naval operations against France and her allies. An additional war which broke out against America in 1812, partly over the issue of impressment, could explain why his ship was in the Atlantic before limping into St Mary's harbour in 1812.

My guess is that William then joined the ranks of naval deserters by lurking among the quiet coves of St Agnes when the time came for the ship to depart. Thus for him the islands served as the refuge described in a contemporary survey for the Admiralty by Graeme Spence: 'Nature has placed Scilly rather as the asylum than the grave of mariners. It saves a far greater number than it destroys.' It's reckoned that many present-day Scillonians, especially in St Agnes, are descendants of 'chance comers from shipping and wrecks' such as William Davis.[6] He was a married man and clearly liked the island enough to encourage his wife Mary to make the arduous journey from London to join him, though she doesn't seem to have brought their two young children with her.[7] Records reveal that the couple produced two more offspring on St Agnes, Edwin Lewis in 1813 and Elizabeth in 1816.

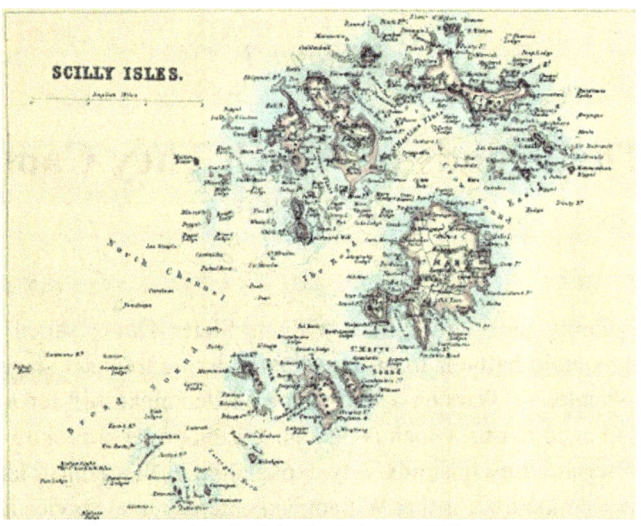

Map by John Bartholomew, 1874

St Agnes is the most south-westerly of the islands, described as 'the last inhabited landfall before America'.[8] Of over 200 low-lying islands comprising the archipelago, only six were inhabited at that time: St Mary's, the largest with a ten-mile coastline, and the outlying St Martin's, Tresco, Bryer, St Agnes and Samson, with a total population of about 1,500. They lack the picturesque forests, groves, rivers, mountains or green pastures of the mainland, so often admired and portrayed by British artists and poets; but they have an allure of their own. As Spence wrote, 'In the summer time the islands are pretty and romantic; in winter time the mountainous waves dashing over the rocks are beautifully terrible.'[9] Many subsequent visitors echoed these impressions. One travelling clergyman, for example, admired these 'granite islands, glowing like gems in the heaving heart of the deep'. He described dramatic granite headlands, rocks and boulders of curious shapes; he found the heathland 'gay with the united bloom of dwarf gorse and heather'; he discovered beaches of the 'purest white sand' often linked by a narrow causeway; and he marvelled at the lustrous, ever-changing colours of the clear sea, deep blue, brilliant emerald green and 'the most gorgeous purple'. He also praised the islands' equable climate, 'just like Nice or Cannes in the garden growth' – but he might not have said the same had he experienced the February frosts and the frequent gales which can play havoc with the tender shoots of flowers and vegetables and render the islands inaccessible.[10]

A vintage postcard shows off the beauties of Scilly.

Despite their small population the islands have had a complicated administrative history. Since the fourteenth century they have been part of the royal Duchy of Cornwall, which still passes automatically to the oldest son of the reigning monarch along with legal rights and privileges and personal ownership of 135,000 acres, including most of Scilly. This lucrative part of the Duchy was leased by Elizabeth I to the Godolphin-Osborne family of Cornwall, who acquired the title Proprietor/Governor. They ruled the islands through a Court of Twelve but were absentee landlords with little interest in Scillonians, whose governance was left to stewards and agents with 'the power to distribute favour or show vengeance in unequal measure'.[11]

Queen Elizabeth's main interest in the islands was to fortify them against the Spanish and it was she who ordered the building of Star Castle on St Mary's and placed a garrison there. After the Spanish threat receded Scilly remained a military base for over two centuries, defending its shores in turn against Moorish pirates and French privateers, serving as the last foothold of the Cavaliers in the English Civil War and housing political prisoners of various hues. The garrison was not exactly welcomed by Scillonians who had to bear much of the burden of supporting it, but many were happy to receive fourpence a day in return for quartering the soldiers. Perhaps as a result of these arrangements there was 'a good deal of inter-marriage ... and many time-expired men settled' on the islands.[12] The Godolphins (who acquired the title Duke of Leeds) kept the lease until 1831, three years before it was sold for £20,000 to Augustus Smith, who assumed the title Lord Proprietor. It was under his energetic regime that my two great-great-grandfathers lived and worked, Edwin Lewis Davis as the lighthouse keeper and John Grenfell Moyle as the islands' only doctor.

Fortunately, there are several accounts which help to throw light on how the Davis family fared when they first arrived. Life on the islands had not changed much since 1750 when Robert Heath wrote his 'Natural and Historical Account' after serving as an officer at the garrison. He stressed their 'intrinsic worth to the nation' and the loyalty of the islanders, as well as various 'vicissitudes of fortune' to which they were subject: the infrequent and dangerous passage from the mainland, the uncertainty of trade, the 'blighting winds' which so often affected garden vegetables, the damp caused by the rock-stone walls of their houses and the lack of schools which caused children to be 'frustrated and lost'. Heath made no secret of their dependence on illicit trading with merchant ships and salvaging from wrecks, which provided commodities they lacked: timber for building and making furniture, fine clothing ('the spoil of their rich neighbours') and 'a stock of rum, brandy, wine and other foreign liquors' for their own immoderate consumption and for duty-free sale. He depicts Scillonians as 'the sons and daughters of God's Providence'; but he also shows pilots and fishermen running 'very great hazards' for these supplies, 'showing undaunted courage and resolution in venturing out, when the seas run mountains high', saving lives, ships and cargoes as often as they scavenged from wrecks. Heath had nothing but respect for Scillonians' ingenuity and fortitude.[13]

Visiting six years later, Dr William Borlase found St Agnes in particular a 'well cultivated little island' of about fifty families, bringing in £40 a year to the Godolphins. He admired its 'pretty coves' but thought the islanders made too little use of the pilchards which abounded in them, concentrating on ling fish which were more easily caught. On the islands as a whole he found some cultivation of barley, rye and root vegetables as well as black cattle and sheep feeding on seaweed when there was not enough grass. Like Heath he could see that there was too little incentive to improve small plots of land which were held on short leases. In the summer, families gathered kelp, which was burned to make fertiliser, earning about £5 over a two-month season and creating a 'heavy stinking vapour' in the process. Borlase also noted and sketched large ships in St Mary's excellent harbour and

St Mary's Harbour, sketched by William Borlase, 1756

appreciated the opportunities they provided for pilots 'especially if the wind blows hard'. But the worthy clergyman made no mention of the smuggling which historians recognise as an 'integral part of everyday life' in the Scillies at this time. The impression Borlase gives is of an easy-going but precarious way of life, in which the islanders were 'left too much to their own free will ... with but the shadow of government'.[14]

Things clearly hadn't changed much by the 1790s, when the Admiralty's survey described the same mode of subsistence. But Graeme Spence laid more emphasis on the islanders' 'daring and venturesome' character and also warned that the 'means of support' were inadequate for the growing population.[15] In the same decade the Proprietor's chaplain, John Troutbeck, published another study, which lifted (without acknowledgement) long descriptions of kelping, fishing, farming and piloting practices straight from Heath and Borlase, presumably finding them still to be accurate. But as a resident of some years, Troutbeck was well acquainted with the 'much misinterpreted' islanders and took the opportunity to express their grudges. He recounts in great detail stories to illustrate neglect and exploitation by the Duke of Leeds's steward. Tenants, who were only allowed a twenty-one-year lease, were dispossessed 'if they happen to disoblige the steward'; a schoolmaster who had been teaching selected boys to write (so that they will 'know how to keep a sea-journal') was not allowed to instruct them in his house when he became lame; islanders were prevented from selling their kelp except through the steward until a petition succeeded in depriving him of this monopoly; and the only mill was left unrepaired so that people had to grind corn in their own homes. Thus, Troutbeck echoes Heath in concluding that 'an overbearing steward may fleece the people as he pleases, to make his own fortune, and no one here can get redress'.

This book was published in the early stages of the long wars against Revolutionary and Napoleonic France and mentions, as an example of Scillonians' 'generosity and benevolence', their saving some 'distressed Frenchmen from perishing among the western rocks in a vessel they had taken from the English'.[16] Since, as the sea shanty puts it, 'Ushant to Scilly is thirty-five leagues', there was inevitably some naval action in Scillonian waters. It was here, for example, that HMS *Indefatigable* under her Cornish captain Sir Edward Pellew, captured the French 44-gun warship *Virginie* in 1796. Soon afterwards Pellew led a cruising expedition off the islands, during which he kept 'a strict lookout for the enemy', correctly predicting that 'Scilly is not likely to be an object for a summer attack'. Pellew also inspected the garrison on St Mary's, where twenty-four invalid soldiers had been replaced by seventy-five regular troops and a home guard known as the Land Fencibles. He found that they comprised 'a Captain, a Lieutenant, an Ensign, five Sergeants and two Drummers, together with 100 Rank and File present for Duty'.[17] As an extra precaution, the captain placed an eighteen-pound signal gun on a restored Civil War gun battery, which was renamed Pellew's Redoubt – but none of these defences would have been sufficient to repel a major French assault.[18]

Also on board *Indefatigable* was the former African slave, Joseph Emidy, whom Pellew had press-ganged in Lisbon to act as the ship's violinist. No doubt Emidy's fiddle helped to divert the crew during a monotonous spell of duty but it seems that it also entertained more exalted company. When invited to dinner at the Star Castle garrison Pellew asked if he could bring the violinist with him. Emidy performed during and after the meal, showing 'a quite remarkable talent for the instrument and an amazing repertoire of classical music, which brought the audience to its feet more than once.'[19] Three years later hostilities came to a temporary halt and both the captain and his black violinist disembarked in Falmouth, where Emidy soon established himself as a skilled teacher and performer in many different instruments.[20]

One of the musician's first flute pupils was the eighteen-year-old Cornishman James Silk Buckingham, who had recently jumped ship from the Royal Navy after witnessing a mutineer being hanged and a deserter flogged around the fleet. Meanwhile war against France had resumed and in 1804 Buckingham accepted an invitation from the captain of a revenue cutter to join an expedition to the Isles of Scilly as part of a general government clampdown on smuggling. He spent a week participating in searches among the islands' intricate channels, keeping watch with telescopes and listening to tall stories told during afternoon drinking sessions. All this led him to conclude that the gentry were heavily involved, along with 'mere tradesmen, shopkeepers and boatmen', and that none of them thought anything of 'cheating the revenue by smuggling and plundering wrecks when thrown upon their reach'.[21]

When William Davis came to St Agnes a few years later, opportunities for such activities had been greatly curtailed by the trade embargo imposed by Napoleon in 1806-7 and Britain's retaliatory economic blockade on France and her allies. Smuggling was also made much riskier by the formation in 1809 of a Preventative Water Guard to patrol coastal waters, which resulted in some culprits ending up in Bodmin Gaol. William, like other islanders, would have to manage as best he could with a rented plot of land, probably growing potatoes for which the army created a great demand. There was no chance of his using his tin-smithing expertise for, as Graeme Spence found, the dearth of fuel and lack of running water made it impractical to work the islands' small tin supplies.[22]

In one way or another, William, with his wife and two young children, managed to survive the dreadful post-war conditions revealed by an inquiry conducted in 1818 in response to a petition from the inhabitants of the four outlying islands. The resulting *Report Detailing the Extreme Miseries of the Off-Islands of Scilly* was written by one of the two investigators, George 'Boatswain' Smith, a Baptist minister well-known for his missions to seafarers. He and a leading Quaker from Penzance visited every house in the islands and were 'shocked by the scenes of human calamity' they found, especially on St Agnes. Many islanders were reduced to eating nothing but limpets knocked off the rocks with a hammer or bill-hook, while others lived on a monotonous fishy diet of 'scads and taties all the week and conger-pie on Sundays'. They had often had to sell their boats, clothes and furniture and were in 'want of fuel or candle'. The worst affected were the many widows who had lost their husbands to 'the frequent and dreadful storms [which] often prove fatal to the men whose business lies on the waters'. Yet, Smith concluded, none of the people in charge, the absentee Duke of Leeds, his Steward ('a petty little lord of everything') and the garrison's Lieutenant-Governor ('a notorious old debauchee') 'cared a straw about the souls and very little for the bodies of the people'.[23]

The investigators attributed the distress to a series of bad harvests, the prohibition on barter with visiting ships, the subdivision of land into very small portions to cater for an enlarged population and a reduced demand for kelp, conclusions which are confirmed by historians. Their main recommendation was that money should be raised to finance a commercial mackerel and pilchard fishery, which would provide small boats, build storehouses and teach people to make nets, so that the 'place would become a scene of business and energy'. Despite these good intentions and the raising of donations amounting to £10,000 (including a token £100 from HRH the Duke of Cornwall), distress continued during the 1820s. It was exacerbated by a drought 'when everything was burnt up by the hot sun' and a 'disease [that] got into the potatoes', as recalled by the Scillonian ballad-singer Robert Maybee.[24] The Duke of Leeds's peremptory demand for payment of arrears in rent only made matters worse, as did a memorandum from Lieutenant-Governor Smythe to Home Secretary Robert Peel advising that any further charity would encourage idleness and improvidence. Meanwhile the fishing scheme was dogged by unreliable pilchard supplies, discord and mismanagement.

It seems that much of the money was diverted to the shipyards on St Mary's even though that island was relatively prosperous and, writes Scillonian historian Forrester Matthews, as 'blind to the sufferings of others' as Lieutenant Smythe, who lived in 'the comfort and security of Star Castle'.²⁵ In the event the redirected money was probably well spent since the shipbuilding industry, then in its infancy, was to provide plenty of employment in decades to come. By the time the 1841 Census was taken, over seventy men could describe themselves as shipwrights or apprentices, while many more benefited from the maritime traffic generated by the importing of timber: 'English oak from the New Forest, red and pitch pine from North America, white and yellow pine from Scandinavia, teak from the East Indies and Africa, and mahogany from Central America and India.'²⁶

One of those to benefit from maritime enterprise was William's son Edwin, who gained enough education from the islands' mission schools to master the science of navigation and the art of writing a sea-journal. After signing on as a merchant seaman while still in his teens he was able to advance rapidly through the service, as shown in his Master's Certificate. But before he reached the age of thirty Edwin, now a married man with two children, abandoned the perils of seafaring to spend the rest of his life in a career which helped to prevent them – looking after the lighthouse on the island of his birth.

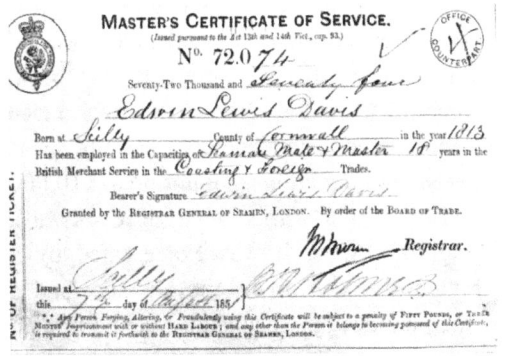

British Merchant Service Master's certificate awarded to Edwin Lewis Davis, 1813.

Trinity House had commissioned the building of a lighthouse on St Agnes in 1680. This would warn ships of the Western Rocks 'lying thicker about this island' and sending in 'more wrecks of ships by the sea than to any other of the Scilly Islands'.[27] It was only the second lighthouse erected in Cornwall and remains one of the oldest in the country. Despite objections that such a beacon would deprive Scillonians of the salvage which made 'some amends for the forlornness of their abode', the squat white tower was erected by the end of the year on the highest point of this low-lying island. Its light was provided by a coal fire in an iron brazier which required 'much care ... to keep a good light' – and there are unproven stories that the first keeper Samuel Hockin let it die down deliberately on the approach of a Virginia trader and even took part in the subsequent plunder.[28] Whether this was true or not, the Elder Brothers of Trinity House decided at the time never to appoint a Scillonian to the post on account of the islanders' 'former piracies' and dependence on wrecks for their livelihood.[29]

No accusations of a misleading light were made about the islands' most famous maritime disaster, the loss of Admiral Sir Cloudesley Shovell's Royal Navy fleet in 1707. On a dark, stormy night, misled by navigational errors, it was smashed to pieces among the Western Rocks. The Admiral's own ship HMS *Association* and four others went down off St Agnes and some 2,000 officers and sailors were drowned. There is, however, an abiding legend to the effect that Shovell was washed up barely alive on Porthellick Cove, St Mary's, and murdered by a woman for the sake of his emerald ring. Yet, many ships were saved by the St Agnes light over the years. In 1757, for example, a vessel carrying Benjamin Franklin to Britain with a list of American grievances against colonial rule was able to change course when the watchman spotted the light 'as big as a cartwheel'. Franklin was so impressed by 'the utility of lighthouses' that he resolved to encourage more to be built in America if he 'should live to return there'.[30]

William Borlase, too, admired the 'fine tower' – so much so that he provided a sketch and a very detailed account of the island's 'greatest ornament' for the benefit of those 'who have never seen one'.³¹ Troutbeck plagiarised this description in his survey but was able to add that in 1790 the coal light had been replaced by twenty-one oil lamps with reflectors revolving by clockwork to give 'a bright and conspicuous body of light in every direction once in a minute'. Nothing, he concluded, could 'contribute more to the safety of shipping than this structure'. But, of course, the weather could defeat any light which the tower could provide, as Graeme Spence so graphically warned.

> All those wrecks happen in thick or foggy weather, with very few exceptions, when the best situated light cannot be seen at more than 600 yards distance; nothing therefore of the fire or light kind can ever point out Scilly in a fog; the Sun of Heaven is not seen in a thick fog, much less a light. ...The strength, irregularity and prevailing Northern direction of the stream will in all probability force [vessels] among those dangerous rocks, where it is hardly possible for them to escape shipwreck.³²

St Agnes Lighthouse, sketched by William Borlase, 1756.

Ten years later James Silk Buckingham judged that St Agnes's 'splendid lighthouse' was very 'well kept and attended to'; but Trinity House records bear out Robert Heath's judgement that it was nerve-racking work to keep a good light going in 'close confinement upon this remote island'. The second keeper, Philip Fisher, complained of 'the endless job' of maintaining a watch, carrying coal up to the lantern, stoking up the fire and 'continually cleaning the windows at night'. In 1740 one of Fisher's successors, Amor Clark, received a severe rebuke from the Deputy Master of Trinity House for taking inadequate care of the lighthouse, ordering the wrong size of grate and drinking so much as to make himself 'unfit for business'. The letter concluded that he must be mad. When Clark died soon after a further censure for showing no clear light, his son took over, only to be charged with using too much coal and with embezzlement. Adding to this dismal record, Keeper Evan Johnson drowned some years later while making the passage from St Mary's.[33]

Eventually Trinity House abandoned its previous embargo and began to appoint Scillonian keepers to St Agnes, while still finding plenty of cause for criticism and complaint. Henry House and Jacob Hicks were dismissed for 'their frequent intoxication and differences of opinion', as were both their successors, who were accused in addition of selling lighthouse oil and stores. Just thirty years before Edwin Davis's posting, Principal Keeper Elias Carter disappeared without trace after frequent reports of violent quarrels with his assistant Thomas Kirby. When searches proved unavailing, it was assumed that Carter had drowned himself after suffering 'the highest degree of invective and enmity' from Kirby, who was dismissed from the service. In 1828 Edwin's fifty-year-old father William Slater Davis took up the post of assistant keeper but his conduct, too, failed to 'merit the Board's approval'. Trinity House limited his pension to £20 a year when he retired in 1832. Nevertheless, Trinity House was willing to appoint Edwin as assistant keeper of St Agnes in 1839.[34]

Augustus John Smith painted by an unknown artist, c.1872

In the early 1830s the islands were still in the grip of the economic depression which lasted, according to modern research, until 1834. It was only then that matters began to improve, after the years of misrule, with the purchase of the lease by Augustus Smith. He was a wealthy young man, bored with a life of leisure and interested in social improvement, who hoped to find in these neglected islands 'an unobstructed field for his projects'.[35] Spending more than he received in rent, the new Proprietor embarked immediately on a programme of public works, 'acting as his own architect, surveyor and clerk-of-works'.[36] St Mary's acquired a new church described by one of its early incumbents as a 'neat building in the gothic style'; all the main islands were equipped with schools staffed by teachers chosen and regularly inspected by Smith; new roads, a pier for St Mary's harbour and a steam-powered flour mill contributed to the greater efficiency of the islands. Smith also converted the old Abbey on Tresco into a country house, which he surrounded with a sub-tropical garden famed for its 'curious plants [which] flourish in our genial climate, requiring only shelter and protection from the violence of the gales'.[37] All this created work for the numerous joiners, stonemasons and general labourers listed in the 1841 and 1851 census returns. No doubt, too, the increasing number of grocers, dressmakers, milliners, shoemakers and publicans profited from the money these employees had to spend.

Postcard of Tresco Gardens, 1906.

Shipbuilding also flourished, bringing rich profits to at least a dozen yard owners and affording more employment for shipwrights, carpenters, ropemakers and sailmakers. No wonder the young Dr Moyle was impressed with the 'bustle, work and prosperity' he found in Scilly on his arrival in 1849: 'The music of the building-hammer and the caulking-mallet resounded continuously through Hugh-town and St Mary's [and] the roadstead was full of big ships of all nations.'[38] Most of this activity was based on St Mary's itself, so that people had to migrate there from the off-islands to take advantage of the new opportunities. They were obliged to move in any case under the new system of landholding enforced by Smith. To prevent the endless subdivision of plots, he decreed that in future a tenancy could pass only to the oldest son, so that his siblings had to find paid employment in the Scillies, at sea or on the mainland – where some ended up in the Penzance Union workhouse, built in 1837 to conform with the austere specifications of the amended Poor Law.[39]

With the jobs he created and the schooling he enforced (three decades before the rest of the country introduced compulsory education up to the age of ten in 1880) islanders would, Smith insisted, be 'a very different race to the home-bred, listless, illiterate, inefficient class of young men and women' he had found 'lounging about the islands' on his arrival. Language such as this did not exactly endear the 'plain-spoken and unmannered' governor to his subjects, who resented many of his authoritarian measures. Among other things, he prohibited young people from marrying before they had a house; he compelled tenants to find their children 'some useful mode of gaining their livelihood'; and as chief magistrate he rigorously enforced the ban on smuggling and plundering wrecks.[40] It's perhaps not surprising that a group of young men on St Agnes felt so aggrieved by such curbs on their freedom that they once captured Smith as he set foot on the island, tied him up in a sail and left him on the shore 'to the mercy of the incoming tide'. Apparently, they thought better of their misdeed and loosened his bonds just in time, running away before he could struggle free.[41] Undeterred, the 'Lord of the Isles' persisted in the effort to improve his domain.

Busy though he was with administrative detail, Smith constantly entertained large numbers of house guests on Tresco, regaling them with shooting parties, splendid picnics and boat-trips to the other islands. He also invited to the Abbey the owners and passengers of yachts moored in St Mary's harbour – especially if they were well-connected. Among those transitory vessels was the new steam-powered royal yacht, *Victoria and*

Albert, which anchored in the harbour on 13 August 1847, with the Queen, Prince Albert and their two oldest children on board. The royal visit was rather a botched affair. It had originally been planned for the previous summer, when newspapers had announced that 'if the weather be favourable for a water excursion, her Majesty will proceed for a short cruise off the Scilly Islands' in the course of her West Country tour. 'Immense preparations were made for her reception' but the royal party did not put in an appearance. It seems that the Queen and Prince Albert ran out of time after showing a 'great interest' in visiting a Cornish tin mine, where they were dragged along candle-lit passages by miners who, judged the Queen, 'seemed so pleased & are intelligent good people'. A steamer was despatched to Scilly from Penzance 'to inform the inhabitants that her Majesty was unable to pay them a visit this time'.[42]

This snub may also be explained by the unfriendly relations which existed at that time between Prince Albert, who was acting for the infant Duke of Cornwall, and Augustus Smith, who was not intimidated by royalty. In a long series of letters about the terms of his tenure, Smith accused Albert of betraying his professed belief in social improvement by supporting him as little as possible: 'The Duchy will give me nothing that they can help.' Suggesting that he might be 'debarred from following up the course of reform' he had pursued for twelve years, he challenged Albert: 'If those who act on behalf of the Prince of Wales during his minority choose to treat such matters as not worth their care ... they must be content to bear responsibility for any mischief that may result in consequence'.[43] This acrimonious correspondence, soon to be published by Smith, did not bode well for a successful encounter.

The 1847 visitation happened almost by accident as the *Victoria and Albert* bore the royal family to the Queen's 'dear, dear Highlands' by way of the west coast. Delayed by fog at Dartmouth on 12 August, the party decided the next day not to put into Falmouth as had been planned but to make for the Scillies and moor there overnight. Thus, to their 'great surprise and delight ...

loyal inhabitants' spotted the royal vessels approaching the islands and being piloted into the harbour. While the Queen recovered from feeling 'wretchedly ill' on a 'nasty rolling' sea and sketched her view of the 'numerous little rocky islands', Prince Albert and the five-year-old Prince of Wales, 'landed in private on the island of Samson, where the latter caught a bird, to his great amusement'. Meanwhile Augustus Smith, informed of Queen Victoria's arrival, used all his powers of organisation to prepare a suitably 'cordial reception' for the first English sovereign to land on Scilly since medieval times.[44]

The Queen's diary records her impressions of the following day:

> After 5 we went in the Barge across the harbour, where, although the sea was very blue, it was rather rough, & landed at a little pier at St Mary's. ... We got into a funny little pony carriage, belonging to Mr Smith & drove through the place, which looks like a little fishing town & then around the fortifications of the Castle, where there is a very pretty walk overhanging the sea, the rocks being covered with fern, heath and furze. The extensive view of the islands is very fine. The little town is built upon a very narrow strip of land with a small bay on either side. We got out at the old Castle, which bears the name of one of the Edwards & the view from the battlements was very fine. Returned from here, just as we came.[45]

This rather patronising and historically inaccurate account fails to mention certain aspects of the loyal welcome which Smith had arranged: a gun salute from the batteries, a reception party of 'principal residents' (not including the lighthouse keeper) and the brilliant illumination of the islands by bonfires and tar barrels which followed the brief royal tour.[46] Many Scillonians, however, caught no glimpse of the Queen because of an unfortunate incident described by an anonymous witness:

> On their way back, Mr. Smith's coachman unluckily took a wrong turn, and directed the ponies' heads down a steep declivity, quite unfit for the

descent of a carriage. . . The Queen and Prince Albert were alarmed, and hastily jumped out, descending the hill on foot, instead of continuing along the proper road, by which means many of the inhabitants lost the gratification of seeing Her Majesty, who returned quickly to the barge, and was conveyed to the yacht.[47]

No account mentions any conversation between the Proprietor and his unhelpful landlord.

Meanwhile Smith had won renown in Cornwall. He often braved the sea passage to attend fashionable events such as the annual Polytechnic Exhibition in Falmouth, where the county's 'Quality' gathered in Barclay Fox's garden.[48] He was a leading member of Cornwall's Masonic Lodge, Geological Society and Royal Institution, and was later elected a Member of Parliament for Truro. In his travels around the Duchy he would take advantage of hospitality at grand country houses such as Saltram, Lanhydrock and Godolphin.[49]

Augustus Smith deserved his reputation for the transformation he wrought in the Isles of Scilly. In an 1850 guide-book, designed to 'draw the attention of tourists to Scilly' with the 'tasteful embellishment' of drawings by Smith's close friend Lady Sophia Tower, the Rev Isaac North attributed the islands' 'recovery from a low and debasing state of poverty' to the 'wise and firm superintendence of the Proprietor'. He praised in particular the efficient schools which enabled Scillonians 'to get their own living and to do their duty in the state of life to which it shall please God to call them'. Smith naturally welcomed such praise and implausibly declared that he had 'contributed nothing' towards the book.[50]

The numerous offspring of Keeper Edwin Davis and Doctor John Moyle would be among those who profited from the new schooling, although many of them had subsequently to leave Scilly in search of opportunities it could not offer. Life was still hard on these bare, windy islands separated by storm-ridden sea passages and frequently cut off from the rest of the kingdom. During bad weather Smith himself complained of knowing nothing of 'what may have happened in the world' and he often found it difficult to recruit schoolmasters, clergymen or household staff who were prepared to come over to work in Scilly. When searching for a new housekeeper, for example, he stipulated that she had to be 'able to live all the year round at Scilly and emulate the parrot in being content'. To live here even today, confessed Francis Hicks, a fellow-descendant of William Davis, who earns his living as a bulb-grower on St Agnes, 'you have to be determined and sometimes bloody-minded.'[51]

Chapter 2

The Moyles of Penzance
1810-1855

Richard Moyle m. Eliza Tippett

1 Lydia	2 Granville	3 John	4 Cordelia	5 Richard	6 Mary Anne
b1811	b1815	b1816	b1818	b1819	b1822
7 James	8 Thomas	9 William	10 Edward	11 Charles	12 Vyvyan
b1824	b1825	b1826	b1827	b1828	b1834

During the early nineteenth century a weekly packet boat laden with letters, passengers and a moderate amount of freight traversed the twenty-eight miles between the Scillies and the Cornish port of Penzance. Often the vessels were prevented from sailing or delayed by 'the excessive violence of the gales' and it was never a comfortable journey, despite advertisements promising refreshments on board and 'very superior accommodation'.[52] Mounts Bay Harbour, sketched by John Grenfell Moyle in his youth, must have been a welcome sight to passengers.[53]

Born in 1816, John grew up near Penzance harbour as third of the twelve children of Richard Moyle, a surgeon/apothecary, and his wife Eliza. The family lived at 16 Market Jew Street, a substantial house leased with nine acres of land, which provided comfortable accommodation for the couple with their offspring

John Grenfell Moyle, View from Paul Hill – Penzance, Marazion and the Mount.

and a few servants, the doctor's surgery, pasture for a horse and an allotment on which to grow produce.[54] The 1841 Census notes the occupations of the street's other inhabitants: artisans (tailors, shoemakers, staymakers, carpenters and straw bonnet makers), tradesmen (innkeepers, grocers, butchers, bakers and confectioners) and porters, carriers, servants and manual labourers. There were also more cerebral workers (a librarian, a scrivener, an accountant, a bank clerk and two school teachers) as well as a few residents of independent means, and two other surgeons. Thus the street reflects the marginal milieu of surgeon/apothecaries who, because they worked with their hands on

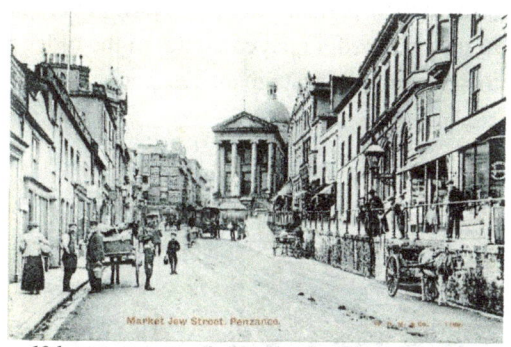

19th-century postcard of Market Jew Street, Penzance.

patients' bodies, slicing like butchers or stitching like cobblers, and sold medicines in the manner of grocers, were not regarded as members of a gentlemanly profession. Richard Moyle had qualified as a Member of the Royal College of Surgeons but occupied a lower social position than physicians who 'hardly touched patients' while charging high fees for their diagnoses and prescriptions.⁵⁵

Penzance in the first half of the 19th century is described in Pigot's Directory as 'one of the most thriving towns in Cornwall'. In addition to being a busy tin port, fishing harbour and market town, it was 'a place of considerable note' for the Cornish gentry, graced by handsome buildings such as the Guildhall and the 'Egyptian House'. The town contained several scholarly societies, a natural history museum, a library and two book clubs, one for ladies and one for gentlemen. It was also developing as 'a favourite resort for invalids', patronised, for example, by the wealthy Fox family of Falmouth. Barclay Fox took his family there in 1849 to stay in lodgings close to the sea, so that his little son George, who had been ill with bronchitis, 'might benefit by exercise in the mild air of that beautiful bay'.⁵⁶ It is not clear whether such visitors and the town's 9,000 or so inhabitants could provide a decent living for all its thirteen surgeons and three physicians as well as an unlisted quantity of quacks.

Doctors' charges were based not only on their qualifications but also on their patients' ability to pay. Fever and dysentery abounded in the cramped, unpaved courts in the older parts of the town with their open drains, stagnant cesspools, and overflowing piggeries – but the poor families stricken by such diseases could not afford doctors' fees.⁵⁷ They could get medical treatment only through charitable dispensaries, the Poor Law authorities or simple altruism on the part of doctors. Richard

Poor children in Penzance, photographed by Gibson & Sons.

Moyle was one of the original surgeons involved in the Penzance Public Dispensary set up in 1810, when it treated 425 patients: 'cured 340, relieved 20, incurable 7, dead 8, on books 48, discharged 2'. In some years the number of patients and deaths rose steeply, as Public Health Inspector George Clark relates:

> Cholera visited Penzance in 1832 and prevailed in the lower part of the town along the margin of the sea and about the roots of the pier – one of the filthiest quarters of the town. In September, October, and November the cholera deaths were 64.

In the neighbouring port of Newlyn, which was served by Penzance doctors, the disease 'carried off above 100 souls' who were buried at night in a special cholera field.[58]

Over Cornwall as a whole, 308 people died of cholera in 1832 out of population of about 300,000. Yet, the impact of the disease was constantly played down by newspapers like the *Royal Cornwall Gazette*, which in September 1832 called on 'the inhabitants of this highly favoured county' to thank the Almighty 'for their merciful preservation from this pestilential scourge'.[59] The people themselves often took more practical precautions such as the cleansing vinegar provided on the boundary of Zennor or the burning of cholera clothes and bedding witnessed by Barclay Fox. Meanwhile doctors did their best to cure victims with such ineffective treatments as 'bleeding from the head, mercurial fumigations and bandaging of the abdomen'. The cholera epidemic caused as much fear as did the Covid 19 pandemic nearly two centuries later, which gathered pace in the county after the lifting of restrictions in July 2021 prompted an influx of tourists.[60]

Cornwall was stricken with another 'fearful visit of cholera' in 1848-9, as Barclay Fox's journal recorded. Falmouth escaped with only a 'mild experience', attributed by Fox to the sanitary measures the town had already adopted, while in the fishing port of Mevagissey nearly a tenth of the population died and half the remaining residents fled.[61] Penzance had not yet made any public health improvements but alarming rates of dysentery and the dread of cholera had prompted the Corporation to look into conditions which might give rise to such diseases. In 1848 an inquiry into the town's water supply heard evidence from doctors, including Richard Moyle. He attributed the 'frequency of cases of fever among the lower orders' to a 'great insufficiency of water for sanitary purposes'. In the same year the town commissioned a full Public Health Inquiry at the end of which the superintending inspector George Clark wrote a damning report. He concluded that despite the town's healthy position 'upon a bay proverbial for its salubrity and beauty, it would be difficult to find a spot so foul in which life is so seriously affected, or which it would cost so little to make pure'.[62] A local Board of Health was immediately set up to take charge of lighting, paving, sewers and water supply, all of which were improved over the next ten years. But these changes came too late to prevent fifty or so Penzance residents dying in the second wave of cholera. No doubt many of the cases were treated without charge at the Public Dispensary where Richard Moyle served for twenty years.

More prosperous patients were also 'assailed by a battery of infections and fevers' which were all too often fatal.[63] Barclay Fox's Journal, for example, recorded his wretched childhood experience of whooping cough, a young cousin's death from scarlet fever and the demise of several acquaintances in outbreaks of influenza. He noted as well his own increasing symptoms of the lethal tuberculosis which was not alleviated by saline waters in Wales, a diet of grapes in Germany, or wintering in Egypt. He often included all too vivid descriptions of the treatment administered by Cornish doctors: a 'most horrible dose' of turpentine for a tapeworm, leeches applied for inflammation of the lungs, half a pint of blood taken after a fall, camomile and mustard plasters to relieve pain, rhubarb administered after a gig accident, and juniper and digitalis for a diseased heart. He also commented on a purge that caused one patient to 'compare the motion of his bowels to nothing but a pump, which destroyed the doctor's gravity' – made him laugh, in other words. Fox was particularly keen to witness surgical procedures such as his pet monkey's broken arm being put in a splint, a 'horrible' amputation, tooth extractions and the cauterisation of dog bites with nitric acid.[64]

Dr Moyle also bled, dosed and operated on his patients, but he left no diary or letters describing these painful and frequently ineffective procedures. Occasionally, though, newspaper reports of court cases or inquests at the Cornwall Assizes provide graphic glimpses of his daily round. Giving evidence in 1820 at the trial of a woman accused of poisoning her husband, Moyle testified that he had disinterred the corpse and taken the stomach to his surgery. Examination of its contents revealed small white particles which test-tube analysis proved to be arsenic. The young doctor was evidently an early British exponent of the benefits of post-mortem examinations, which had become 'almost a fetish' in Paris and Vienna. On the strength of Moyle's testimony the wife was found guilty and sentenced to death. In the interests of further medical research the remains of her body were to be 'given for dissection'.

Thirty years later Richard Moyle appeared in court to defend a fellow practitioner who had been accused of incompetence. He recounted tasks they had tackled together: 'a very difficult case of midwifery' in which they saved the woman but not the child; 'a very severely lacerated foot and leg from an accident in a mine'; and 'removing a cancerous breast'. At this stage of Moyle's career he may have been using new painkilling methods like ether and chloroform when he performed operations like these in patients' homes.[65]

For such demanding work a diligent surgeon-apothecary could make about £400 a year in a mixed practice. On this sort of income Richard Moyle was able to support his large family, to keep a few servants, to collect books and paintings and to run a small horse-drawn gig so that he did not have to ride a horse or resort to Shanks's pony when visiting more distant patients – but it 'scarcely bought gentility'. Like Elizabeth Gaskell's Mr Hoggins of Cranford, Moyle was 'inadmissible to society ... on account of his boots, smelling of the stable, and himself, smelling of drugs'.[66]

Even so, I found numerous references to his name in the local press among the 'influential merchants and gentlemen' urging improvements such as a new pier and the extension of the railway network into Cornwall. He founded the Penzance Natural History and Antiquarian Society in 1839 and subscribed to the town's Royal Geological Society, attending their meetings and balls along with the local élite – who would probably not have invited him for luncheon or dinner in their own homes. He was also a contributor to numerous charitable causes like one set up to relieve the widows and orphans of Mounts Bay fishermen. In 1839 he was elected Mayor and during his year's term of office wrote a letter to the Home Secretary, which suggests a broadly conservative political stance. He expressed his fear that the 'proverbial loyalty' and 'almost universal contentment' of his town would be overturned by the 'seditious and inflammatory language' used at a local meeting organised by members of the Chartist movement, who dared to demand one man one vote.[67]

Not all doctors were as satisfied with their place in society. Another general practitioner complained that after thirty years of 'rigid economy and painful application to a laborious profession ... among the lowest of the people' he did not earn enough to maintain himself, his wife and six sons and daughters 'as gentlemen and ladies'. And Anthony Trollope's well-observed Dr Thorne is 'still a poor man' after many years of wearying labour, worrying about how to provide for his niece Mary.[68] Dr Moyle had larger responsibilities. The nine sons and three daughters, who are listed in a family pocket-book I inherited, all survived childhood, no doubt with the help of his medical expertise.[69] Now they had to be launched into the world.

* * * *

The two brothers closest in age to John Grenfell got off their father's hands quite early in typical Cornish fashion – by going to sea. Granville entered the Royal Navy in 1830 when he was fifteen and Richard joined the Merchant Marine in 1832 at the age of thirteen. There is no record of either boy's education but they may well have been set on a marine career at a local school, Regent House Academy. It was run by Richard Barnes, who walked on crutches, made 'constant use' of the cane and taught 'a smattering of classics

Richard Moyle's offspring listed in his pocket-book.

and mathematics, and a knowledge of navigation learnt from his father, a master mariner'. The schoolmaster is thus described in the *Reminiscences* of former pupil George Boase who went on to Penzance Grammar School. Here Boase met the doctor's fourth son, whom he lists as 'James Moyle – dead'. This accords with a family record to the effect that James joined the merchant navy and perished in 1844 on his first voyage.[70] Meanwhile, two of the daughters found suitable husbands; the oldest Lydia married Captain Thomas Mathias of the Royal Navy and Cordelia a Penzance gentleman, Richard Long, some twenty years older than herself. Mary Anne was still living at home in 1841 and no doubt made herself useful in a house which still contained five young boys as well as a busy surgery.[71]

The only son to follow his father's profession was John Grenfell, third in the family after Lydia and Granville. Since he was clearly a clever boy it's likely that he was sent to the Grammar School in advance of the younger brothers remembered by Boase – though the annual fees of eight guineas were a serious drain on the doctor's pocket. John would have received no scientific grounding under the direction of its headmaster Rev George Morris, a good classical scholar and one of the town's best chess-players, who made no secret of writing his sermons when he should have been attending to his pupils. But similar negligence on the part of Morris's predecessor had not held back the school's famous student Humphry Davy, the chemist who invented (among much else) the Davy lamp for use in mines and 'laughing gas' which could help to relieve pain in surgery. Davy thought himself lucky to have enjoyed so much idleness at school: 'What I am I have made myself.'[72]

Like other port towns, Penzance had lots of fun to offer a lad in those days, as Boase and Humphry Davy's younger brother John vividly recall. Mr Phillpott the pastrycook 'did considerable business with the rising generation', who relished his Chelsea buns and gingerbread cakes known as 'lillybangers'. The Grammar School's 'grassy playground' was ideal for games such as rounders and cutters-and-smugglers, while out of school the 'great amusement was war', waged with slings and stones against the boys of Newlyn or Mousehole. Feast days were celebrated with wild torch processions and with fireworks made from steel filings acquired from a 'very obliging blacksmith'. Best of all, the Midsummer and Corpus Christi fairs offered peepshows, menageries, boxing booths and sword-swallowers 'observed with amazement by medical men'. Quieter amusements included 'boyhood excursions' or 'solitary rambles' along the cliffs, with 'the ever-varying blue sea' on one side and 'furze-clad hills' on the other. Down below, the beaches offered opportunities for shrimping or collecting specimens from rock-pools 'abounding in animal life'.[73]

John doubtless spent his spare time in such pursuits (many of which sound remarkably like my own childhood pastimes in a Devon seaside village) as well as reading in his father's library, which was full of medical and scientific books. And from an early age he depicted the scene around him in pencil drawings of local landscapes or rock formations along the Penwith coastline and in more ambitious oil paintings. One of his youthful works, *View of Penzance,* won a prize at the first exhibition of the Cornwall Polytechnic Society in 1834, which was attended in Falmouth by such county grandees as Sir Charles Lemon, Sir Thomas Dyke Acland and Charles Fox.[74] That picture has not survived but another of his paintings, which can be dated to his teenage years, today forms part of the collection of the Penlee Gallery in Penzance; it portrays parishioners gathering outside the temporary church at Alverton, which stood from 1833 to 1835 on the outskirts of the town.[75]

John Grenfell Moyle, Alverton Temporary Church, *c 1835*.

At some point in the 1830s John had to start taking life more seriously, since he was obliged to serve an apprenticeship of several years before going on to any formal medical training. He probably did this in his father's surgery, which would have contained specimens resembling those which startled a lady visitor to Doctor Thorne's study: 'a pair of human thigh-bones which ... he was in the constant habit of handling with much energy' and a 'little child's skull which grinned at her from off the chimney-piece'.[76] Like John Keats, who trained as a surgeon apothecary in London, John Moyle performed such tasks as bookkeeping, cleaning the surgery, dressing wounds, drawing teeth, making up medicines and preparing leeches to be used for bleeding patients. He also accompanied the doctor on home visits, seeing for himself the conditions which had contributed to the severity of the cholera epidemic.

In 1839 John travelled to London to take up his place at the new University College, a secular body denounced by Dr Arnold, headmaster of Rugby School, as 'that Godless institution in Gower Street' where 'Jew, Mahometan, Hindoo, or Benthamite may all be … taught physical science together' – which would hardly matter since 'physical science is not education'.[77] The journey involved a three-day drive by stage-coach, or a slightly quicker one by the night-mail from Bristol or Bath, with all the attendant problems of dust, mud and rain, especially for those sitting on the box with the coachman. Only after 1840 was it possible to do part of the journey on Brunel's Great Western Railway, a speedier option which John may well have chosen later in his course. He studied not for a medical degree, which would have taken four years and cost his father hundreds of pounds, but for a diploma with the influential Royal College of Surgeons. He attended daily lectures, often held in the College's Hunterian Museum among its anatomical specimens, surgical instruments and skeletons.[78] In the College's purpose-built hospital he observed operations as well as the dissection of corpses and body parts provided by grave robbers, exem-

Robert Schnebbelie, A lecture at the Hunterian Anatomy School, London 1839.

plified by the 'resurrection man' Jerry Cruncher in Dickens's *A Tale of Two Cities*. At the end of the course students took an oral examination before a Court of three surgeons who then voted on whether to admit them as Members of the Royal College. John gained this title within two years, so that in 1841 the Census recorded him as 'John Grenfell Moyle, 25, Surgeon', living with his parents and six siblings in Market Jew Street. No doubt he was working with his father at this time but it was not long before he followed in the wake of his sea-faring brothers by enlisting as a ship's surgeon on a vessel sailing for Bombay.[79]

It would have been quite easy for John to find such a passage. Just around the coast from Penzance in the busy port of Falmouth vessels constantly landed from, and sailed to, countries all round the world. 'Ship News' in the *Royal Cornwall Gazette* regularly reported on such traffic. There were East Indiamen laden with exotic goods such as silk, spices and indigo; steam packets carrying mail to the Far East on the new 'Overland Route' via Egypt, taking two months rather than six; fast clippers bearing emigrants to Australia and returning with cargoes of wool; and schooners transporting precious metals from South America, such as the consignment stolen in the famous gold dust robbery of 1839. Often their captains and surgeons brought home tropical plants and specimens for the gardens of south Cornwall, where they flourish to this day. The Fox family, for example, was delighted with the gift of a carnivorous coral collected by Captain Fitzroy, on his epic voyage with Charles Darwin on HMS *Beagle* – this curious 'flower animal' found a place in their grounds at Penjerrick, where it can still be found nestling in the undergrowth.[80] Even though the P&O Steam Packet Company moved its base to Southampton in 1843 and some feared that 'the tide of prosperity may now be set against the port of Falmouth', this fine Cornish harbour remained part of a global trading network.[81] All substantial vessels carried surgeons such as John, who were ranked and treated as officers.

Family accounts record that John made two voyages with the

East India Merchant Service, 'taking troops to India and bringing home time-expired men and families', for which he would have been paid quite well – the standard rate was £5 a month all found on East Indiamen. It's likely too that he received hospitality from his uncle and exact namesake, a Fellow of the Royal Society of Surgeons who practised medicine in Bombay. But it was no longer easy for crewmen to gain riches by private trading on such travels, as appears from the experience of Dr Allan Woodcourt, the hero of Dickens's *Bleak House*. Having put in 'a great deal of work for very little money' in the service of London's poor, Woodcourt goes on 'a long, long voyage' to recoup his fortunes and those of his widowed mother who had spent all she could spare 'in qualifying him for his profession'. Woodcourt failed in this respect: 'He had gone out a poor ship's surgeon and had come home nothing better.'[82]

Nor did John Moyle make his fortune, as is suggested in an obituary written by someone 'intimately acquainted' with him for nearly fifty years. It seems that the Indian expeditions gave John the opportunity for some independent travel, during which he had cause to fall back on his artistic talent:

> While touring in the south of France, owing to the delay of a letter, the treasury ran out and the finances were reduced to nil. But at the hotel his portfolio procured him the needful, till remittances came to hand.[83]

Such Gallic paintings have not come to light but one or two may yet hang on the walls of the French hotel which gave John Moyle board and lodging.

As well as such adventures and new scenes to depict with his pencil and brush, he gained valuable medical experience. A ship's surgeon was essentially a general practitioner attending to everyone on board – passengers, crew and troops. After taking a morning sick call he visited patients, fumigated the medical bay, checked the sanitary conditions of the whole ship and tended to any injuries incurred during the day. Even in peacetime a ship was a dangerous environment, especially when the weather was stormy or the sailors were drunk, and their logbooks frequently record accidents such as falls from the mast, men overboard and shipboard fires. A midshipman called William Barlow recounted on his maiden voyage that he had to hold down a man whose hand was amputated after a six-pounder exploded while it was being loaded. He also witnessed the result of a shipmate's falling down a hatchway – his nostril was entirely cut 'as if it had been done with a knife'. Some years later, when he was still only nineteen, Barlow himself fell from the foretop mast, hit his head on a bolt and died of the injury despite the best efforts of the surgeon.[84] John doubtless had to use his surgical skills in such incidents on his two voyages to Bombay, as well as treating occupational conditions like scurvy, venereal disease and the effects of over-indulgence in grog. In addition, he had to deal with the infections which spread rapidly in the close quarters of a ship, both familiar ones like smallpox, typhus, dysentery and cholera, and diseases more common in the tropics such as yellow fever, malaria and plague. Any such outbreaks required the ship to be quarantined when it reached port, an exercise which the surgeon had to supervise. As a young man with an inquiring mind, John used this maritime experience to increase his medical knowledge and expertise, which would stand him in good stead for his Scillonian future.

John Grenfell Moyle as a young man.

* * * *

Meanwhile the five younger brothers left at home began to make their way in the world. Thomas is remembered as a fellow-pupil of Penzance Grammar School (also known as Penare Academy) by George Boase who thought he was dead, whereas in fact he had gone off to Australia.[85] I know that William also attended Penare Academy as I inherited a prize medal for English Elocution which he won there in 1843 at the age of seventeen. I discovered that

Medal awarded to William Moyle by Penare Academy.

another of his prizes was sold at auction a few years ago: a similar medal awarded in 1842 for his prowess in speaking French. A surviving programme of recitals by the 'Young Gentlemen of Penare House Academy' in 1843 provides further evidence of his oratorical skill. Master W Moyle was the leading light of the show, giving the Introductory Address and acting scenes by Shakespeare, Molière and Terence in English, French and Latin respectively.[86]

His good speaking voice, as well as a recommendation from the school, no doubt helped William to gain a clerical post in the Fleet Street branch of Praed's banking house which had strong Cornish connections. The general ledger shows that he began work there on 15 October 1845.[87] Meanwhile Edward, who was just a year younger and had participated in the same school recital, still lived at home while working as a customs clerk in the port. Charles possessed his brother John's artistic skills, which he put to use in the drawing office of the Bank of England. The youngest son, Vyvyan, was sent to live with Rev George Morris, who had retired from the headmastership of the Grammar School to become Vicar of St Allen near Truro.[88] He coached the boy in classics, though such teaching as he imparted in religion and morality was to prove sadly ineffectual.

John had returned from his second sea voyage by 1845, when he painted that year's Regatta at St Michael's Mount. He also witnessed the brief royal visit of September 1846. This included a tour of the tidal island which, according to a report in the *Daily News*, the Queen wanted to buy from the St Aubyn Family. This

John Grenfell Moyle, The Departure of Queen Victoria and Prince Albert from St Michael's Mount, *1846.*

rumour proved to be false but the expedition gave John Moyle the opportunity to execute one of his best-known paintings, *The Departure of Queen Victoria and Prince Albert from St Michael's Mount*, in which he depicted the Mayor and Corporation of Penzance 'so faithfully ... that every occupant in the boat could be easily recognised'.[89] As we have seen, the royal yacht did not undertake the planned passage to Scilly on that occasion. In June 1849 John himself made that journey, which marked an epoch in his life. He went to St Mary's to act as locum during the absence of William Lemon Blewett; when that doctor died later in the month while on holiday, John was appointed as surgeon both for the general population of all the islands and for the troops based in the garrison.[90]

Although leaving his mainland past behind, John obviously cherished memories of his Penzance boyhood. A year after his arrival he conjured up the carnival traditionally held at Mount's Bay on Midsummer's Day in his painting, *Quay Fair*.[91] Against the background of billowing sails in the harbour, dancers perform

John Grenfell Moyle, Quay Fair, *1850.*

on a stage, families share picnics, an 'Overboat' wheel turns, two lovers canoodle, a sailor dances the hornpipe while a hurdy-gurdy girl plays – and a boy picks a handkerchief from the pocket of one of her gentleman admirers. This is the only misdemeanour in a happy scene, which bears a striking stylistic resemblance to earlier depictions of such festivities. But the young John Moyle's benign, rose-tinted viewpoint contrasts sharply with the disorder and villainy shown in William Hogarth's satirical *Southwark Fair* or the raucous jollity of Thomas Rowlandson's colourful *Bartholomew Fair* and *Greenwich Fair*. The Penzance panorama is also different in mood from the lonely landscapes which John would be inspired to paint in the Isles of Scilly.

The Moyles of Penzance

* * * *

After the departure of most of their offspring, Richard and Eliza Moyle continued to live in Market Jew Street, together with Edward, their unmarried daughter Mary Anne, one servant and two apprentices, one of whom was his sixteen-year-old nephew, Granville Borlase Moyle, from the Bombay branch of the family.[92] This was a more comfortable period for the 67-year-old 'esteemed practitioner' as he could charge more for his services and had fewer dependants to drain his purse. Thus he was able to afford Oxford University fees for his youngest son, Vyvyan, who entered Pembroke College in 1853 destined, like most of its graduates, for the Church.

It was at this stage in his life that Richard Moyle made the acquaintance of Wilkie Collins, who embarked on a walking tour of Cornwall in August 1850 which resulted in a publication he called *Rambles Beyond Railways*, illustrated by his travelling companion Henry Brandling. Like other writers of his time, Collins was attracted to the West Country as a source of literary material. His aim was to tell his readers something about a part of the country which was 'still too little visited and too little known' and in so doing he gives a fascinated outsider's view of the environment in which Richard Moyle's family grew up. Despite being taken as a pedlar, a 'trodger' or as a mapper for the proposed new railroad, the genial Collins managed to befriend not only the educated Dr Moyle but also sundry locals from whom he elicited plenty of illuminating information as well as some 'quaint legends'.[93]

He witnessed the relative prosperity of certain local industries as well as their fragility, which threatened Cornish livelihoods. At many seaport towns and villages on the Penwith peninsula he observed the pilchard fishing which still gave 'active employment to a hardy and honest race who would starve without it'. He invited readers to 'catch the infection and cheer with the rest' at the spotting of vast shoals, the casting of huge 'seine' nets from the shore, the hauling of a 'teeming, convulsed mass of shining, glancing, silvery scales' to the surface, and the loading of the fish into boats, baskets and barrows. The 'noisiest and most amusing of all the scenes' was the salting-house, where 'screaming, talking' women and girls piled the pilchards up on layers of salt 'at threepence an hour'. Collins reckoned that at Trereen (now Treen) cove in Mount's Bay the inhabitants caught 1,440,000 pilchards.[94] What this vivid spectacle unwittingly foretold was that overfishing would soon reduce the shoals. The resulting decline of seining and of ports like Penzance which exported the fish affected the entire population. There would be less work for a young man such as Edward Moyle in Mount's Bay harbour.

An even more exciting experience for Collins and Brandling was their visit to a copper and tin mine at Botallack, near Land's End, another flourishing but precarious industry. The descent of 420 feet down perpendicular ladders, the climbing, crouching and crawling through passages, the 'hot, moist, sickly vapour floating about us' and the 'sound of the surf lashing the rocks above us, and of the waves breaking on the beach beyond' was almost too much for the pair: 'Just over our heads we observe a wooden plug of the thickness of a man's leg; there is a hole here, and the plug is all that we have to keep out the sea.' Covered as they were with 'a mixture of mud, tallow, and iron-drippings' they declined the chance to penetrate to even deeper galleries where miners were hacking away at seams of tin and arsenic. Having knocked off a tiny morsel of copper as a memento, they were glad to return to the surface and breathe in 'the cold, health-giving purity of the sea breeze'. Like Queen Victoria in 1846, Collins was full of admiration for the 'industrious and intelligent' miners who earned on average about

Engraving of Clarkson Stansfield, Botallack Mine, 1836.

ten shillings a week for their labour. But he began to fear for their future when he was told that the price of copper had fallen recently, that the 'treasures of the earth' were beginning to run out and that 'the mine ... had failed to pay the expenses of working it'.[95]

Collins became even more aware of the dangers of mining when, in the company of Dr Moyle, he visited a fourteen-year-old boy who had slipped down the shaft of Boscaswell Downs mine near Penzance, falling seventy-eight feet but miraculously suffering nothing worse than multiple cuts and bruises. Two months later the boy was back at work in the mine, according to his 'medical attendant', whom Collins described as a 'gentleman whose life had been passed in Cornwall, and who was highly and deservedly respected by all among whom he resided'.[96]

Richard Moyle gave Collins further 'kind assistance' in his research, plying him with stories from his casebook about the superstitions surviving in his remote part of the duchy. One told of a boy wounded by a pitchfork whose family believed, in accordance with a local tradition, that his recovery was accelerated by their keeping the offending tool 'bright and clean'. The doctor also recounted the tale of his finding arsenic in a man's body, as a result of which his wife was hanged for murder. For Collins's benefit he added 'horrible stories' of the aftermath:

> Certain people declared that they had seen a ghastly resemblance of the murderess, robed in her winding-sheet, with the black mark of the rope round her swollen neck, standing on stormy nights upon her husband's grave, and digging there with a spade in hideous imitation of the actions of the men who had disinterred the corpse for medical examination.

Further 'awful misgivings arose' when villagers feared that the guilty woman had been baptised with water from a well near the church, which was supposed to make the child secure from ever being hanged. Only when the register proved that she had been christened at a neighbouring church was 'the wonderful character of the parish well' vindicated – to such an extent that 'the peasantry of the neighbouring districts began to send for the renowned water before christenings'.[97]

Collins was no doubt pleased to have such lurid legends which would help to sell his book but he also included more rational aspects of Cornish behaviour, such as the attendance at 'good National Schools' and mass vaccination against the scourge of smallpox. While relishing many a 'gloomy story of shipwreck and death' related with 'awe and horror' by the 'peasantry', he was glad to be assured by Richard Moyle that the crime of deliberate 'wrecking' was now unknown in Cornwall. In fact, reported the doctor, sailors were often 'rescued from death by the courage and humanity of the population of the coast'.[98]

Richard and Eliza Moyle no doubt enjoyed entertaining visitors with the grisly myths of old Cornwall but they themselves were struck by tragedy in the next few years. Their son Charles came home from London in the throes of a severe illness, from which he died in 1850 'deeply regretted aged 20 years'.[99] In 1852 and 1854 their daughters Lydia Mathias and Cordelia Long lost their husbands. Cordelia married again, her new husband being a surgeon who had trained with her brother John, chief witness at the wedding, but she herself died only three years later. Meanwhile the ageing doctor continued visiting patients over a wide area, travelling as much as fifteen miles a day in his two-wheeled carriage. It was an unstable vehicle which regularly featured in accident reports in local newspapers. On Friday 17 April 1855 Richard Moyle stepped into his gig to drive to Sancreed, a village about five miles away. The *Royal Cornwall Gazette* reports what happened next:

> His mare suddenly became restive, and turned round from in front of his house towards the stables opposite. It was then seen by bystanders that the bridle had slipped from her head, and all command over the animal was lost. ... She dashed down Market Jew Street at a gallop. Outside the 'King William the Fourth' public house, she came into collision with a cart, and Dr Moyle was thrown some distance away, fell heavily on the ground, and the vehicle turned over on him. ... It

was ascertained that he had sustained severe injuries in the head, and compression of the brain. Notwithstanding all the professional aid of the town and neighbourhood was applied Mr Moyle gradually sank and died at 11 o'clock on Tuesday night.

A coroner's inquest confirmed the 71-year-old doctor's death from 'concussion of the brain', adding that his fellow practitioners would 'long remember his attention and skill as a professional man, and his genial disposition and kindness in private life'. The second edition of Collins's *Rambles* added a note informing readers that 'death has removed Mr Moyle from the scene of his labours, to the lasting and sincere regret of all who knew him'.[100]

With the loss of its breadwinner the Moyle household broke up. The rented house in Market Jew Street was given up and the *Cornish Telegraph* advertised the auction of its contents:

> A Piano Forte, by Broadwood; numerous Oil Paintings, embracing subjects of local, historical, and scriptural interest; about Three Hundred Volumes of Books, on medicine, surgery, general science and of standard and miscellaneous literature; a large Oatbin, Saddle and Bridle, &c, &c.

The following week another auction took place at the doctor's house of the 'valuable Household Furniture' belonging to his widowed daughter Lydia Mathias, who was presumably living there with her three young sons. The items on offer included not only her fine dinner services and two hundred 'standard and interesting books' but also Commander Mathias's ship's compass and some of the boys' playthings – a child's bagatelle board and a rocking horse.[101]

Precious family possessions were frequently dispersed in such sales brought about by dire necessity – as they were in the case of my husband's forebear Edward Brendon. He was a solicitor with a practice in Callington, Cornwall, who died of a fever in 1820 at the age of twenty-nine. He left a widow and three children, as well as creditors who were invited to 'prove their debts' before a London lawyer.[102] Among his assets was a grandfather clock, fashioned for him by a local carpenter who might otherwise have been employed making coffins. It was a simple instrument, its internal mechanism brought in from the Midlands, and its face crafted specially for Edward with the letters of his name in place of numerals. Fortunately, the clock was bought by his more prosperous brother George and it has come down to us. It stands in our hall, where the chimes remind us hourly of the fragility of Victorian family life, wrecked so easily by sudden misfortune.

Clock made by William Hender of Callington c1820.

Chapter 3

A Penzance Diaspora
1855-1914

I found it difficult to locate Richard Moyle's widow among official records and local newspapers since there were so many Eliza (or Elizabeth) Moyles living in Cornwall at that time. She should not be confused, for example, with one Eliza Moyle who was an inmate of Redruth workhouse or another imprisoned for 'keeping a bawdy house'. In fact, she moved to a small house in Leskinnick Terrace, just round the corner from her old home, and lived there until her death on 4 January 1861. Her will, leaving 'effects under £1000', was witnessed by her youngest son, Vyvyan Henry Moyle, who was probably a beneficiary.[103] After attending his mother's funeral at St Mary's church he returned to Yorkshire where he pursued the astonishing clerical and criminal career which is traced in the next chapter. His unmarried sister Mary Anne, who is later described as an 'annuitant' or pensioner, may also have inherited a modest sum. By the time the ten-yearly census was compiled in spring 1861 she and John Grenfell were the only offspring of Richard and Eliza Moyle still registered in the county of their birth. This chapter will also leave Cornwall in order to trace the family's fortunes as it dispersed over this country and further afield.

Now in her mid-thirties, Mary Anne was the one most affected by the break-up of the household. She had no doubt helped out at home but was trained in no profession or occupation other than the genteel womanhood idealised in Victorian times. Cast adrift from her role as 'angel of the house' she became one of the 'odd women' characterised in George Gissing's novel of that name, in which the Madden sisters suffer a fate strikingly similar to Mary Anne's. They, too, are doctor's daughters whose father is called out to an urgent case: 'Dr Madden was driving at full speed, alone in his dog-cart, towards the scene of duty', when his horse 'stumbled and fell, and its driver was flung forward into the road', dying from his injuries a day or two later. His motherless unmarried daughters must now support themselves as best they can on small pensions drawn from his invested capital, supplemented by any work they can get as ladies' companions or nursery-governesses. They join the ranks of half a million spinsters, for whom there was no established role in the society of their day.[104]

Notes in the family book, census returns and parish records suggest a similarly uneasy life for Mary Anne Moyle. She probably lived with her widowed mother, as was expected of an unmarried daughter, becoming homeless again with Eliza's death in January 1861. When the census was taken in the spring, she was still in Penzance, listed as a 'visitor' (rather than a resident) in St Mary's Terrace together with George Fenton, a clergyman from Leeds, and two more spinsters – his 37-year-old sister Georgiana with her lady companion who was ten years older. Their assembled presence is explained by Rev Fenton's marriage in August of that year to Mary Gregory of Penzance, whom Mary Anne must have known since childhood. The Fentons stayed on in Penzance where the birth of three children is registered but Mary Anne was sadly 'left on the shelf', to use the callous phrase of the day, and moved away after attending her mother's funeral and her friend's wedding.

Tracing her afterwards was difficult because Mary Anne (or Ann) was such a popular Christian name in Victorian times. I had to be careful not to mix her up with various namesakes emigrating to America or getting married and settling down in the duchy. A clue was provided by the entry beside Mary Anne's name in the family notes later compiled by her niece Emma Moyle: 'Resident Bootham York 1884. Friend of the wife or sister of Archbishop of York.' I have not been able to find evidence for such a friendship but it may well have been fostered by Mary Anne's youngest brother Vyvyan who (as the next chapter will show) was well acquainted with Archbishop William Thomson, whose wife Zoe 'gathered around her the right women of every class'. Zoe's biographer claims that, while some accused her of 'caring only for the great ones of the earth', her 'milk of human kindness ... flowed equally over the poor, the dowdy and the dull'. Thus 'she would take any amount of trouble to help a poor protégée', writing endless letters to gain her a post or a pension, 'her strong will generally leading to a triumphant result'.[105]

I eventually found 'Mary Ann Moyle' from Penzance in the 1881 Census for Bootham, where she is listed as the inmate of its 'Old Maid's Hospital'. This was a row of almshouses endowed by

Census reference for Wandesford House, Bootham, York.

Mary Wandesford in 1739 'for the use of ten poor gentlewomen who were never married and who shall be of the religion which is taught and practised in the Church of England as by law established, who shall retire from the hurry and noise of the world into a religious house of protestant retirement'. On visiting York I found a fine classical building, now called Wandesford House, just outside the city walls, which still offers shelter to 'single women over fifty years of age in physical or emotional hardship'. I can't help concluding that it was the patronage of Zoe Thomson which gained Mary Anne admission to one of the Hospital's small dwellings, comprising a ground-floor sitting room, with a range for heating and cooking, and a first-floor bedroom. Mary Anne Moyle was not a feminist or a pioneer like some of the brave characters in Gissing's novel, who set up training schools to enable single women to achieve financial autonomy and social dignity. I hope, however, that she belied Zoe Thomson's belief that 'wifehood and motherhood were the only paths to feminine happiness' and was able to enjoy some independence as 'Head' of her own household together with the companionship of the other 'old maids'.[106]

Author's photograph of Wandesford House.

When Mary Anne died in York in 1886 she left the modest sum of £57 14s 6d, her will being witnessed by her younger brother William, the London bank clerk who lived in a succession of boarding houses in and around Islington. His frequent moves are understandable for, as Trollope's civil service clerk John Eames discovers in his search for respectability, decent rooms 'at forty-eight pounds a year, paid quarterly, are not to be found readily in London'. As a bank clerk William had 'a relatively cosseted career within London's clerical circles', earning about £200 a year, which was just about adequate for him to maintain the gentlemanly demeanour required by a company like Praed's.[107] He could not easily have afforded to support a family and seems to have heeded advice such as that given to John Eames that he would need £500 a year to 'get along' as a family man'.[108] Thus William, who worked at Praed's until his retirement, remained a lifelong bachelor.

Unusually, he possessed a passport, another memento which I have inherited.[109] It was issued by the Foreign Office on 21 July 1864 for 'travelling on the Continent', entitling William 'to pass freely without let or hindrance and to ... every assistance and protection of which he may stand in need'. But this document is something of a mystery. The earliest stamp indicates that on the very next day William set out for the Kingdom of Prussia, which was currently engaged in war with Denmark. Another shows that he entered France on 27 July 1871 just after a terrible series of events: a disastrous war with Prussia ending with a long siege of Paris and military defeat; a punitive treaty involving the loss of two provinces, Alsace and Lorraine plus a five-million-franc indemnity; and revolution in the form of the Paris Commune brought to an end with savage reprisals. William's third visit was to Germany in August 1889 after it had become a unified country. It's just possible that these were simple summer holidays. But travel was still expensive – a typical Cook's tourist, for example, 'would have had an income of between £300 and £600 a year'. In any case, 'a sensible, law-abiding Englishman ... could travel abroad ... without a passport or any sort of official permission' until after the First World War.[110] It's more likely that William was using the proficiency in languages he had shown at school to travel on behalf of the bank, to help clients in times of trouble or (in the case of Germany) during precipitous economic growth. In such circumstances he might well have needed the demonstrable protection of the Foreign Office.

Passport issued to William Moyle in 1864.

Even though William had no children the passport has passed down through the family. This, in addition to his signature on Mary Anne's will, shows that some of the siblings kept in touch with each other, scattered though they were over the British Isles and across the oceans.

* * * *

Moyle is just one of the Cornish surnames to appear frequently in British colonial records, evidence of the 'Great Emigration' from the county between 1840 and 1900. Nearly quarter of a million Cornish men and women fled poverty, sought adventure or looked for a new start in life, taking with them not only surnames but place names such as Truro and Penzance, plus a partiality to wrestling matches, brass bands, sea shanties, Methodism, pasties and saffron cake. Wilkie Collins suggested that emigration was more common from Cornwall than from any English county, giving as an example that five per cent of the population of the Penzance Poor Law Union 'left their native land for Australia or New Zealand in 1849' because of a local potato-blight.[111] He had already glimpsed the decline of copper mining and in its turn the price of the tin fell; cheaper deposits of the metal were found overseas and by the end of the nineteenth century Cornwall's tin mining industry had severely contracted. Among the victims were the uncles recalled in A. L. Rowse's childhood memoir. They all flocked to South Africa from Tregonissey when the local mines closed down: 'If it meant aching hearts at home, many separations and much grief, there was also much fun, the enjoyment of camaraderie, the sticking together of Cornish folk, 'Cousin Jacks', out there.'[112]

The business of emigration thus became deeply entrenched in Cornwall. Government agents, local newspapers, lectures, clergy and gentry encouraged the process. Victorian sages such as Carlyle and Ruskin championed emigration as a solution to poverty and unemployment at home as well as a contribution to the power of Greater Britain overseas – the empire and colonies. Letters from distant friends and family conjured up tempting prospects: 'Penryn is nothing to Adelaide,' wrote one emigrant, 'we can buy everything we want.' Farmers, merchants, tradesmen, craftsmen and sailors joined the throng of those embarking on emigrant ships at West Country ports.[113] So, it's no surprise that four of Richard Moyle's sons and his apprenticed nephew set off to try their luck in foreign lands.

A Penzance Diaspora

The first to settle abroad was the oldest son, Granville Richard, whose naval career saw more hope than glory.[114] He enlisted as a midshipman in 1830 and in this post-Napoleonic era there were few opportunities to show valour, win quick promotion or earn prize money. It took Granville six years to pass his exams, after which he served as mate on HMS *Niagara*, sent to patrol the Canadian Lakes where French-speaking independence fighters, with American support, were seeking vengeance for the destruction of one of their boats.[115] These duties allowed some time for shore leave, during which Granville met the Canadian-born Martha Atkinson, whom he married in June 1842 in Kingston on Lake Ontario, where the couple set up home. By the time their first daughter was born a year later Granville had been promoted to the rank of lieutenant and sent off with the Pacific fleet on HMS *Dublin*.

Portrait of Granville Richard Moyle, 1840s.

He took with him, in his sea-chest, reminders of his Cornish family: two leather-bound volumes of the *Works of Walter Moyle Esq*, tangible pieces of evidence passed down to me.[116] One is inscribed by Richard Moyle in December 1842, clearly a present in honour of his son's promotion, and the other bears Granville's own bookplate and a price mark of fifteen shillings. Both books are battered and stained, with every sign of having been subjected to the hazards of a Pacific voyage. The Walter Moyle they celebrate was a country gentleman who lived near St Germans, Cornwall from 1672 to 1721, a descendant of the Elizabethan philanthropist Sir William Moyle, whose almshouses are still to be seen in the village. Walter was a distinguished literary and political figure who earned a long entry in the *Dictionary of National Biography*, but he was not a direct forebear of Granville since all his children died without issue and his property was left to his brother. Nevertheless, some of the Penzance Moyles made much of this grand connection and the crest on Granville's bookplate depicts a mule similar to the one below Walter Moyle's portrait.[117]

Granville Moyle's bookplate and engraving of Walter Moyle.

Pencil markings in both volumes suggest that Granville took a close interest in Walter's diverse activities, which ranged from high politics to 'collecting and preserving' insects and birds. He must have been amused by the contrast between the 'lewd Covent-Garden life' Walter lived in London, with its jokes about catching the pox from whores, and his insistence on public morality as a magistrate in Cornwall. Walter's letters reveal that he spent happy hours in 'Will's coffee house, the merriest place in the world', in the company of leading poets and playwrights such as Dryden, Wycherley and Congreve – and yet he instructed the good folk of Liskeard to avoid the dangers of 'Lewdness and Debauchery'.[118]

Granville would have appreciated most Walter's vigorous championing of the Royal Navy, whose wooden walls were a bastion of freedom, whereas a standing army was the 'last refuge of tyranny'. As a Whig MP and a man of letters, Walter defended Britain's naval and mercantile interests. He took 'great pains in forwarding a Bill for the encouraging of Seamen, the speedy Manning of the Royal Navy' and better treatment of sailors; he supported the 'Adventures and Discoveries [to which] we owe the Increase of our Trade and Navigation'; and he encouraged the search for a North-West passage and exploration of the South Seas. It was in much the same spirit that in 1843 Lieutenant Moyle joined the expedition aboard HMS *Dublin* to protect British trade in the unstable Pacific region and to ship precious metals back to Britain. After all, as Walter had written:

> Trade renders us Masters of the Silver and Gold of the East and West without our toiling in the Mine [and] breeds us multitudes of able-bodied and skilful Seamen to defend the Treasures they bring home ... whose manner of Life will never suffer them to be debauched or enervated with Ease or Idleness.[119]

These sentiments foreshadow those expressed in the unpublished diary of Granville's shipmate, Marine Lieutenant Gerrard Montague, who describes their shared experiences on the voyage. The *Dublin* called at South American ports such as 'miserable' Arica in Chile, where 'the valuable production of the mines ... is the only cause of its having been a place of any importance to foreigners'. At San Blas in Panama the Admiral and the Captain were 'anxiously collecting freight ... to the amount of 1,200 dollars'. Montague often drew attention to the political and social instability of such places as Valparaiso in Chile from which the President had fled after a revolution. He described Peru as a 'country almost without government', the inhabitants of which 'are a lazy, indolent and trifling race'. The presence of the *Dublin* and other British men-of-war usually managed 'to frighten the natives into submission without bloodshed', though they did not succeed in preventing the French from depriving the 'poor helpless Tahitian Queen of her dominions' in 1844.[120]

The mission on which Granville served was not without its discomforts and dangers. The 'old *Dublin* pitched and rolled' so much in heavy seas that the ship was damaged and half the sailors were sick. Moreover, at least six men lost their lives by falling overboard or from the mizzen top mast. But the officers at least enjoyed themselves with sight-seeing, shooting expeditions and dinner parties and balls to which local 'people of distinction' were invited. The scenery was often spectacular and on one occasion an 'immense stream of light' was observed, which turned out to be a comet, 'larger and more beautiful than any that have appeared for a number of years'. Granville must have been intrigued to come across an equally 'rare phenomenon' in Walter Moyle's second volume, where he records being cheered, during a dull, gout-ridden time in the country, by the sight of a meteor emitting a 'prodigious blaze of light'.[121]

Painting by Emeric Vidal of a ball on board HMS Dublin *in 1835.*

The Pacific voyage ended in 1845 and Granville returned to Kingston, where three more daughters were born. According to the *Naval Biographical Dictionary* of 1849 this was the end of Granville's naval service. In fact, it was coming to a climax. As the British census of 1851 shows, he was posted (still a lieutenant) to HMS *Trafalgar*, a 120-gun ship of the line commissioned off Sheerness. The family had moved to this port on the Isle of Sheppey by the time *Trafalgar* was sent to the Black Sea in 1854 to support British troops engaged in the Crimean War against Russia. Granville was on board as the French and British navies shelled Odessa for twelve hours and went on to support ground troops during the year-long siege of

Russia's naval base, Sebastopol. As so often happens in wartime, he experienced months of tedium punctuated by moments of terror.

A midshipman's log records much routine cleaning and watering as well as the *Trafalgar*'s participation in a bombardment of Russian coastal batteries. On 17 October 1854, as the *Times* also reported, the firing on both sides 'soon became terrific'.

Anonymous engraving of the Trafalgar *and the* Retribution *at the Siege of Sebastopol, 1854.*

> At the distance of six miles the sustained sound resembled that of a locomotive at full steam but, of course, the roar was infinitely grander. The day was dead calm, so that the smoke hung heavily about both ships and batteries and frequently prevented either side from seeing anything. From about two till dark (nearly six) the cannonade raged most furiously.

Trafalgar was stationed near the end of the line, further away from Russian guns than most of the twenty-seven ships in the Allied fleet. Thus she escaped the worst effects of the enemy's 'red-hot shot', whereas the decks of other vessels 'were cut up like ploughed fields [and] fires broke out in all parts'. Even so, *Trafalgar*'s main shroud was shot away and her rigging severely mauled. Granville was not among the 340 Allied casualties suffered that day; nor was he a victim of infectious diseases such as cholera and typhus, which were far more deadly. Further assaults forced the Russian army to withdraw from Sebastopol in September 1855, but the *Times* judged that modern artillery had exposed the weakness of 'those wooden walls on which the supremacy of Great Britain rested'.[122] In fact magnificent three-decker sailing ships like *Trafalgar* were obsolete. At Sebastopol paddle-steamers had to tow them into position and after the war they were taken out of service to be converted to screw propulsion. Granville had witnessed the end of a naval era.

He himself now took a fresh direction. After being paid off he returned with his family (now including a son) to settle in a fine house in Kingston, Ontario, where he was employed by the Anchor Insurance Agency.[123] He remained a reservist in the Royal Navy, however, and retained the full dress-uniform which has passed down to a descendant, who has posted photographs of its many accoutrements on *Ancestry*. Granville also acted as Treasurer and Secretary of the Cataraqui Cemetery Company. And it was in that same cemetery that he was buried after he 'died suddenly' aged 44 in January 1859. His new life, brought to the premature and unexplained end, was announced in Canadian and Cornish newspapers.[124] Granville's widow lived on in Ontario province where she witnessed the marriage of two of her daughters. A stained-glass window in Toronto's Old City Hall celebrates the contribution that British immigrants, many of them Cornishmen like Granville Moyle, made to the growth and prosperity of Ontario.

'Woodlands' Residence of Mrs Granville Moyle, Kingston, Ontario.

Granville's seafaring brother, Richard Edwards Moyle, also found his way to foreign fields. As an apprentice and, after 1851, a master mariner, he was engaged in 'foreign trade', though his certificate of service does not specify which routes he plied. In

1848 he married the daughter of another Penzance seaman, Jane Painter Millett, with whom he went to live near London's West India Dock, the departure point for many long-distance voyages.[125] From 'mercantile jacks' in Sailortown, the waterfront area so vividly described by Dickens in *Dombey and Son*, the couple undoubtedly heard about the discovery of gold in Victoria, Australia which was attracting migrants from all over the country in the 1850s. This was probably what led Richard to abandon his life as a mariner to seek his fortune. I found the couple listed as a 'Gent' and a 'Lady', unassisted emigrants aged 34 and 33, boarding the *Calphurnia* headed for Melbourne in April 1853 and arriving in the city's Port Phillip in August.[126]

The Moyle name is liberally scattered among the passenger lists of the many ships rushing to Australia that same year – and several can be safely identified as further members of the doctor's family. His nineteen-year-old nephew and apprentice, Granville Borlase Moyle, became part of the 'epidemic of abandonment', giving up his 'irksome' medical studies to follow his 'wandering spirit'. In January 1853 he boarded the *Emigrant* as a cabin passenger, whose arrival was recorded in the *Melbourne Argus* when the ship docked five months later.[127] At about the same time his cousin Thomas Greenway Moyle, the doctor's fifth son, embarked on the *Roxburgh Castle*, which had recently docked after an eventful maiden voyage from Melbourne with seventy passengers and a large freight of gold on board. *The Illustrated London News* reported that: 'On the passage the *Roxburgh Castle* rescued the crew, 21 in number, of a merchant ship on fire, which afterwards burnt to the water's edge.'[128]

This near-disaster is some indication of the many hazards endured on wooden sailing vessels during these Antipodean voyages, which took them around the Cape of Good Hope on the outward journey and Cape Horn on the way home. The *Roxburgh Castle* was herself later wrecked on the Goodwin Sands. The demand for speedier passages inspired a competitive spirit among the captains of these 'clipper' ships, designed as they were to clip over the waves. Thus when Edward Edwards Moyle, the last of the emigrant brothers, made the voyage in 1861 as a second-class cabin passenger aboard the *Swiftsure*, celebrated for living up to her name, he arrived at Port Phillip in three months despite the ship's labouring heavily in 'a hard gale' a few hours out of Plymouth. The Penzance customs clerk had reinvented himself, appearing on the passenger list as a 'trader', and no doubt his hopes were high. After all, the *Swiftsure* (as well as many other vessels) regularly arrived in London laden with 'a large and valuable shipment of gold' along with 'homeward bounders' who had made good.[129]

In reality, historians find, 'the majority of gold seekers were ultimately unsuccessful' and the quest often brought much physical and emotional hardship.[130] A prospector had to apply and pay for a mining licence and claim a patch of ground which might or might not yield rock containing the magical colour. Sometimes nuggets were found on the surface or in the mud at the edge of creeks but more often the search involved the back-breaking drudgery of digging, often aggravated by extreme weather, solitude, hunger, disease and violent conflict with other miners. The four young Moyles who emigrated to the Antipodes met with widely varying fates.

There is no trace of Richard Edwards Moyle among the thousands arriving from all parts of the globe on Victorian gold-fields such as Ballarat and Bendigo. Instead, he is listed on the 1856 Electoral Roll of Pentridge, a suburb of Melbourne best known for its large prison hastily built in 1850 to accommodate the crime wave associated with the gold rush. Richard was employed by the government as an 'overseer' in Pentridge Prison on a salary of £100 a year, which gave him the right to vote – though his wife Jane was not, of course, enfranchised. It's likely that Richard's appointment came about through the influence of John Giles Price, a member of the slave-trading Price family of Trengwainton House in Penzance, who was at that time inspector-general of penal establishments in Victoria. Cornish emigrants tended to stick together even if they came from different backgrounds.

The overseer's job was not an easy one. At this early stage of the prison's development the convicts were housed in insecure wooden stockades and in hulks moored offshore rather than in the regulated, circular Panopticon for which Pentridge later

John Giles Price, 1856.

became famous. Conditions were even more squalid than in the rest of Melbourne, known at that time as 'Smelbourne' because of its pervasive odour of human excrement. Richard probably had supervisory duties both on the hulks and on land, where gangs of convicts were employed to build roads and used every opportunity to attempt escape. The regime imposed by Price was as merciless as his earlier administration of convicts in Van Diemen's Land and Norfolk Island. It aroused bitter resentment among the prisoners as well as questions in the local press. In 1856 the *Melbourne Argus* wrote:

> Is it the fact that the Penal Department is conducted on the principle of excessive and relentless cruelty towards the criminals placed under its management? Are the subordinate officials authorised to practise on the prisoners in their charge experiments of the amount of torture that human nature can bear? Is the Head of the Department authorised to extend the term of imprisonment of refractory criminals at his pleasure, and to subject them to whatever modes of punishment an acutely cruel imagination can devise? Is that functionary, in fact, an irresponsible despot, not less absolute within his own province than an Eastern satrap? These are some of the questions ... eagerly asked by the public at the present moment.[131]

It was in the course of an inquiry set up to answer these questions that a shocking event took place. On 26 March 1857 enraged inmates of the hulks attacked Price with rocks and iron bars, beating him so savagely that he died of his injuries. In the very same month the *Argus* announced another death at Pentridge, that of 'Richard Edwards Moyle, aged 37, third son of Richard Moyle, Esq., surgeon, late of Penzance, Cornwall'. It's probable that he had been smitten by the 'colonial fever' (later identified as typhoid) which often came in with the emigrant ships, festered in the overcrowded conditions of Victoria during the 1850s, and was especially prevalent in penitentiaries. All alone, Jane made the sad journey back to Penzance, where the 1861 Census found her living in respectable Chapel Street with her widowed mother and two spinster sisters – and no children. When she herself died the following year, there was no one left to tell the tragic tale of this fleeting Australian venture.[132]

At the time of Richard's death, his cousin Granville Borlase Moyle was living in Victoria but there is no evidence that he attended the funeral. He himself survived long enough to leave more in the way of a memorial than a bare newspaper announcement. In fact, he became a prominent Victorian citizen whose somewhat embroidered narrative of his life formed the basis of a long obituary in the local press when he died in 1914 at the age of eighty.

One established fact is that by 1856 Granville Borlase had purchased a miner's right and was thereby registered to vote in Moliagul. This was a thriving gold mining village north-west of Melbourne famed for the discovery of the 'Welcome Stranger', the largest nugget ever unearthed.[133] No such luck came Granville's way but he was, by his own account, 'fairly successful' on various diggings before settling down in Kilmore, the oldest inland town in Victoria. Here he married a widow, Mary Ann Painting, and had two daughters as well as a son who died in infancy. He had not made enough in gold to live as a leisured gentleman but nor did he return to the medical profession, preferring 'to please himself what he did for a living'. In 1884 Granville Borlase announced in the *Kilmore Free Press* that he was opening a fruit and grocery store in Sydney Street which would keep 'a good article at a moderate price' under the superintendence of his daughter.[134] He was still a 'dealer' in 1903, according to Kilmore's electoral register, but in 1905 he is listed simply as a labourer.

West side of Sydney Street in Kilmore, Victoria in 1861.

All this was a far cry from the obituary's deferential account of Granville Borlase's lineage, which apparently dated back to 'the time of William the Conqueror'. He was said to possess a family crest with a Latin motto and to be connected to 'members of English society' including the Duke of Argyle. There is no more evidence for such social distinction than there is for Granville Borlase's academic prowess as 'a finished Hebrew scholar'. More realistically, he was recognised as 'one of Kilmore's old identities', 'generous almost to a fault and well respected and esteemed by his acquaintances, of whom he had a wide circle'. He was survived by his daughters, three grandchildren and one great-grandchild – three generations of new Australians.[135]

Thomas Greenway (the fifth son of Dr Richard Moyle) left a rather different mark on his adopted land. He initially described himself as a miner, like most of his fellow emigrants aboard the *Roxburgh Castle*, since he was setting out to dig for gold in Victoria. It seems that he did not strike lucky but nor did he 'disappear in the gold rush' as the family notes state. Instead, he discovered another means of supporting himself, using the painterly skill he shared with at least two of his siblings. Thomas worked as an artist on commission for mining companies which wanted to record their claims, or for private individuals who had hit pay dirt. As he didn't settle down, marry or beget a family T.G. Moyle survives not on electors' lists or official registers but as a signature on the corners of paintings which portray, in scrupulous detail, the rapidly changing Australian scene.

Thomas created, for example, the only pictorial record of one particularly tragic attempt to transform the Outback. In the autumn of 1861, a group of settlers from Victoria led by Horatio Wills trekked to Cullin-la-ringo in Queensland with a long bullock train and 10,000 sheep which they hoped to graze on the 64,000 virgin acres they claimed. The size of the venture aroused the resentment of neighbouring Gayiri Aboriginals, who attacked the party on 19 October, killing nineteen men, women and children, including Wills himself. The massacre was widely reported, especially in the victims' home state, but the newspapers make no mention of a graphic painting of the 'Wills Tragedy', executed for

T. G. Moyle, The Wills Tragedy, *1861.*

H.N. Bailey, a Ballarat resident whose name and address are written on the reverse. It is signed by T.G. Moyle and captioned 'The Arrival of the Neighbouring Squatters, Men collecting and burying the Dead, after Attack by the Blacks on H.R. Wills Esq.

Station Leichhardt District, Queensland'. This event was followed by a more appalling bloodbath. A party of heavily-armed settler vigilantes slaughtered up to 370 Gayiri in what is now seen as 'a pivotal moment' in Queensland's frontier wars.[136] Thomas's painting is now considered an important historical work, although the *Dictionary of Australian Artists* could reveal little about the painter.[137]

The only clue it had about his origins was a water colour painted during the hot and dusty Ballarat summer of December 1866, in which Thomas conjured up the cool blues and greens of a view he had known well as a boy and which was often depicted by his brother John Grenfell: Mounts Bay as seen from Gulval Cairn.[138] It therefore placed Thomas firmly in the bosom of the

T. G. Moyle, Mounts Bay, St Michael's Mount and Penzance.

far-flung Penzance family evoked in this chapter. It reflects a nostalgia for the home country which he shared with many of the recent emigrants he encountered in this part of Australia and it sold for a substantial sum in 1998.

For his bread-and-butter work Thomas travelled around Victoria to carry out commissions, depicting, for example, Great Northern Junction Gold Mining Company's claim at Dead Horse and Ballarat Extension Company's field at Rose Hill. During the 1870s he produced a large view of the Lord Malmsbury Gold

Mining Company's claim at Spring Hill, Creswick and in 1881 a pen, ink and watercolour drawing of Sergeants Freehold Quartz Gold Mining claim at Redan, Ballarat. The latter is a particularly detailed view which illustrates typical features of a mine: a huge pile of the quartz in which gold is often found, the minehead frame flying the company flag, new offices and houses, smoking chimneys and dark clouds which suggest the pollution they generate.[139]

T. G. Moyle, Sergeants Freehold Quartz Gold Mining Company's Claim, Redan, Ballarat, 1881.

Sometimes Thomas was commissioned to paint the more domestic buildings created by those who had made good in the

T. G. Moyle, George Ward's Queensland Hotel, Roma, 1887.

goldfields and wanted to show it. George Ward's Queensland Hotel in Roma is a typical example. Workaday images like this are currently displayed in art galleries and museums, prized for the 'naive charm' with which they convey Australia's gold rush era.[140]

At the time they enabled Thomas Moyle to earn his living though they did not win him the respect of contemporaries. Living in Queensland in his later years he took to painting public events, such as the big handicap at Roma race-course. He sent a photograph of this work to the *Western Star and Roma Advertiser*, which found the scene 'faithfully depicted' and painting 'commendable', adding a patronising regret that the artist had not gained 'the mystic appendage of the Royal Academy'. A year later the newspaper was a little kinder towards 'our district artist, Mr Moyle, who has made himself famous by his representations of the Roma races, local buildings, and the far-famed race for the Salisbury Cup.' It announced a new painting of the Roma Volunteers under review, which was to be raffled 'amongst other gems' the following week.[141] None of these late works seem to be on public view today but they are no doubt treasured in Australian households. When Thomas Greenway Moyle died in Bundaberg, Queensland, in 1892 he was simply listed in the cemetery register as a 67-year-old artist from England. His burial in an unmarked grave suggests a lonely and impoverished death. Like other early Australian painters, whose creations are now valued, he had the misfortune not to be properly appreciated during his lifetime.

The most elusive of the doctor's emigrant sons is the seventh, Edward Edwards Moyle. Luckily his surprising middle name, which comes from his mother's family, helped me to trace him among the many other Edward Moyles inhabiting Cornwall, Australia and New Zealand at this time. As there is no sign of his presence in Victoria after his arrival at Port Phillip in May 1861, I guessed that he decided to seek his fortune in New Zealand. The discovery of gold in Otago on the South Island in the very month of his landing in Australia suggests that he joined thousands of other hopeful prospectors flocking there. Like characters evoked in Rose Tremain's *The Colour*, he would have experienced the 'pure and absolute chaos' of a new gold rush as well as 'the drudgery of the body and of the mind' involved in the struggle to hew gold out of the wilderness. Stocks dwindled after 1864 so that the erstwhile customs clerk had to find other means of supporting himself – for, as other settlers reported, this was a land where 'it was no disgrace to a man to take any kind of work'.[142]

The lengths and depths to which Edward resorted I found in two inquest reports of 1872 and 1873, which give direct and unexpected evidence of his Antipodean life. Both come from the Waikato area in the North Island to which he had obviously travelled in search of employment and they tell a sad story. On 31 October 1872 a coroner's court at Rangiriri heard testimony from a witness named as 'Edward Edwards Vivian Moyle' who had been summoned to attend a sick child 'in the belief that he was a medical man'. He had advised the mother to bathe her son's feet in mustard and water, administer a powder of burnt egg-shell and sugar which he concocted and finally to give him port wine. None of these remedies prevented the eight-year-old boy's death from inflammation of the chest. Edward's sworn deposition claimed that he was a 'legally-qualified medical man but not in practice'. He also said that he had left his diploma from the Royal College of Surgeons in Nelson on South Island.

In explaining that he had not been acting 'as a registered medical practitioner', Edward gave a picture of the life he had been leading in New Zealand:

> I have resided at Mr. Ralph's about four months. I am employed to make bricks. Previous to going to Mr. Ralph's I was employed by Mr. Spencer at Taupiri as a carpenter. I was formerly a private in the 4th Waikato Regiment.

There was clearly plenty of casual labouring work available with the arrival of ever more immigrants and consequent house and road building. This very expansion had led to the 1863-6 Waikato land wars against the indigenous Māori and the forming of militias such as the one Edward claims to have joined. Veterans were entitled to a grant of fifty acres confiscated from the defeated Māori but the land was often swampy and infertile. If Edward had received such a grant he had obviously not succeeded as a farmer and was now masquerading as a doctor, adopting the language and demeanour he had observed in his father's Penzance surgery. In the event the jury did not convict Edward of fraud but did express regret for 'the circumstances which prevented proper medical aid being procured for the deceased'.[143]

Henry Winkelmann, Mount Eden Jail, 1876.

Just seven months later an inquest was held in the same area at the Mount Eden Stockade[144] on Edward Moyle, aged 45, an inmate of the prison, whose age and self-styled previous profession identify him as the doctor's seventh son. It recorded that:

> Deceased had formerly been an apothecary, and was committed by the Waiuku Bench of Magistrates for three months' hard labour, for having no lawful means of support. His entrance to the Stockade took place on May 24, 1873. Captain Eyre, Governor of the Gaol, was sworn, and deposed to deceased being in a filthy and unhealthy state on being received into prison and also to his having been in the hospital nearly the whole of the five weeks he had been under his charge.[145]

The question before the jury was whether the prisoner died as a result of mistreatment or from natural causes.

A fellow inmate swore that despite being in 'a very weak state' Edward had been put to hard labour (drawing the go-cart) and allowed to remain 'in wet clothes under the open shed during the day'. Captain Eyre, on the other hand, testified that Edward had 'received every kindness and attention from the authorities' and a hospital orderly stated that he had 'received every attention from the gaol authorities'. A post-mortem revealed that Edward had died 'from serious apoplexy' and the jury's predictable verdict was that this had not been caused by any ill-treatment in the gaol.[146] The death was registered in Auckland but was not announced in the Cornish or Australian press. Edward's siblings had no way of knowing that he ended his life in a state of starvation and destitution in a New Zealand gaol designed to resemble Dartmoor prison. The family book simply and erroneously notes that he was 'in New Zealand 1884'.

Newspapers in all three places were, however, filled with reports of a court case involving Dr Moyle's youngest son, Rev. Vyvyan Henry Moyle, whose first name Edward had adopted when pretending to be a doctor. If he had been in a fit state to buy and peruse the *Daily Southern Cross* on 1 April 1873 Edward might even have read a report of his brother's trial and conviction. Meanwhile, the other surviving brothers and sisters, Thomas in Australia, Lydia in Portsea, John in the Isles of Scilly, Mary Anne in York and William in Islington, could hardly have missed this sensational story of 'Wholesale Forgery by a Clergyman'. Vyvyan's notoriety also made it possible for me, his descendant and near namesake, to trace the criminal career to which the next chapter is devoted.

Chapter 4

'The Reverend Delinquent'
1861-1908

Rev Vyvyan Henry Moyle m. 1865 Wilhelmina Wade

1 Wilhelmina   2 Vyvyan Henry Copley
b1869   b1872

When Vyvyan travelled from Cleveland to Penzance to attend his mother's funeral on 11 January 1861, he no doubt met those of his surviving siblings who remained in the country; Mary Anne and Edward were still in Penzance while John, William and Lydia did not have too far to come. Despite being the youngest member of the family, the newly ordained curate played a leading role in the gathering. He probably arranged, and could even have conducted, the service at St Mary's Church; he acted as his mother's executor; and he also took it upon himself the day after the burial to add an inscription on the back of John's early painting of Alverton Temporary Church, which had been replaced by St Mary's. He

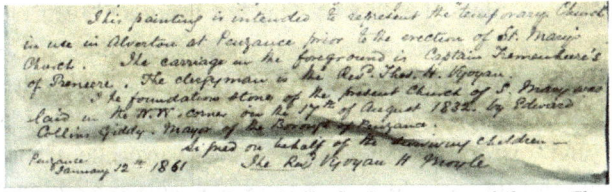

Vyvyan Moyle's inscription on the back of his brother's painting of Alverton Church.

named the owner of the carriage and the clergyman shown in the picture and noted the foundation of the new church in 1832, signing 'on behalf of the surviving children'.[147]

I think Vyvyan further marked the occasion by visiting the innovative photographic studio which had just been set up in Penzance. The Scillonian mariner, John Gibson, used it between voyages to take portraits with a camera said to have been bought abroad.[148] There the clergyman posed in his new vestments for a picture I have long had in my possession and can now place in context. With his luxuriant beard (which was apparently red) he looks considerably older than his twenty-six years and also highly respectable. None of his siblings could have had any cause for concern.

Rev Vyvyan Henry Moyle photographed by John Gibson.

Reports in Northern newspapers certainly give the impression that Vyvyan made an admirable start to his clerical career. He dealt skilfully with the 'subject of total abstinence' at a temperance meeting in Redcar; he delivered 'a popular view of Church Architecture' at Newcastle Church Institute; he accompanied North Ormesby Sunday Scholars on a visit to York where they were 'greatly pleased with what they has heard and seen'; he had a 'large attendance' for his lecture on 'Nineveh and its discovered remains in connection with Holy Scriptures' at Bilsdale; he gave an 'able and masterly' account of the pyramids of Egypt to 'a very large and respectable audience' at the Newcastle Church of England Institute, in which he 'earnestly exhorted his hearers not

'The Reverend Delinquent'

to give way to scepticism'; and he organised an Art and Industry Exhibition in North Ormesby designed 'to improve the tastes of the working-classes'. All this was in addition, as was later to be noted in court, to his presence 'at the bedside of the sick parishioner, at the hospital, or at the humble fireside of the cottager'. In fact, he was seen as 'one of the most esteemed clergymen in Cleveland', noted for his 'warm piety, great ability, zeal, energy and exceeding self-devotion'.[149]

As a curate Vyvyan earned less than £100 a year and yet he managed to give the impression of being 'a man of some wealth', the descendant of an 'old Cornish family, seated for some generations in Penzance'. On the strength of this reputation, as well as his marriage to Irish heiress Wilhelmina Wade in 1865, and his initiation into the Grand Lodge of Freemasons, he mixed 'in close intimacy and friendship with the leading gentlemen of the district'.[150] These probably included Archbishop William Thomson, described by the *Pall Mall Gazette* as 'a man of the world' possessed of the 'pushing ability' to secure elevation to the see of York at the early age of 42. Thomson also had a 'keen interest in social, economic and political questions' and was to be seen 'at every large public meeting in the diocese', such as those addressed by Rev Moyle.[151]

It was certainly through his patronage that in 1868 Vyvyan was appointed vicar of the new parish of Eston, an ironstone-mining township on the outskirts of Middlesbrough. He now had an annual stipend of £290, but this was still insufficient for keeping up the appearances and making the charitable donations expected of clergymen, many of whom fell into debt or bankruptcy. Archbishop Thomson had to confiscate the parishes of at least ten parsons who had accumulated debts ranging from £95 to £10,000.[152] Rev. Vyvyan Moyle obviously wanted to avoid such ignominy but at the same time felt, like the incumbent of Anthony Trollope's *Framley Parsonage*, that 'he was intended by nature for the society of rich people'. As was soon to be revealed, he was prepared to use any means to achieve this end.[153]

Some of his monetary ventures were undoubtedly benevolent. He raised £2,000 to clear the debt of North Riding Infirmary, for example, and 'it was solely through his exertions' that North Ormesby parish gained a new church, 'a handsome brick structure in the Early English style'.[154] At the same time, he lived extravagantly, moving his family into Normanby Manor House, which he filled with luxurious furnishings, a collection of Old Masters and three resident servants.[155] The archbishop's son, Basil, remembered that on his father's official visitation to

Normanby Manor House, now a doctor's surgery and a listed building.

the parish he was met at the station by 'a smart brougham and pair with a liveried footman – the sort of equipage that was beyond the reach of people with an income of less than £5,000 a year'. After that surprise the visitation proceeded normally, with satisfactory replies being given to the archbishop's questions.[156] Vyvyan also had a fashionable address in Hyde Park – though he often stayed in such smart London hotels as the newly-built Langham in Portland Place (featuring a hundred water closets, thirty-six bathrooms and the first hydraulic lifts in England). He received 'honours from various learned societies' and at the same time became involved in numerous business schemes, including the Tees Dock and Railway Company, which he was perfectly able to justify in terms of his social and clerical duties. Chairing a meeting of the Mutual Society in Middlesbrough in June 1872 he explained that 'as a clergyman he believed he was in his proper place in bringing before the public a good society for investors and also for every class of persons who wished to use and gain capital'. After purchasing shares in the Eston iron manufacturers, Messrs Jackson, Gill & Co, he 'advocated the extension of various systems which were projected for the benefit of the lower classes'.[157] It all sounded plausible.

'The Reverend Delinquent'

However, suspicions were aroused by the enormous scale of Vyvyan's investment. On 30 December 1872, as he left Normanby House to catch a train, he was arrested on a charge of forgery. Vyvyan immediately admitted the offence to the police officer, who remembered his exact words: 'I am guilty, Heaven knows. I shall never attempt to deny it. I don't know whatever made me do it.' That same day, while held in a cell beneath Middlesbrough Town Hall, he procured stamped writing paper and penned a letter to Archbishop Thomson, resigning the benefice of Eston, on the grounds that he was 'leaving the district' and referring to the almost 'insuperable' difficulties under which he had laboured. Quick to dissociate himself from the scandalous case and anxious to be spared 'the costly and difficult proceedings necessary for depriving the Vicar of his living', the archbishop at once accepted Vyvyan's resignation.[158]

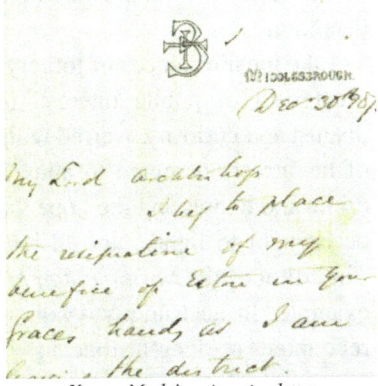

Vyvyan Moyle's resignation letter.

On 7 January 1873 a very crowded court heard the extraordinary charge that the vicar had forged £20,000 worth of share certificates in Jackson, Gill & Co and had used these as security to raise a loan of £11,400 from the Mutual Society's London office. Further evidence of the forgery was produced at several more court hearings 'crammed in every corner' of Middlesbrough Town Hall. Metcalfe & Co, jewellers and engravers, revealed that Vyvyan had pretended that he was about to give a lecture on heraldry, designed a seal and ordered a die; Waterlows stationers said that he had instructed them to print five hundred scrip certificates; and the Secretary of the Mutual Society gave detailed evidence of his offering these bogus documents as security. 'It was all a sham from beginning to end.' The case was then committed to the March York Assizes and the prisoner, already 'much altered in appearance', was refused bail despite pleas that his mental health would be seriously affected by further detention.[159]

Like most instances of forgery at the time, Vyvyan's attracted a great deal of public interest, in which 'sympathy and anger, disgust and curiosity, warred with each other'.[160] The first account of his arrest attempted to allay local fears by playing down the crime and expressing the hope that 'mitigating circumstances will be brought to light'. Not all journalists were so compassionate. The editor of the *Northampton Mercury* took spiteful pleasure, for example, in accusing Vyvyan of an earlier swindle. The paper recounted at length that in 1871 the 'reverend borrower', possessed of 'rather a romantic turn of mind', had raised a loan of £5,000 from a young lady in London whom he entertained to dinner at the Crystal Palace. When inquiries revealed that he did not own the mining shares which he had used as security, an attorney and a detective visited his 'apartments in the fashionable quarter of St James's, finding him in a gorgeous dressing-gown reading the morning papers in slippered ease and comfort'. The lawyer insisted on the money being paid back to the 'fair creditor', even accompanying Moyle by train to Yorkshire, where 'the divine entered a house which was evidently occupied by a wealthy gentleman', emerging eventually with the necessary cheque. The forged share certificates were destroyed and, on this occasion, the 'reverend defaulter' escaped prosecution.[161]

Before the forgery case for which he did stand trial, there were reports which suggested that 'some of the highest dignitaries of the Church' were 'interesting themselves on behalf of the prisoner', who had lived in 'close intimacy and friendship with the leading men of the district'. The *Leeds Mercury* went so far as to speculate under a headline 'Discovery of Accomplices' that others may have been engaged 'in the perpetration of these alleged frauds'. Vyvyan's name was quite often linked with that of the archbishop, who had apparently wanted to appoint him as his

'The Reverend Delinquent'

private secretary and had made 'numerous offers of preferment'. Several newspapers claimed that 'at the time Mr Moyle was apprehended he had in his pocket a letter from the Archbishop of York offering him the rectory of Stokesley at the annual value of £1,200' – though no such document is to be found in the episcopal archive. With such a benefice Vyvyan would have enjoyed an income judged by Trollope as 'sufficient for a gentleman's wants'.[162]

Instead he lost everything. In February 1873 a new incumbent was appointed to Eston parish and Wilhelmina had to move out of Normanby House with her four-year-old daughter and baby son (named respectively after their parents). Advertisements for the well-attended four-day auction of its contents give some indication of the style to which the vicar and his family had become accustomed and contrast sharply with the modest sale which followed his father's death in 1855. The items included first-class furniture, oil paintings, china, cut glass, goose-feather beds, a library of books, a grey pony, a phaeton, a harness and two milch cows. A little later Vyvyan resigned from the honorary post he had held as chaplain to the First North Riding Yorkshire Artillery.[163]

The 'misery which had fallen on his wife and family' was one of the mitigating circumstances pleaded by William Digby Seymour QC in defending Vyvyan when his case was heard at the York Assizes on 24 March 1873. The Irish barrister, who was known for his flamboyant language, also used 'glowing terms' to describe 'the great zeal the prisoner had displayed in his mission work in the borough of Middlesbrough', suggesting that he had in the process over-taxed both his brain and his private resources. As Vyvyan made no attempt to deny the charge of forgery, covering his face with his hands and weeping bitterly throughout, his learned counsel could only plead his disturbed state of mind when he found himself heavily in debt. Neighbouring vicars and the MP for Stockton then testified to Vyvyan's 'high character'.[164]

Seymour's eloquent pleas that his client had acted in a moment of weakness contradicted the evidence. The eminent prosecuting counsel, Fitzjames Stephen QC, needed only a few words to convince the judge that 'the case disclosed great premeditation and contrivance'.[165] Lord Chief Justice Bovill, who had expressed 'his strong disapprobation' of the burst of applause which greeted Seymour's appeal for mercy, summed up the case:

> I find it was a most deliberate act on your part. ... You endeavoured to enrich yourself by speculation, you involved yourself in pecuniary difficulties and embarrassments, and instead of boldly facing these difficulties, you unfortunately resorted to crime to cover your position.

Determined that this case should serve 'as a warning to others', the judge used all the 'terrors and penalties' available to him by inflicting 'a punishment equal to that awarded to those who are not in so favoured a position'.[166] Until 1837 the hangman's noose was still the normal penalty for the forgery of bank notes, shares and wills, a crime which was thought to undermine 'confidence in the practices and institutions that sustained a commercial society'. A reforming Whig government removed the death penalty for forgery despite the misgivings of the Tory leader about 'the facility of committing the crime [and] the difficulty of detection'. It was replaced with transportation to Australia, but this practice came to an end in 1868.[167] Thus Vyvyan Moyle was sent down for seven years of penal servitude. He left the court 'overcome with emotion'.

The sentence involved a nine-month period of 'separate confinement', followed by hard labour at a convict prison and release on licence for up to a quarter of the stretch if the prisoner behaved well. Vyvyan's Home Office record reveals that his seven years' time followed this pattern – and it also provides more personal details than I have found for any of his siblings. A photograph in Pentonville's prison register shows him in his

'The Reverend Delinquent'

prison uniform and he is further described as a fair-complexioned man with brown hair and blue eyes, five feet six inches in height, 159 pounds in weight and proportionate in build. His medical notes further reveal that he was losing his hair ('alopecia'), short-sighted ('myopic'), infested with roundworm ('ascarids'), rheumatic and prone to palpitations. He was also described, somewhat surprisingly, as 'fat' and his general health was 'not very good'. Still, his mind was judged to be 'sound' and his reading and writing skills 'superior'.

Vyvyan's wife was listed (though not named) as next of kin, to be contacted 'care of Mr W. Moyle, 29 Holford Sq. Islington, London'.[168] This is the first sign that Vyvyan had had any recent contact with his siblings and it suggests that his brother William befriended Wilhelmina in her vulnerable situation. He was not in a position to give her much financial help, nor could he have taken the family in, living as he did in one of a series of respectable boarding houses. The address given for William in 1873 is within easy walking distance of Pentonville Gaol, to which his brother was transferred in May.

Prison visits were strictly rationed under the 'separate system' practised in Pentonville, which pioneered this method of incarceration. It was based on the principle that by being deprived of all 'sources of animal pleasure and excitement' the convict would hear 'the still small voice' of conscience and be 'brought to himself'.[169] Inmates were housed in single cells, spending their days in total isolation, silence and useful labour, visited only by the chaplain and prison officers. During exercise periods they

Vyvyan Moyle in Pentonville Prison.

wore peaked caps so that they couldn't see each other and in chapel they sat in separate high-sided stalls from which they could see only the chaplain and their guards. By the time Vyvyan arrived some of these rules had been relaxed after medical officers noticed that 'separate confinement ... had a tendency to produce or to develop mental disease among prisoners.[170] He may therefore have been spared the peaked cap and have attended chapel in more normal circumstances. But he would still have spent nearly all his time alone in his cell, doing his assigned work as a tailor and reading the Bible. Home Office records show that during his time at Pentonville Vyvyan was allowed to receive correspondence as well as two visits from his wife, who had found accommodation in the area. His conduct was described as 'very good'.

Once this phase of his correction was completed, in January 1874, Vyvyan was taken to the public-works prison on Portland Island to work alongside other offenders in the hard productive labour which was an intrinsic part of his sentence. Inmates had already built the island's colossal breakwater and were now engaged in digging tons of Portland stone a week from quarries owned by the Admiralty. This dangerous, back-breaking work was enforced by means of iron discipline, which provoked frequent attacks on warders similar to those witnessed by his brother Richard at Pentridge Prison in Australia. Soon after Vyvyan's arrival, for example, there was a minor mutiny on Good Friday, in which ten prisoners rushed guards as they were marched in from exercise. Deaths among inmates were frequent in this 'heart-breaking, soul-enslaving,

Victorian photograph depicting hard labour at Portland quarry.

brain-destroying hell upon earth' and they were more likely to occur among 'educated men of sedentary habits ... than the uneducated of the labouring classes'. Such was the verdict of a Medical Officer submitted to an 1878 investigation into penal servitude, which heard further evidence that the system bore more heavily on 'gentleman' convicts than on others.[171] This may well have been the case with the Rev Moyle but he would not have been able to express his misery in the censored letters he was permitted to write to his wife.

A letter from Wilhelmina Moyle to the governor of Portland on 15 July 1875 reveals that Vyvyan was now entitled to 'a visit every four months' but claims that she had 'neither strength nor means' to make the journey as frequently as that from her new London address. Not having seen her husband since the previous October, she requested double time for the visit she was due to make 'as the journey is so long and I cannot go again this year'. She was granted a forty-five-minute slot and travelled to Portland on 20 July 'owing to the kindness of the Rev George Wilkinson who pays [for] my journey'. When she got there it seems that the couple did not have a great deal to say to each other, as the prison's careful records show that only twenty-five minutes were taken. Wilhelmina visited her husband once more during his time in Portland, perhaps with help from the same kindly vicar, who had visited Vyvyan himself in January 1875.[172]

In the event Moyle was spared prolonged tortures at Portland. In February 1876 a surgeon's report found him in a 'delicate' state of health, suffering from 'chronic rheumatism and ascarids' and 'totally unfit for any public works'. He was transferred to Woking Male Invalid Prison, established in 1859 to treat those weakened or injured by hard labour – or, in some cases, of self-harm. In one of the 'large and lofty' cells of 'Woking Palace', as it was often termed, Vyvyan was set to work at the more congenial task of bookbinding.[173] Here it was much easier for him to maintain contact with Wilhelmina, who paid ten visits and kept up a regular correspondence. She must have known about, and perhaps even encouraged, a petition organised by some of Vyvyan's friends in July 1877, seeking to secure a free pardon or remission of his sentence. They argued that 'he had no intention to defraud' and that his mental and physical health were impaired by prison. The Home Office ordered a report on the prisoner's condition, on the basis of which the Home Secretary did not see fit to 'advise any interference with the sentence passed'. But unlike other prisoners who recuperated in Woking, he was not sent back to Portland. Eventually, Vyvyan's consistent record of very good or exemplary conduct earned him the right to release on licence in October 1878. He had served a term of five and a half years.[174]

The prison authorities were not alone in being convinced that Vyvyan was a reformed character. There are accounts, notably by Archbishop Thomson's son Basil, that a 'florid man in clerical dress', easily recognised as Rev Moyle by his red beard, visited Bishopthorpe Palace in York soon after his release. Whether or not he was forgiven his sins, Vyvyan remained an ordained clergyman of the Church of England and it was even claimed later that 'he obtained a curacy in Berkshire within one year of the expiration of his sentence'. However, the census of 1881 describes him as a 'clergyman without cure of souls' living with his wife and children at Brook House in Burghfield, Berkshire, next door to labourers and gardeners. This would suggest that he was an unemployed vicar; yet the emphatic crossing-out of this description casts a veil of mystery over his record.[175]

If Vyvyan was receiving no income from the Church of England he could still hope to live off his wife's remaining resources, over which the law gave him control. It is true that the Married Women's Property Act of 1870 had allowed married women to keep their own wages, investments and legacies – but it did not apply retrospectively: existing wives like Wilhelmina remained under 'coverture' with no property rights and no legal responsibility for their children. This situation was just about to change as a result of a determined feminist campaign. A second act in 1882 rendered every married woman 'capable of acquiring, holding, and disposing by will or otherwise, of any real or personal property as her separate property'. Wives also gained equal responsibility for the maintenance of their children. Loyal as Wilhelmina had been during her husband's imprisonment, she took advantage of her new-found financial independence in the 1880s to leave Vyvyan and to set up her own household with her son and daughter in Bexhill.[176]

The resourceful priest soon found other means of support. In 1885 the Bishop of Oxford was sufficiently convinced of his contrition to appoint him to St Clement at Ashampstead in Berkshire. But Vyvyan was disappointed to find, as he explained in his *Notes on the Ecclesiastical History of Ashampstead* (1895), that both the population of the parish and its glebe lands were 'greatly diminished', so that his stipend was 'miserably low, not £70 per annum, out of which have to come rates, taxes and vicarage repairs, and even some portion of the tithe is very irregularly paid'. This was not enough to satisfy a man of Vyvyan's compulsive extravagance but luckily he found a wealthy, 65-year-old widow to help out. Emma Porteous from Gibraltar, who is described as his cousin in the 1891 census but is not to be found in the Moyle family tree, moved into the vicarage and apparently put her considerable means at his disposal. There is, however, no evidence for the vicar's claim that he made 'on an average £250 a year by literary work' for the nine-page booklet on Ashampstead was his only publication. It's true that he had discovered some remarkable but 'much injured' thirteenth-century frescoes in the nave, which had been plastered over during the Reformation, but this work can hardly have been a bestseller – though he promised that a large parochial history was on the way.[177]

The statement about Vyvyan's literary earnings was made before a bankruptcy court in November 1894 and was quoted in an article on 'The church scandal at Ashampstead' in the monthly periodical *Truth*, which regularly revealed frauds. The article, which appeared in January 1899, outlined the whole history of this 'irreclaimable scoundrel'. It asserted that the vicar, who 'had never resided in the parish for more than a few weeks in succession', had reduced Mrs Porteous to a state of 'abject poverty ... having scarcely a rag to her back, being partially crippled, covered with sores, and half starved'. Furthermore, he had run up large debts and spent forty-two days in a debtors' prison, with parole on Sundays so that he could take a service – at one of which he preached a sermon based on the text: 'owe no man anything'. Now he was being hounded by City moneylenders such as 'the notorious Victor Honor' for a sum of £625. Like other journals which reported the case, *Truth* was unable to tell how or whether Vyvyan's bankruptcy was resolved. But it held the Bishop of Oxford responsible for allowing a man with such a record to occupy a benefice:

> Unless the Bishop of Oxford lives in his palace at Cuddesdon with his eyes and ears closed to all that is going on in his diocese, some rumours of the scandal at Ashampstead must surely have reached him years ago. ... Many will agree that such neglect of duty is far more scandalous, and far more mischievous to the Church, than ... illegalities in matters of ritual.[178]

The bishop in question was the eminent historian William Stubbs, who may well have been distracted by writing his weighty *Constitutional History of England* (1891-98); but a month after the article appeared he instructed the Archdeacon of Berkshire to conduct an inquiry. Vyvyan chose not to appear on the grounds that he would probably be arrested 'owing to various writs for rates and taxes that were out against him'. A former churchwarden at Ashampstead, who had resigned in disgust, confirmed that 'since Whitsuntide ... there had been no services on eleven Sundays, including Christmas Day'. The vicar had even failed to turn up for funerals so that on one occasion 'the corpse was left in the road for four hours till a neighbouring clergyman arrived'. Another witness spoke of his connection with the local Beekeepers' Association, of which he had been Honorary Secretary and Vice-President; he had apparently 'obtained honey for sale but did not account for the proceeds'. Even more seriously, it emerged that 'money received for the restoration of the church and the harvest festival was not paid over'. This must refer to the donations made by generous parishioners 'in these days of agricultural depression', for which he had expressed 'warm thanks' in his booklet.[179] The evidence provided sufficient grounds for Bishop Stubbs to deprive Vyvyan of the benefice later that year. When the 1901 Census was compiled he was living in Wood Green near Alexandra Palace, registered as a clergyman of the Church of England but apparently without a parish. 82-year-old Emma Porteous was under the same roof, still listed as his cousin and described as 'living on own means', reduced though these evidently were by the depredations described by *Truth*.

Vyvyan's immediate family had spent the 1890s more fruitfully. His son, Vyvyan Henry Copley Moyle, had taken a degree in Modern History at Lincoln College, Oxford, financed presumably by the newly independent Wilhelmina. Despite the scandal which by now surrounded his Christian names and surname, he had gained a curacy in Cheshire and was currently vicar of Horsham, where he dropped the Vyvyan from his name in the census return, obviously hoping to disassociate himself from his father. He headed a household consisting of his mother and his 31-year-old sister Wilhelmina, who never married. Like Grace Crawley, daughter of the Barsetshire curate accused of theft, she bore the stigma of 'papa's sorrow and disgrace'. 'By the stern laws of the world,' writes Trollope, 'the son and daughter must pay for the offence of the father or mother.'[180]

As the century ended and a new monarch came to the throne, seventy-year-old Vyvyan had nowhere to turn. An undischarged bankrupt with a criminal record and writs out against him all over the place, he could no longer borrow and there was no social security available apart from the dreaded workhouse. All his siblings had died by this time, apart from 74-year-old William, who had retired from the bank and was boarding with two spinster governesses in Dorking. William's pension would hardly have enabled him to rescue his brother.[181] By hook or by crook Vyvyan survived until 1905 when his name hit the headlines as the participant in another major fraud.

The story was especially newsworthy because of the involvement of Vyvyan's partner in crime, Charles Deville Wells, celebrated in music-hall song as 'The Man Who Broke the Bank at Monte Carlo'. Wells was a swindler and bogus inventor who had gambled at the roulette table with his ill-gotten gains in 1891, winning £40,000 in five days and jeopardising the casino's financial security. Over the next thirteen years he spent the money on such items as a luxury yacht complete with ballroom, gambled again and lost, went bankrupt, devised further fraudulent schemes and served eight years' penal servitude in Portland Prison. Thus Wells, who was now known as William Davenport, found that he had plenty in common with Vyvyan Moyle when they met on London's South Bank in 1904. They soon fell into discussion about an exciting new venture.

Together they formed a company called the South and South-West Coast Steam Trawling and Fishing Syndicate. Vyvyan was a plausible director since, as he explained to potential investors, he 'was born near an important marine fishery centre and so from childhood knew the lucrative nature of the industry'. He even claimed to have had yachting and trawling experience, for which there is no evidence. But it was his clerical background which was especially useful to Davenport, who reckoned that his cassock and title would inspire trust. In reality the syndicate had no assets other than two unseaworthy vessels and a rented office in Stamford Street containing 'a ship's wheel, fishing nets and a sea of literature'. On this flimsy basis it advertised extensively in newspapers, inviting the public to buy shares on which healthy profits were promised from the sale of fish for human and animal consumption.[182]

One of the pair's publicity stunts was performed at a stand in the 1905 Naval, Shipping and Fisheries Exhibition commemorating the centenary of Trafalgar.

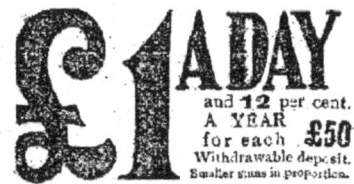

Advertisement placed in Daily Mirror, *17 July 1905.*

With the aid of a Japanese doll, Vyvyan demonstrated an artificial respiration machine designed by Davenport. According to an accompanying leaflet written by a doctor, this could restore life to 'apparently dying (and even actually dead) beings'. This remarkable claim, as well as Vyvyan's 'weighty manner and clerical dress', apparently impressed spectators. Those who made further inquiries received a glossy pamphlet and a hand-written letter from the vicar, urging them to invest: 'The profits are very good and with good reason, for there is *no rent to pay for the sea* and no stock to buy or feed. The fish feed themselves and are *awaiting capture*.' Vyvyan would imply that he himself had bought shares in the scheme and had persuaded 'old and valued friends', including a viscount and a prominent member of the City of London Corporation, to do the same. Further to demonstrate his credentials, he mentioned a book he was writing and expressed the syndicate's charitable intention to sell 'snacks of fish to poor people in London'.[183]

Such letters, as well as personal meetings with the two promoters in Stamford Street, proved so persuasive that by the autumn of 1905 they had sold £5,000 worth of shares, though these were recorded in no account books. A dressmaker from Tonbridge Wells, for example, sent Davenport £50 in £5 notes, practically the whole of her savings. She confessed that it was

Moyle's letter which had convinced her: 'I am a member of the Church of England and the fact that he was a clergyman influenced me a great deal.'[184]

Soon, however, newspapers began to investigate the syndicate, expressing a gleeful delight in what they uncovered. A correspondent of the *Financial News* visited the company's office and found everything 'extremely fishy', while another journalist discovered that the 'picturesque address *Sea Shell*' given in Davenport's letters was in fact 'an empty house – or an empty shell'. But no reporter linked either man to his disreputable past until 9 November, when another article in *Truth*, entitled 'Fisher of Men', reminded its readers of the revelations about Moyle's career it had published in 1899, characterising him as 'a scoundrel of the very blackest type'. As both pieces were written by the magazine's owner and editor, the Radical politician Henry Labouchere, it might be thought that they were part of an anti-clerical campaign. But, while there was no independent evidence of Moyle's 'robbery and desertion' of 'helpless old' Mrs Porteous, there could be no doubt about his fraud, bankruptcy and neglect of parochial duty, all of which had been upheld by a court of law or ecclesiastical commission. It was this record which, Labouchere suggested, should prompt the police to do 'a little fishing in Stamford Street on their own account'.[185]

That is just what happened the very next day. Keeping watch on the premises, Detective-Inspector Knell saw Vyvyan emerge, followed him and arrested him on a charge of conspiracy to defraud. As several newspapers reported, the vicar's response was to blame everything but himself: 'I expect "Truth" is the cause of this trouble. Why don't you arrest Davenport? He is the head of the concern.' He refused to give an address and when searched was found in possession of three £5 notes, £4 in gold and £50 worth of money orders – as well as a copy of the article 'Fisher of Men'. Davenport was indeed arrested after a search of the office 'failed to show that any genuine business had been carried out'.[186] Both the accused were remanded before an initial hearing later in the year at Tower Bridge Police Court, where they continued to argue that the syndicate had been a genuine fishing business. By now it had become known that Davenport was none other than 'Monte Carlo Wells' and the case attracted increasing press attention all over the world as the pair awaited trial at the Old Bailey.[187]

THE MAN WHO BROKE THE BANK AT MONTE CARLO.
William Davenport, of Gambling Fame, and the Clergyman Who Is Accused of Being Associated with Him in a Shady Get-Rich-Quick Scheme.

The two defendants in court.

On 5 February 1906 four witnesses gave detailed testimony about how they had been persuaded by the defendants to buy shares in what seemed a genuine company with a fleet of vessels, accounts of previous profits, authentic-looking mortgage bonds and an impressive list of investors. They had even received a few instalments of interest. But by now it had become clear that the ships had never been to sea, that there were no balance-sheets, that the bonds were worthless, that payments simply came from other people's deposits and that both men were undischarged bankrupts. In the end Davenport pleaded guilty to 'obtaining moneys and securities by false pretences with intent to defraud' and Moyle simply to conspiracy. For these crimes they were sentenced respectively to three years' penal servitude and eighteen months' hard labour. The judge added that he was so horrified by the re-admission to the Church of a convicted felon like Moyle that 'but for his age' he would have pressed for a more serious charge than conspiracy.[188]

The two convicts were taken from the court to their respective prisons, Davenport to Dartmoor, a forbidding edifice providing full penal servitude, and Vyvyan to Wandsworth, designed on the separate system principle. The Governor of Dartmoor Prison at this time was none other than Basil Thomson, who came to like his new inmate. He thought Davenport 'the pleasantest and most unselfish of rascals', and wondered why he had been given 'the heavier sentence of the two'.[189] However, the eighteen-month term in Wandsworth certainly took its toll on the septuagenarian Moyle.

It's true that the Prison Reform Act of 1898 had mitigated the 'hard labour, hard fare, hard bed' regime publicised by Oscar Wilde who spent two years in Pentonville, Wandsworth and Reading gaols. Vyvyan did not have to do hours of pointless labour on a treadmill or a hand crank; instead, he worked on more productive tasks such as shoe-making, book-binding or tailoring. But once again he was consigned to silent separation, despite evidence that the system frequently drove prisoners mad. Discipline was still so rigid that William Morrison, the deputy chaplain of Wandsworth, concluded that 'self-respect is systematically destroyed and self-expression prevented by every phase of prison existence', so that the inmate was rendered 'less fit for useful social life'.[190]

Morrison undoubtedly got to know Vyvyan, who conformed to this judgement after being released from Wandsworth. A story published in a Queensland newspaper in December 1907 indicates that he adopted an alias and sank to new depths:

> An astounding career as clergyman and criminal is that of George Newstead, 74, who, wearing clerical attire, was charged at Clerkenwell on Friday with trespassing on the property of the Midland Railway Company and annoying passengers. Mr Crimp, who prosecuted, said that the prisoner was warned off the station but he returned and accosted a passenger, telling him that he was a clergyman at St Albans, and had no money for his return fare. Detective-Sergeant Pike [told the story of the Fishing Syndicate trial and revealed that] Newstead was then known as the Rev. Vyvyan Henry Moyle.[191]

Vyvyan did not, of course, have a parish in St Albans and appears to have possessed no home or means of support. Who knows how

'The Reverend Delinquent'

he spent the next few months before April 1908, when he was admitted by the police to Westminster Union Workhouse and discharged shortly afterwards to the Cleveland Street Sick Asylum? This pattern was repeated in August, with an admission to Southwark Union workhouse and a transfer to the Infirmary.[192] On both occasions he was described as ill.

The most puzzling entry in the workhouse records appears in the column on the Southwark entry form headed 'Relations or Friends'. Clearly and fully listed are Vyvyan's wife Wilhelmina Charlotte, described as elderly and living with her daughter Wilhelmina Charlotte Elizabeth and her son, Rev Vyvyan Henry Copley Moyle, at Iping Rectory, near Midhurst in Sussex, all of which is confirmed by the 1911 Census. The elder Vyvyan must have supplied these details during an interview with the master and they show that he was in some kind of contact with his wife and offspring. What they don't reveal is whether he received any assistance from them in his dire need. On a stipend of £240 a year the rector of Iping could not have provided much financial aid. Nor could he have taken the disgraced clergyman into the commodious rectory without scandalising both parishioners and church dignitaries. But perhaps the old vicar was beyond help, prison having rendered him 'unfit for the tasks and duties of life'. It seems that all he could do was to wander the streets of London, seeking refuge in its workhouses and infirmaries along with the city's numberless down-and-outs. He was still in Southwark Infirmary when he died on 12 September 1908 of diabetes and an abscess on his foot; the death was registered not by his son but by the superintendent.

Vyvyan Henry Copley Moyle, Rector of Iping 1902-12.

Vyvyan was buried in the leafier and quieter setting of

Brookwood Cemetery in Surrey, very close to Woking Invalid Prison in which he had once been confined. It is the largest necropolis in the country, established in 1849 to accommodate the surplus of London's deceased population. It had its own railway station next to Waterloo and dedicated trains carried the coffins in first-, second- or third-class carriages. Third-class funerals were designed for those buried at parish expense who were allowed no permanent memorials. This was the fate of Vyvyan Henry Moyle, whose body was borne to its final resting-place on 16 September 1908. Contrary to the company's official policy, he was buried in a mass grave with five other paupers in one of the areas reserved for Southwark parishes.[193] Relations could pay to upgrade a third-class grave if they wished to erect a memorial but Vyvyan's wife, son and daughter did not choose to do this. Nor is there any evidence that they ever visited the green pastures in which the black sheep of the family now lay. Instead, the virtuous son left the country to become Chaplain of Hong Kong Cathedral. Over a period of twenty-five years in the colony Rev H. Copley Moyle 'endeared himself to members of all communities', 'never missed a duty at Sunday service' and became an 'energetic golfer and tennis player'.[194]

Coffin ticket for Brookwood Cemetery.

There is no mention of the imprisonment and destitution of Edward or Vyvyan Moyle in the family book compiled by their niece Emma. Either she didn't know about these poignant sagas or she thought them too shameful to include. I have reconstructed them from census and home office records as well as from press reports which were widely available at the time. Accounts of Vyvyan's first trial appeared, for example, in the *Royal Cornwall Gazette* and the *Western Daily Press*. In the 1870s and 1880s John Grenfell Moyle, who was Vyvyan's oldest surviving brother and Emma's father, must have read such articles, busy though he was

'The Reverend Delinquent'

as a Justice of the Peace and the only doctor on the five Isles of Scilly. We can only wonder whether his magisterial or his medical judgement prevailed when considering the newspapers' stern view that 'the continual putting forward of insanity ... as the invariable cause of crime is a most dangerous principle in practice, whatever psychological arguments may be adduced in its favour.' Contemplating his fall from grace, the benevolent doctor had, I suspect, some sympathy with 'the reverend delinquent'.[195]

Chapter 5

Island Duties and Delights
1840s and 1850s

Edwin Lewis Davis m. Jane Legg 1816-1847
|
1 William Legg   2 Mary Jane   3 Thomas Legg
b1838   b1840   b1841
4 Edwin Lewis 5 Sarah Elizabeth 6 Jemima Ann
b1843   b1845   b1841

By the time John Moyle took up his medical practice in 1849 Edwin Davis had already served ten years on St Agnes as Assistant and, from 1843, Principal Keeper of the lighthouse.[196] As it was a land light, Edwin lived on the island all the time with his family rather than sailing out for spells of duty at sea. Even so, St Agnes was an isolated station and Edwin would be fortunate if he could avoid the troubles that, as we have seen, afflicted some of his predecessors.

Conditions at the lighthouse had improved somewhat over the years. It had now been fitted with thirty lamps with parabolic reflectors, revolving every minute and giving a bright light. On a visit to St Agnes in 1801 the lighthouse engineer Robert Stevenson judged them to be the 'most advanced in design and efficiency' and claimed that they made the keeper's work 'very easy'. Yet, as Edwin later explained to Royal Commission inspectors, 'the care and labour required about thirty different

Island Duties and Delights

lamps and a like number of silvered reflectors' was incomparably greater than that of 'arranging the lamp and dusting a glass lens'.[197] Stevenson also failed to mention a grisly hazard noted by the vicar of St Agnes, George Woodley, in his *View of the Scilly Isles*: the large number of birds attracted by the bright lantern which 'fall stunned or lifeless in the gallery'.[198] Soon after Edwin's arrival rape seed oil replaced the foul and smoky whale oil previously burned by the lamps. But despite the greater efficiency of the light, the Western Rocks continued to pose a threat to those 'that go down to the sea in ships'. This was made all too apparent in a disaster graphically recorded by Rev Woodley as well as by many newspapers.

On 4 January 1841 in the midst of a terrific storm the captain of the *Thames* steamer from Dublin spotted the revolving Scilly light but mistook it for the static Longships Light off Land's End. As a result he changed course and ran into Jacky's Rock three miles from St Agnes. The alarm was raised and a pilot boat left the island with 'ten brave fellows' ready to render assistance, while 'crowds of women were out on the hills, wringing their hands, and loudly bewailing the anticipated fate of their nearest relatives'. A female passenger and two stewardesses were hauled off the *Thames* and taken amid 'a heavy gale with very severe hail storms' to St Agnes, where they found refuge in the lighthouse. Before any further help could reach the remaining sixty-four crew and passengers:

> They perished under the most heart-rending circumstances; near the land, and in the view of a great number of their sympathizing fellow creatures, who could only deplore a catastrophe which it was out of the power of man to avert or mitigate.[199]

The following day boats were able to reach the uninhabited island of Rosevear where they retrieved several dead bodies among the wreckage and rescued a single survivor, a seaman who had found shelter in a porter barrel and was able to explain the circumstances in which the *Thames* was lost. Mary Meyler, one of the rescued stewardesses, recognised some of the corpses, which included the wife of a soldier and her 'little infant which she was suckling'. From the lighthouse, where she was 'receiving every kindness', she wrote to her parents assuring them of her own safety and asking them to pray for the valiant captain of the *Thames*, who had insisted on women being rescued first. Although the keepers had not braved the dangers which earned medals for the pilot boat's crew, they were actively involved in a calamity which their light had not been able to prevent. They and their families gave shelter and comfort to the survivors and helped to prepare the victims' bodies for their passage to St Mary's for burial in the churchyard. Later on, the ship's figurehead of Old Father Thames was salvaged and is now displayed among many other such sad mementoes in Tresco Abbey gardens. Shipwrecks were part of the tenure of Edwin's existence during his long occupation of the lighthouse and he was to witness many another such 'melancholy occurrence'.[200]

Figurehead of SS Thames.

The more normal duties of land-based keepers were spelt out in 1839 by the Secretary of Trinity House. They were to 'light the lamps every evening at Sunsetting and keep them burning bright and clear till Sunrising' while maintaining 'perpetual watch throughout the night', with no bed or sofa allowed in the watch room. During the day their jobs were to clean and polish the lamps, ensure 'economy and good management' of the oil and other stores, see to any repairs and keep 'a journal of all occurrences and observations'. I witnessed for myself the enduring stipulation of 'a proper discretion in the admission of Visitors to view the Establishment' when in 2022 I went to visit my distant cousin who lives in the lighthouse. It was only our shared relationship to Edwin Davis which persuaded him to allow me to mount three narrow staircases to the comfortless, stone-floored watch room.[201]

The author with her cousin Francis Hicks in St Agnes Lighthouse.

Trinity House's final instruction to keepers was to observe a 'constant habit of cleanliness and good order' as well as 'temperance and morality', endeavours in which Edwin was aided by his wife Jane (née Legg) from St Mary's. Their life was a struggle, even though Edwin's modest wage of £65 a year was supplemented by free accommodation, 'a suit of clothes annually, and coal, oil and furniture for dwelling'.[202] On this he had to maintain three children under two and three more born within six years of his appointment. Yet he was better off than most of the 250 or so inhabitants of St Agnes, who had to depend very much on their own resources. They ground corn with round stone hand-mills, grew potatoes and other vegetables, caught fish, kept pigs, gathered bracken to use as fuel, made and repaired their clothes and prepared smelly fish or seal oil to provide artificial light.[203] A spot of quiet beach-combing or smuggling may have helped them to make ends meet.

The rigours of Scillonian life proved too much for Jane, who fell seriously ill in July 1847, causing Edwin to be granted a month's leave of absence. It was a busy time at the lighthouse because of a welcome decision by Trinity House to replace the shared cottage judged by one predecessor as 'little better than a hogstye', with a pair of two-bedroom residences attached to the lighthouse for the keeper and his assistant. Designed as 'substantial, neat and comfortable' dwellings with rubble-stone walls and no 'unnecessary expenditure for ornament' and built at a cost of £986, they were more commodious than most homes on

The cottages attached to St Agnes Lighthouse, with 20th-century conservatory.

the islands. Construction work was delayed by disputes with the Duchy of Cornwall over the rent to be paid by Trinity House. Furthermore, the builders made a gruesome discovery – a skeleton buried at a depth of two or three feet. There was no official inquest but older islanders recognised peculiarities of its teeth and identified it as that of Keeper Elias Carter who had disappeared in 1809. They concluded that he had been murdered by his quarrelsome colleague, Thomas Kirby, and hastily interred near the lighthouse – but the truth of the matter will never be known.[204]

Sad to say, Jane herself died on 22 October 1847 at the age of thirty-two without being able to benefit from the new accommodation. Edwin now had to cope not only with his lighthouse duties but also with all the household chores, as well as moving his family into the completed cottage. His first recourse was Trinity House to whom he wrote 'praying some assistance'. Their donation of £5 helped him to meet the costs of Jane's medical treatment and of a simple country funeral and burial in St Mary's churchyard.[205]

Edwin may also have prayed for help at the 'place of worship' he was required by Trinity House to attend 'upon each Sunday in turn'. He had the choice of St Agnes parish church, rebuilt by the SPCK in 1817, or the Bible Christian chapel, both of which had large regular congregations. The Bible Christian movement, a West Country offshoot of Methodism, benefited from the active participation of women whom they often employed as itinerant preachers. Since it was 'such a strange thing for a woman to preach', they always attracted crowds, as did Mary Ann Wherry of Tintagel who was sent to the Isles of Scilly in the 1820s. Her sermons on St Mary's and the off-islands were clearly effective: 'The Word of God came from her lips with startling power to many as she told them of a living Christ and a personal salvation.' To consolidate her mission and those of other brave women, male ministers were dispatched 'to oversee the work' in Scilly.[206]

Keeper Edwin Davis in the 1850s

As the Davis name appears in a list of over forty Bible Christians on St Agnes Edwin clearly attended their chapel, which was housed in a dilapidated former school room. There, like others of the faithful, this 'larger than life', quick-tempered man renounced the Devil and all his works, among them 'drunkenness, swearing and sabbath-breaking'. Brother Way who visited the island in January 1842 was impressed by the sobriety he found:

> I am happy to say that on St Agnes Island there are only three adults and four children but what are Teetotallers. Not a drop of intoxicating liquor, as far as I can learn, has been drunk by the inhabitants during the Christmas. Never was such a Christmas spent on the island before, since the memory of man.[207]

If this verdict was correct there would have been precious little trade at the three public houses which have been identified by a local historian but not identified as such by the census-takers in 1841. Whether or not Edwin imbibed any of the 'spirituous or malt liquor' still free from tax at this time, he was sufficiently devout to gain the approval of the twenty-two-year-old Bible Christian missionary, Martha Hutchings.[208]

Martha was born as one of the ten children of a poor agricultural labourer in Seavington St Mary, Somerset. Her adult accomplishments suggest that she had received some education, probably at one of the small day schools in the village, supplemented perhaps by the Methodist or Church of England Sunday School. During the Bible Christians' Crewkerne Mission to bring the 'poor and wretched sinners' of that neighbourhood to the 'means of grace', Martha was converted at the age of seventeen.[209] She became 'very earnest in her work' and in 1847 was engaged on a two-year mission to the Isles of Scilly when she encountered the recently widowed Edwin and was moved by his 'great distress'. 'After much prayer and in the full assurance that it was of the Lord' she married him on 22 December 1847, just two months after the death of Jane. As far as Edwin was concerned, 'Martha must have seemed like an answer to a prayer,' wrote her great-great-granddaughter. She became the affectionate wife described by a son-in-law: a 'cheerful and large-hearted' woman who discharged the 'duties of her responsible and difficult position' with 'discretion and kindness'. Together she and Edwin became known as 'hearty supporters of the cause'.[210]

It was not until September 1850 that the Duchy of Cornwall signed the lease for the new keepers' premises and the couple could move in, along with Edwin's six children. Aged between twelve and five, they are described as 'scholars' in the 1851 Census, which meant that they went down the hill to the tiny St Agnes School. Lord Proprietor Smith stipulated that parents paid a penny a week for a child going to school and tuppence if he or she stayed away. Unsurprisingly, therefore, an inspection in 1848 found that most Scillonian children between the ages of two and thirteen were at school. The 'intelligent and well-informed'

Island Duties and Delights

young master on St Agnes described by Her Majesty's inspector had been trained under the new pupil-teaching scheme at Norwood in London and was 'extremely fond of teaching and of his children'. Even so, the results he was able to achieve with them were somewhat mixed:

> English Grammar soundly taught to the first class. History, geography, and arithmetic, fair; writing from dictation fair; vocal music well taught; religious instruction is principally Bible history.[211]

By the standards of the day, Edwin's offspring had a good start in life.

Since no servant is mentioned in the census Martha evidently did the cooking, cleaning, washing, mending and nursing for the whole family, like so many other working-men's wives. But eleven-year-old Mary Jane, with 'ready obedience to [her stepmother's] wishes', helped in the house and the older boys, William and Thomas, no doubt carried out heavier tasks such as fetching coal, growing vegetables and fishing.[212] Their assistance was particularly necessary at the time the census was taken in 1851, when Martha was listed, along with the two babies born since her marriage, at her parents' home in Somerset. It's not known whether she managed another visit or whether she ever saw Beulah House, a tiny chapel built by the Bible Christians of Seavington in 1859.

Bible Christian Chapel, Seavington St Mary, 1859.

Meanwhile John Moyle had arrived in St Mary's to take up his post as the sole doctor on the Scillies. He made a calm midsummer crossing from Penzance in June 1849 to be greeted with a panorama he would never forget. Forty years later he recalled:

> The islands resting so picturesquely and reflecting their charming tints in a quiet sea, gilded with a sunset glow, looking so beautiful that I exclaimed "These are the Golden Hesperides! – the Eldorado of my imaginings!"[213]

His romantic response helps to explain why he stayed for so long and spent so much time depicting the beauties of the islands in paint.

John Grenfell Moyle's house in The Parade, St Mary's.

He soon set up home in the Parade, St Mary's, where he is listed among the tradesmen (rather than gentry) in the local Directory.[214] The spacious Regency house (now divided into flats) provided plenty of room for his surgery and a resident housekeeper. The Parade also afforded the 'cheerfulness and comfort' noted by Rev Isaac North in his 1850 guidebook. From here John looked after the health of the residents of all five islands, sailing between them 'attired in a pilot's jacket and large boots and carrying his medical instruments and medicines in his pocket'.[215] In addition he tended the soldiers of the Royal Invalid Artillery, who had retired for light duties at St Mary's Garrison, as well as sailors from vessels docked in the port or wrecked offshore.

He had some idea of what to expect as he had supplied Rev North with records to help him assess the medical condition of the islands. The mortality registers for 1838-47 showed that they were 'remarkably free' of typhus. Other epidemics also occurred less frequently than on the mainland, though they killed 42 people

Island Duties and Delights

over the period. Had the registers for 1848-9 been available they would have shown that Scilly did not entirely escape the cholera outbreak of those years, which took the lives of four master mariners on St Mary's. By far the most common fatal disease was phthisis (or tuberculosis), which caused 68 deaths and was attributed by North to the 'variation of the climate'. In general, though, the parson found the islands to be 'exceedingly healthy' containing as they did 'many persons considerably above eighty years'.[216]

Among John's patients were the lighthouse keepers, Edwin Davis and his Scillonian assistant Richard Scadden. In the records of Trinity House I found an agreement it reached with the doctor in August 1851: he would 'give his professional attendance and find medicines' for the men in its employment for one shilling per head a month. Such a private insurance scheme was unusual at a time when doctors habitually sent out bills at Christmas, hoping to be paid by midsummer, and when the 'gentlemanly ethic' prevented much 'open discussion of the business side of medicine'. The arrangement benefited both parties, giving John an assured income and the keepers treatment at a reasonable cost, which seems to have been borne by Trinity House. It is not clear, however, whether the doctor's contract covered the Keepers' wives and Edwin's growing brood of children. The insurance soon proved its worth when Scadden broke his arm, the setting of which would normally have cost about ten shillings. The arm was still in such a 'weak state' the following year that Scadden declined 'the offer of promotion to Principal Keeper at Longships', a post on a storm-tossed tower light which would have been demanding even for a fit 48-year-old man.[217]

Despite 'the cares of his profession', John found time to do research on the natural world and on medical science, both topics of intense inquiry in his day. In January 1854 he gave the first of a course of public lectures organised by Rev Treacher and Lord Proprietor Smith, delivering 'a most interesting and instructive' talk on 'Water, its chemistry and its wonders'. His listeners clearly enjoyed the way John traced an individual's use of water 'through his normal daily course, from his rising in the morning to his going to rest at night', although they may have been disappointed that his experiments to demonstrate by microscope the element's 'many wonders' had to be deferred 'due to the lateness of the hour'. Cheers lasting for five minutes 'by the largest audience we have lately seen in Scilly rang through the spacious classroom'. John himself attended further lectures on such topics as Mechanics, Maritime Commerce or the Catacombs of Rome. In March 1855 he contributed a second one of his own, this time on 'The Senses', and gave more talks subsequently. It was all, in the opinion of the *Royal Cornwall Gazette*, 'a considerable advance for the islanders'.[218]

John kept in touch with a network of professional and amateur scientists in the outside world. He corresponded with the Royal Institution of Cornwall based in Truro, sending data about rainfall and temperatures in Scilly. In particular he noted the surprisingly cold temperature of the sea surrounding the islands, an observation I can endorse from the experience of swimming there. Interestingly enough, John's uncle, Matthew Paul Moyle, surgeon-apothecary at Helston, also contributed to the Society's meteorological research. In addition, Matthew won local renown and an entry in the *Oxford Dictionary of National Biography* by his investigations into the dangerous atmosphere in mines, prompted by attending to the injuries of underground workers.[219]

Both Moyle doctors pursued their scientific interests at a time when patients tended to think that 'laboratory training *unfits* a man for his work as a physician'. Many resembled the inhabitants of George Eliot's Middlemarch, who preferred 'the old treatment, which has made Englishmen what they are' to new ideas 'about ventilation and diet'. John was undeterred by any disapproval he encountered. Speaking in November 1855 at the Natural History and Antiquarian Society of Penzance founded by his late father, he explained the link between the high rate of consumptive disease on the islands and their mild damp air. While emphasising that the

Island Duties and Delights

death rate from all causes was considerably lower than in the rest of the country, he thought that 'the sea damp and the prevalence of high winds' prevented Scilly from developing as a health resort like Penzance. In any case, he added, the invalids would have 'no amusements and no choice of diet and there is a great lack of accommodation for genteel patients'.[220]

John did, however, meet visitors who risked such discomforts. That same year Wilkie Collins followed up his earlier Cornish rambles with a sailing voyage in the company of his wealthy friend Edward Smyth Pigott, from the latter's country house in Weston-Super-Mare to these 'last morsels of English ground'. They stayed for one night at the islands' only hotel which was run by the master of the packet service Frank Tregarthen and his three daughters, who made the sailors feel 'really and truly at home'. And, adds Collins in his light-hearted account of the cruise, 'who should the resident medical man turn out to be but a gentleman whom I knew?' John must have met Collins in Penzance in 1850 and during this unexpected reunion they no doubt lamented Richard Moyle's fatal accident earlier in 1855. It seems that they also discussed the islanders' health as Collins writes of the prevalence of consumption. Unlike the doctor, however, he blamed it on Scillonians' 'distrust of fresh air and unwillingness to take exercise'.[221]

It was not long before Augustus Smith, discovering that the author of 'Rambles Beyond Railways' was 'in port in a small yacht', took charge of the two literati (both of whom were friends of Dickens) and bore them off to the Abbey with its 'gardens of the most exquisite beauty'. He guided them around the islands, pointing out 'all that he had done, and was doing, for the welfare and happiness of the people committed to his charge'. Smith may have omitted his most recent and rather less successful venture, which involved relocating the ten impoverished inhabitants of Samson and replacing them with a herd of deer, who promptly swam away from their new home. Collins was duly impressed with the 'social conditions of the islanders' whom the proprietor had 'succoured, reformed, and taught'. He also admired the 'natural panoramas of land and sea' observed on his thirteen-mile walk around St Mary's – a feat which apparently amazed 'a respectable inhabitant who laughed at the idea as incredulously as if we had proposed a swimming match to the Cornish coast'. He and Pigott clearly enjoyed the hospitality of their 'kind entertainer' and conversations with their medical companion.[222]

Two years later John met another literary pair, who felt so strongly 'beckoned like syrens to the dangerous shores' of the islands that they were undeterred by any of their deficiencies. In March 1857 'Mr and Mrs Lewes' emerged from a delayed six-hour crossing, on which they had been semi-delirious, icy-cold, and afflicted with 'the sensations which fly around sea-sickness', and found, to their relief, 'comfortable lodgings, clean as a Dutchman's' above St Mary's Post Office in Hugh Town.[223] The landlady they knew as 'Mrs Scadden' appears in the census as Mary Scadden, the spinster sister of Assistant Light Keeper Richard and Postmaster William Scadden, but in her role as a business woman she used the courtesy married title. For a different reason the travellers were also engaged in a masquerade. The writers George Henry Lewes and Marian Evans had recently set up house together in London but George was married to someone else and Marian was a single woman, who had decided that the name Mrs Lewes was less likely to shock polite Victorian society – and provincial landladies. It was soon after her stay on St Mary's, where she wrote her first work of fiction, that Marian assumed a third identity. In order to be taken more seriously as a novelist she adopted the masculine pen name for which she soon became famous – George Eliot.

The attraction of the islands for the couple was not its cuisine, its climate or the company of its inhabitants, whose 'burdensome acquaintance' they intended to avoid. They were drawn rather by a new-found interest in natural history and biology for which Scilly's granite rocks and treasure-strewn beaches would provide 'a land of marvels'. Equipped with jars and bottles, they walked over the downs and along the shores, collecting specimens – seaweed, marine spiders, sponges, crustacea, sea anemones and fish such as those described and sketched by Lewes: a pipe-fish with its 'miniature greyhound's head' and a feathery star-fish:

Specimens sketched by George Henry Lewes in St Mary's.

> Sudden joy leaps into our hearts at the sight of this creature ... I could not satiate myself with looking at my prize. All the way home the bottle was constantly being raised to my loving regard, that I might feast myself upon the wavering grace of those pink and white feathers.

Back in their lodgings Lewes would examine his specimens through his powerful new Smith & Becks microscope, dissect them and perform experiments. Fired by current scientific discourse, he found that nothing could be 'more interesting than to watch the beginnings of Life, to trace the gradual evolution of an animal from a mass of cells ... and to note how Life is, from the first, one incessant struggle and progress'.[224]

Because of their fascination with the islands' zoology the conspicuous, oddly-dressed couple were glad to make the acquaintance of John Moyle, to whom Wilkie Collins had provided a letter of introduction: 'he became a delightful friend to us, always ready to help with the contents of his surgery or anything else at his command'. John frequently visited them in the evenings to smoke a cigar and work with the microscope, bringing them books about Scilly. By day he went out hunting specimens with Lewes, leaving Marian free to read Mrs Gaskell's *Life of Charlotte Bronte*, hot from the press, and to finish writing the first of her own *Scenes of Clerical Life*. On Lewes's birthday John took advantage of his friendship with Augustus Smith to arrange a visit to the Abbey for lunch and a tour of the gardens, where Lewes showed a particular interest in the plants from South Africa, Australia and California. Both the writers appreciated the doctor's 'inexhaustible obligingness', while he, apparently indifferent to their adulterous state, long treasured the memory of their visit.[225]

John had more in common with his new friends than an interest in biology. They shared an intoxication with the sheer beauty of the islands. Lewes's heart 'bounded like a leopard on his prey' as he regarded the 'many reefs and creeks along the wavy shores', the furze rendering the downs 'all aflame with their golden light' and the 'stupendous aspect' of the granite rocks. Marian's journal is also illuminated by joyful recollections of Scilly.

> The colouring of the rocks was very various and beautiful – sometimes a delicate greyish-green, … then a light warm brown; then black; occasionally of a rich yellow, and here and there purplish. … The waves that beat on this coast are clear as crystal, and we used to delight in watching them rear themselves like the horses of a mighty sea-god, as they approach the rocks on which they were broken into eddies of milky foam.

John had been capturing these wonders in paint ever since his arrival on Scilly, as he continued to do throughout his long career. In *Holy Vale* (1849), for example, he depicts a scene such as the writers describe. It reflects an observation Marian made on these

John Grenfell Moyle, Holy Vale, *1849.*

seaside travels, which her biographer Jenny Uglow considers to be 'very close to her theory of fiction': 'What is it that light cannot transfigure into beauty!'[226]

The visitors stayed on St Mary's for seven happy weeks filling 'our bottles and our souls at once' and combining science with culture in the spirit of their time. But the discomforts, which John had noted as putting a brake on tourism, took a toll on their health and morale. The blustering winds and frequent rain meant that they were 'constantly ailing'. They were sickened by the 'monotony of beef and fried pollock' provided by Mrs Scadden, who 'like almost all peculiarly domestic women has ... rudimentary ideas of cooking', not improved by Marian's daily 'culinary lectures'. Lewes couldn't find any of his favourite Harvey's sauce in St Mary's and had to send to Penzance for a jar. The visitors' patronising description of their landlady reflects their attitude to most Scillonians, whom they found 'gentle and dignified' but dull company. They described their neighbour Mr Buckstone, for example, as 'stupid, good-natured and unaffected' and his wife as 'a silly, ill-bred woman'. Marian was grateful, however, for an excursion led by Mr Buckstone to Garrison Hill, which gave them a view of the 'venerable' St Agnes lighthouse 'painted bright white to increase its conspicuousness', and to Rat Island, from where they could see an additional lighthouse being built on Bishop Rock. On the whole they kept their distance from all the islanders apart from 'the admirable surgeon', viewing them with an amused condescension. In the end, wrote Lewes, 'the Granite Beauties turned a cold boulder on me, and I resolved to weary them no longer.'[227]

Marian had completed 'Mr Gilfil's Love Story' while 'sitting on the Fortification Hill one sunshining morning'.[228] She intended to use the islands as a background for a novel on the Napoleonic Wars but never actually wrote it. Nor did any of her novels have a seaside setting. She did say, though, that marine research had taught her to 'look at man in the light of a shell fish', deploying scientific techniques in observing and recording everyday human life. A few Scillonian names feature in her works: Mrs Lemon's school in *Middlemarch* carries an echo of a St Mary's name which amused her and the Scadden surname makes an appearance in *Felix Holt*. Furthermore, it is difficult not to see a resemblance between Dr Moyle of Scilly and Dr Tertius Lydgate of Middlemarch, both assiduous local doctors who hoped to keep 'in the track of far-reaching investigation' through the 'careful observation and inference' of their daily work, thus enlarging 'the scientific, rational basis' of their profession.[229]

John was to spend the next three decades caring for the health of Scillonians who, as Lewes observed, were 'justly proud' of him. He used proceeds from the sale of his paintings to finance free treatment for poorer islanders, although he did send bills to the Vestry of St Mary's Parish when he attended paupers under its charge. The islands had not been included in the harsh new system of Poor Law Unions but the old-fashioned parishes were often just as reluctant to provide relief to the needy. Vestry records reveal that John's bills were paid grudgingly 'when they have funds in hand' and only on condition that the doctor 'attended to the rule ... that he should get an order from the overseers before attending a pauper medically'. This arrangement became so cumbersome that eventually the Vestry offered 'a sum of five pounds a year as a fixed salary for dispensing medicines and attending medically to paupers in St Mary's'. John accepted this arrangement (adding 'ten shillings extra for each pauper confinement') even though it was hardly likely to cover his costs, which could amount, for example, to £3 for setting a fractured thigh and dressing a wound for a single pauper patient.[230]

The doctor also kept an eye on matters of public health, such as the state of the wells on which Scilly's water supply depended. He would report to the parish authorities if the water was 'in an impure condition' or if the wells were 'dangerous to children' because of being uncovered, regularly recommending that they be 'cleansed, fenced and paved out of the poor rates'. He arranged for the inspection of drains and for investigations into the causes of bad smells. These measures helped to prevent the return of cholera and, in one case of a suspected outbreak, John made arrangements for quarantine.[231]

A year after the visit of Henry and Marian, the doctor married Eliza Nance, who belonged to a large clan of farmers and seafarers on St Martin's. She had grown up on that island in a cottage similar to the one occupied by a member of the Nance family, which was beautifully photographed by John Gibson's son Alexander. Her childhood had been spent with two mariners' widows, her grandmother and her mother Honor, who supported the family by knitting and spinning.[232]

Alexander Gibson, Mary Nance's Kitchen.

By the time John met and fell in love with her, Eliza was lodging with a seaman's wife on St Mary's and working as a dressmaker. According to a reminiscence from their grandson Trevellick Moyle, the couple married 'rather secretly' in April 1858; they made their own separate ways to the church alone and had only the parson and the verger present at the service. This simple wedding reflected the bridegroom's modesty and distaste for show. Eliza and her mother now moved into John's house in the Parade, where two daughters and a son were born by 1861 and another sea widow was employed as a temporary nurse.[233]

On St Agnes Edwin Davis was still keeping the light in the 'good order' observed by the Royal Commission of 1861, despite the commissioning of a new lighthouse on the steep crag four miles offshore, known as Bishop Rock because of its 'supposed similarity to a bishop's mitre'. An iron screw-pile structure was erected but even before the lantern had been fitted, a storm swept it away on 5 February 1850.[234] Trinity House then commissioned the building of the granite tower which Lewes and Marian had seen in progress. This 'difficult undertaking accomplished without loss of life or serious accident to any person employed' was completed by October 1858. It was hoped that this 'King of Lighthouses' would prove to be 'one of the most extremely useful of all the lights'. But it did not make St Agnes redundant. Edwin even gained a £5 increase in his salary in return 'for taking charge of oil and stores belonging to Bishop Light'. These perilous waters could never have too many navigational aids.[235]

Lithograph of the incomplete lighthouse swept away from Bishop Rock.

Danger lurked not only out in the ocean but in the choppy waters traversed by the islanders every day. In October 1858, for example, both the lighthouse keeper and the doctor were involved when two men and a little girl were 'plunged into the sea' from their boat in St Mary's harbour. The men were soon saved but the child sank to the bottom and was not rescued, it was reported, for 'a full ten minutes'.

> She was apparently quite dead. Mr Davis, the lighthouse keeper, at once commenced treating her as prescribed by the simple instruction of the Royal National Lifeboat Association. In the meantime a medical man had been sent for. He continued with the same plan; and after three hours of steady perseverance, they had the great reward of seeing their humane efforts crowned with success.

Island Duties and Delights

Edwin was obviously trained and practised in life-saving techniques and quick to take the lead in an emergency.[236] He and the islands' only 'medical man' had saved a Scillonian life.

Alfred Tennyson presented the doctor with a less testing case. In September 1860 the Poet Laureate's pursuit of King Arthur took him to the furthest 'limit of the West in the land of Lyonesse, where, save the rocky Isles of Scilly, all is now wild sea'.[237] He stayed for a few nights in Tregarthen's Hotel with his companion, the anthologist and critic Francis Palgrave, who remembered Tennyson's reading 'a portable copy of Homer as we wandered over the wild rock-island'. Perhaps it was his absorption in the maritime adventures of Ulysses which caused Tennyson to stumble, with the result that John 'had the honor of doctoring a scratch on the Poet Laureate's leg'.[238]

Aloes in the garden of Tregarthen's Hotel.

He recuperated in the hotel's garden writing in his diary about its 'West Indian aloes thirty feet high, in blossom and out all the winter'.[239] Here Tennyson also penned his long narrative poem 'Enoch Arden'. It was a work akin not to nebulous myths of Lyonesse but to the harsh realities of Scillonian life.

In plain and homely language the poem tells the story of Enoch Arden, 'a rough sailor's lad, made orphan by a winter shipwreck', who marries his childhood sweetheart and works both as a fisherman and as a merchant mariner 'abroad on wrathful seas'. At first his journeys take him mostly 'landward' but after a spell of idleness necessitated by a broken limb he decides to sign on as boatswain with a China-bound vessel, hoping that this will save his growing family from 'low, miserable lives of hand-to-mouth'. He seeks to reassure his fearful wife before he leaves in words uttered by many a Cornish seaman:

> Annie, this voyage by the grace of god
> Will bring fair weather yet to all of us.
> Keep a clean hearth and a clear fire for me,
> And I'll be back, my girl, before you know it.

But ten years pass with no news of Enoch, who has been shipwrecked on the homeward journey and cast ashore on an island 'loneliest in a lonely sea'. Despairing of ever seeing him again Annie (unlike Homer's faithful Penelope) succumbs to the pleas of a persistent suitor. She marries the prosperous village miller who has loved her since childhood and gives birth to another baby. Eventually Enoch sights a passing ship which rescues him and brings him at long last to the 'harbour whence he had sailed before'. Soon discovering what has happened in his absence, he hides away and dies a year later broken by 'grief and solitude'.[240]

To modern readers this may seem a melodramatic tale but such maritime tragedies pervaded the life and imagination of Britons in the days when the sea was still a key element of the country's existence. Examples are legion. Rev Hawker of Morwenstow in north Cornwall gave Christian burials to some forty unknown sailors. Their bodies (or body parts) were found on the beach beneath the cliff-top hut where he kept anxious watch and wrote poems expressing his dread of 'the storm – the blast – the tempest shock'. Charles Dickens visited wreck scenes compulsively and used them as copy for articles. In one of them he describes the noble efforts of a Welsh clergyman to identify corpses from the wrecked *Royal Charter*, so that he could write to the relations of those he buried. And in *Dombey and Son* Dickens evokes the agony of those who lament when 'told of all hands lost' and their joy when the sailor-hero Walter Gay returns. Elizabeth Gaskell had special cause to be haunted by stories of those who vanished without trace after her brother disappeared on a sea voyage in

Island Duties and Delights

1828. Sailors appear as 'figures of loss and longing, hope and fear' in several of her novels, including *Sylvia's Lovers* of 1863 in which the heroine suffers a fate remarkably similar to that of Tennyson's Annie Arden.[241]

Scillonians were acutely conscious of disappearing seamen for they had so often to deal with those 'found drowned' on their beaches. In October 1854, for example:

> The bodies of two men were washed ashore, wrapped in hammocks or canvas, as if they had been put overboard or buried at sea. One appeared to be a young man, and the other an elderly man with short grey hair, but no marks to distinguish who they were. Coffins were provided and the bodies decently interred, and all expenses defrayed by Augustus Smith, Esq, the Lord Proprietor.

Islanders were haunted by fears that their own seafarers could be cast on foreign shores 'without a grave, unknell'd, uncoffin'd and unknown'. Tennyson may well have been inspired to write 'Enoch Arden' by tales he heard beside Scilly's rugged shores.[242]

Chapter 6

Disasters and Misdemeanours
1860s and 1870s

Edwin Lewis Davis m. Martha Hutchings 1847

1 William Legg 2 Thirza 3 Charles Royer 4 Eliza 5 Eva Mary
  b1848   *b850*   *b1852*   *b1853* *b1855*
6 Emma 7 Samuel 8 Martha Mary 9 Alberta 10 Lewis Edwin
 b1858 *b1859*   *b1860*   *b1864*   *b 867*

On the most remote of Scilly's shores the Principal Keeper's cottage was full of new life. By 1861 eight more children had been born there, only one of whom died in infancy. Even Martha's undoubted skills in domestic management must have been put to the test as she cooked, clothed and cared for a brood ranging in age from twelve years to eight months and kept the house in the 'very clean' condition found by Trinity House inspectors in 1861.[243] She kept no servant but the Keeper's salary would probably have enabled her to use the services of one of the island's three washerwomen. Remarkably, she found time to organise family worship three times a day in accordance with Bible Christian practice.

The overcrowding in the cottage was relieved by the departure of Jane's six offspring to take up occupations for which their education at home and at school had fitted them. The oldest son, William, had enlisted with Trinity House and was currently

Disasters and Misdemeanours

Assistant Keeper at Gunfleet Lighthouse in the North Sea. The other two boys, Thomas and Edwin, had taken up the career favoured by Augustus Smith and were at sea on Scilly-built merchant ships. Their eighteen-year-old sister Mary Jane had married the new Assistant Light Keeper, George Boulden, and moved into the next-door cottage. The remaining two daughters, Sarah and Jemima, were using their home-trained skills as dressmakers, plying their trade on St Mary's from the household of Edwin's sister Elizabeth and her husband, Captain Tobias Legg.[244]

As well as saying family prayers, Martha played the organ in the parish church on Sundays. It seems that she was happy, like other Scillonians, to attend services at both church and chapel, while the children, in their home-made and hand-me-down Sunday best and boots from the local shoemakers, went off to morning and afternoon Sunday School.[245] This meant that they could enjoy an annual treat on St Mary's: a procession with banners and music followed by a sermon 'in simple language adapted to the capacities of children' and an 'ample supply' of tea and cakes. Cornish newspapers did not carry full reports of such offshore events and none of the Davis children wrote a childhood memoir but I expect they joined in with further seasonal fun, some of it peculiarly Scillonian.

Shrove Tuesday was known as Gravel-night because boys threw stones at house doors hoping to be bought off with pancakes. On Good Friday islanders released paper boats on to the water and collected

John Gibson, May Day in Hugh Town, *1876.*

limpets. May Day was celebrated by the crowning of a May Queen, dancing around a maypole, the blowing of home-made whistles and gorging on rounds of bread spread with thick cream and treacle.[246] There was a fair in Hugh Town on Whit Monday.

Midsummer Night saw bonfires and torch processions. Church bells were rung on Guy Fawkes night. During Advent, masked and blackened Goose-dancers appeared in strange costumes, girls dressed as ships' captains and boys as women. Many families had a pig or a hen to kill and feast on at Christmas.

Some years were marked by further celebrations. In 1857 Augustus Smith made much of his election to parliament:

> The grand dinner at St Mary's, in honour of my return as a M.P., came off with much eclat; no less than 160 persons [including John Moyle] sat down at their own cost to the banquet laid out in the Infant Schoolroom. At St Agnes they had also a grand tea drinking of their own, with tar-barrel bonfires, etc, in the evening. The whole affair, as so spontaneously taken up, has shown a very gratifying feeling on the part of the islanders.

In 1863 Smith organised similar festivities to salute the marriage of the Prince of Wales: tea and cake for the pupils of St Mary's as well as 'the brats of St Agnes, St Martin's and Tresco', followed by games on the Abbey green and a march by the children 'headed by the drum and fife band of St Agnes'.[247]

Such feast days were often marked by a full or half-day holiday but St Agnes school records for this period frequently reveal less enjoyable reasons for children's non-attendance: 'work in the fields', 'a very wet day', 'carrying oil and stores for the Light house'; 'mistress being unable through indisposition to keep school'; 'mistress could not get from St Martin's in time to open school'; 'school closed to be whitened'. No wonder one inspectors' report judged that pupils were 'neither ready, industrious nor persevering'.[248] When free from school or work youngsters could find plenty to do, for their isolated environment offered its own delights: the sea to swim in, rock pools to explore, beaches to roam, cliffs to climb, and uninhabited islands to visit for family picnics. J. C. Trewin, who grew up near the lighthouse on the remote Lizard peninsula, vividly conjures up such childhood experiences:

> Sloe-blossom, vernal squills and silver-white campions, lonely Novembers and hot gold Julys, the tide's constant tune. Each jut and pinnacle of rock, the familiar line of village roofs, the proud sense of belonging.

Like him, the Davis children could well have found comfort at night in the revolving lighthouse beam as it 'hovered upon wall and ceiling, faded, returned, faded, returned, and would do so until daybreak dimmed it'.[249]

Despite the endless chores, monotonous diet and cramped living conditions, the lives of these children were 'set in a much brighter atmosphere' than those of their grandparents. This was largely thanks to the greater prosperity wrought by Augustus Smith. The historian James Anthony Froude, an expert yachtsman who sailed to Scilly in 1857 and was scooped up from the harbour to spend a day with the Proprietor, was impressed with what he saw. Froude did not publicise his impressions until four years after Smith died, when he used the 1876 annual lecture of the Edinburgh Philosophical Institution to 'show Radical Scotland how beneficent a fairy a landlord still might be'.

> Throughout the compass of the British Islands you will not find an equal number of people on an equal area, on an average, so well clothed, so well fed, so well lodged, so well educated. ...The whole place wears an air of quiet industry, prosperity, order and discipline. These results Mr Smith arrived at by the arbitrary exercise of his power as a landlord. He was a Radical who looked to ends rather than means.[250]

Edwin Davis and his family were among many who gained from Smith's benevolent despotism.

* * * *

Despite all improvements the craggy isolation of the islands meant that disaster could strike at any time – as it did for the Davis family in 1863. When Edwin came to relieve his assistant keeper and son-in-law George Boulden at midnight on 20 February he found him missing from his watch and 'nowhere to be found'. The next day a search was made and when 'some persons alleged that they had discovered traces of him by some precipitous rocks ... it was supposed that he had thrown himself into the sea'. Local newspapers carried detailed stories of the 'suspected suicide'. Typically, too, they expressed pity and gave sympathetic explanations for Boulden's being 'depressed in mind', gathered from his family and neighbours and perhaps from the doctor.

> He is said to have been unwell, in a very unsettled state of mind for some time past, arising from the religious excitement caused by the revival meetings recently held at these islands, which meetings he attended at every opportunity and became a religious convert. He subsequently manifested some aberration of intellect, by destroying some articles of his children's dresses, and also some of his own, as superfluous and unbecoming of Christians. Poor Boulden bore a very good character, and the unfortunate circumstance has caused considerable sorrow and regret among the inhabitants.[251]

This was not an unlikely sequence of events for, according to historian Olive Anderson, there was often a 'link between despair of personal salvation and thoughts of suicide'. But it was only after George's body was found washed ashore on 6 March that an inquest could be held to determine whether his death was due to natural causes, accident, homicide or *felo de se* (the illegal act of killing oneself). A verdict of suicide would mean that George could not have a Christian burial and that any property was forfeit to the Crown – unless the jury decided that it had occurred 'in a fit of mental aberration', as had been suggested in the press.[252]

The inquest was held on St Agnes before the coroner, Thomas Lemon Hall, a shipowner and merchant of St Mary's who had been elected to the post as a person of standing, there being no requirement of professional qualifications at that time. A jury of local fishermen, pilots and farmers, nearly all of whom bore the common Scillonian surnames Hicks and Legg, viewed the body and heard evidence from the coastguard who had found it, as well as from other witnesses. Among them were Edwin Davis and Dr John Moyle.[253] It did not take the jury long to decide on the simple verdict of 'Found Drowned', which avoided both the stigma and the penalties of suicide. Unlike those convicted of the crime, who lie in unconsecrated ground, George Boulden was buried in his parish churchyard. The headstone bears an inscription adapted from *Revelation* XIV:13 which may have consoled his 'grieving friends': 'Blessed are the dead who die in the Lord for they rest from their labours.'

Grave of George Henry Boulden in St Agnes churchyard.

Trinity House provided more practical help, paying Edwin £7 15s towards the expenses of searching for George's body and attending the inquest.[254] The pregnant Mary Jane and her three young children now lost their home as well as their breadwinner, and George's short period of service meant that she was not entitled to the widow's pension which Trinity House usually provided. She appealed to the Committee for assistance in her 'distressed condition' and was granted a donation of £10, which helped her to begin a new life in Landewednack near George's original home on Cornwall's Lizard peninsula.[255]

The light of St Agnes continued to shine throughout and beyond these sad events. But the rocks of Scilly remained 'as hard as iron', in the words of a bronze-faced old man interviewed by *The Cornishman*: 'They have no sympathy with the luckless ship that chances to be driven on them, at a time when the waves are lashed with fury by the force of the tempest.' The article concluded that over a period of nineteen years, even with the added protection of Bishop Rock, there had been twenty-five 'total wrecks on the Islands, eight of which were attended with loss of life'.[256]

Further fatalities were sometimes prevented by Dr Moyle's being 'on the spot', as he was after the *Friar Tuck* was wrecked in a gale off St Mary's in December 1863. The crew was taken ashore with the rocket apparatus pioneered by Captain George Manby, which fired a rescue line to the ship. A subsequent attempt to move the vessel nearly caused the death of Francis Banfield, the islands' ship agent, and one of his employees. Both men were thrown on to the rocks and 'taken up insensible' but the doctor 'rendered every assistance, and under his skilful treatment both sufferers are progressing favourably'. John also attended to shipboard accidents. On one occasion he had to amputate the hand of a sailor who had caught it in the cog wheels of the engine: 'The operation was performed under chloroform and the man is going on favourably.' A later report told of a Greek boatswain who suffered 'a fractured skull, a severe scalp-wound and fracture of the shoulder' when the windlass capsized. The doctor was 'soon in attendance so that he and two other injured men were 'progressing favourably'.[257]

John was also heavily involved in the deadliest Scillonian disaster of this period. This occurred during the evening of 7 May 1875 when the ocean liner *Schiller*, a German steamship on a voyage from New York, ran into dense fog. While most passengers danced at a birthday party, others volunteered to look out for the lights at Bishop Rock and St Agnes. They could not discern these through the gloom and no one apparently heard the Bishop's fog bell which Keeper James Daniel set at 8.40 pm to sound at six strokes per minute. So, the *Schiller* came to within half a mile of the lighthouse, struck the Retarrier Ledges and shattered amid tremendous waves and treacherous currents. Only two lifeboats were successfully launched, while most of the passengers and crew clung to the wreckage before being washed into the sea. Meanwhile the *Schiller* fired signal-guns which were heard on shore but mistaken for those of a vessel announcing her arrival. No one except the keepers on Bishop Rock knew what was happening but, as a letter to the *Times* later pointed out, there was 'no means of communication with St Mary's, where the lifeboat was kept'. The correspondent saw 'no reason why the lighthouse-men – a most intelligent class – should not work a simple telegraph instrument as easily as a pointsman does on a railway'. As it was, Keeper Daniel and his colleagues watched helplessly as bodies floated by: 'No one knows what was felt in the house by all hands to see so many of our dear fellow creatures suffering and dying so near to us.'[258]

It was not until the first light of morning that the alarm was raised, at which point a pilot boat from St Agnes hastened to the scene. Its crew discovered the mast of the sinking ship, picked up five survivors and rowed to St Mary's to summon further assistance. 'From every inhabited island boats put out, manned in some instances by mere boys, and cruised around the wreck for hours, rescuing the majority of those whose lives were saved.' About forty of the mostly German crew and passengers were taken to land and consigned to 'the skilful care' of Dr Moyle. Up to 330 people lost their lives, among them many children, who fell 'an easy prey' to the billows.[259]

Over a hundred of their bodies were washed ashore, for each of which an inquest was held and a funeral conducted. It was a harrowing time for Rev J. H. White, the island chaplain 'who had many painful duties to perform'. So it was for the doctor, for the pilots, for the coroner and for Algernon Dorrien Smith, the new Lord Proprietor who had moved to Scilly the previous year after inheriting the position from his uncle Augustus. None of them would ever forget the tragedy. Nine years later Rev White hanged himself after telling a friend that 'life was unbearable'. It's hard to believe that his 'very depressed state' was unconnected with the *Schiller* funerals. The inquest verdict of 'suicide during a fit of temporary insanity' meant that he was entitled to the Christian burial he had given to so many others.[260] Dorrien Smith's wife Edith believed that the cries 'of those unhappy people struggling for their lives within a few miles of us' would ring in her ears all her life. Doctor Moyle kept the *Times*'s long and vivid account of the disaster and pasted it into the scrapbook which I would eventually inherit. He also recorded 'The Burial of the Bodies from the *Schiller*' in a 'talented and truthful painting' described in detail by the *Royal Cornwall Gazette*:

> The old church in partial rain – the picturesque churchyard – the open graves showing the coffins bestrewn with flowers – the clergyman standing beside reading the Burial Service, attended by a large concourse of persons who were present on the occasion to testify their sympathy – and the back ground framed by a correct representation of a grand pile of rocks, viz. Cara Lee, – and in the distance a sister steamboat passing up channel – all combined, tends to make it a picture of such importance as cannot fail to commemorate the sad catastrophe and to reflect great merit on the artist.

John apparently included 'some very excellent likenesses' of many local people, including a Mr Davis. Meaningful though the painting was to Scillonians, it was sold to a Mr Ridyard of Birkenhead and I have not managed to view it in any form. An engraving which appeared in the *Illustrated London News* must suffice to depict the procession of 'two-wheeled island carts drawn by the little shaggy island ponies' which served as hearses and of the 'interments in the little stone-walled island churchyard'.[261]

The burial of those drowned in the Schiller *in Old Town, St Mary's.*

* * * *

Disasters and Misdemeanours

Edwin Davis was among the mourners for the *Schiller* victims and it is likely that his thoughts turned to the male offspring of his two marriages, four of whom had become master mariners. Three years earlier his second son Thomas, had died aged thirty-one on board his ship at St John's, Newfoundland. The next boy, Edwin junior, was still at sea. Martha's oldest sons, John Hutchings and Charles Royer, had followed their half-brothers into the merchant navy and were now sailing the seven seas. Of particular interest to me is the career of Charles, my great-grandfather.

In November 1865 he was apprenticed at the age of fourteen to the Scillonian ship owner John Banfield and then served on board the *Anne Laity Banfield*, carrying a cargo of flour and wheat as well as several emigrants to Australia. After completing his apprenticeship in 1867 Charles took the exams which were now compulsory for promotion in the merchant navy, progressed to first mate and then master mariner rank and was soon commanding ships on voyages across the world. These young Davis men had made use of their navigation classes to 'follow the sea' and to be promoted to officer status, thus fulfilling the Proprietor's boast that none of the boys from his schools 'remained before the mast'.[262]

Charles's Master Mariner Certificate.

Charles and his brothers doubtless wrote to Edwin and Martha but no family correspondence survived the cramped conditions of the lighthouse cottage. One extant letter, written by a local shipping agent, gives just a glimpse of Charles's captaincy and of dangers on board the 528-ton *John Banfield*, the largest vessel ever built in Scilly. In 1872, during a voyage from New York to Antwerp, she put into St Mary's with sad news:

Poor Alex Hartley the carpenter fell from the topmast head on the 1st of February. The ship in a heavy gale fell on her side. Alex and 2nd Mate were cutting away the top gallant mast when Alex fell and split open his head, killed on the spot [and] buried the next day. They all liked him so much on board, he had behaved so well on the voyage. Cap Davis told me he never heard a bad word or idle expression escape his lips ... and that when the weather was fine he would during the dog watch be with the apprentices singing hymns and frequently they would read a portion of God's holy word. Cap Davis would have a Meeting on board every Sunday evening at sea and he says the Carpenter always availed himself of the opportunity of attending. ... Cap Davis called in with me to see poor Lydia his Mother who is in great trouble about him as they were so attached. ... Cap Davis said he was a fine young man much beloved and he [had] hoped to have him on another voyage as he was such a religious young man and he hoped he was gone home to Heaven.

The letter certainly testifies to the influence of Charles's childhood home.[263]

Another glimpse of the brothers' seafaring life is afforded by a photograph, accompanied by a family story. Charles sits on the right beside two of his older brothers, Edwin and John. Behind them stands their teenage brother Samuel. The photo can be dated to the 1870s even though the bearded and weather-beaten sailors look older than their years. The story goes that the three master mariners and the cabin boy were photographed in Calcutta, where

From left to right: Edwin, Samuel, John and Charles Davis.

they had all met by chance while taking refuge from monsoon storms. My guess is that they were staying at the Sailors' Home, which provided board and lodging for the British Merchant Marine. After this fraternal reunion they all resumed their respective voyages.[264]

Charles's ship was the *Macduff,* one of the celebrated clippers which plied between Britain and Australia, carrying passengers on the way out and returning home with cargoes of wool and sometimes gold. These speedy journeys were fraught with dangers, some of which had befallen this vessel shortly before Charles took charge: an outbreak of smallpox, a collision with a fishing boat and a man overboard. On this passage from London to Melbourne (July-October 1878) the main problem was the health of the captain himself. The *Melbourne Argus* reported that 'consumption appears to have set in and marked him for its own'.

The Macduff *entering Williamstown harbour, Melbourne.*

By the time the *Macduff* reached Melbourne Charles was in 'a very weak and exhausted condition' and died, aged only twenty-seven, as the ship lay in Williamstown harbour. It is not known when Charles contracted tuberculosis but it can only have been exacerbated by years spent in vessels 'swept from end to end by every roaring sea'.[265]

The newly constructed telegraph line to the Scillies conveyed the 'intelligence of the arrival of the ship *Macduff,* Capt. Charles Davis, from London; also the sad news of the death of the captain ... a son of Mr Edwin Davis, lightkeeper, St Agnes. Great sympathy is felt for the young widow and friends.'[266] The 'young widow' was Ambrosine (née McFarland), a fellow Scillonian, whom Charles had married early in 1877. Their son Harold (my 'Grandpa') was born in

December of that year, six months before the *Macduff* sailed, so that he had no memory of the seafaring father whose story he often told me. Nor was he ever able to visit Williamstown Cemetery where Charles was buried while 'all vessels hauled their flags at half-mast in memory of the deceased'.[267]

Headstone of Captain Charles Royer Davis.

John Grenfell Moyle m. Eliza Nance

1 Emma Grenfell	2 Jessie	3 Edwards Nance Vyvyan	4 Mary
b1858	b1860	b1861	b1863
5 Annie	6 John Grenfell	7 Janie	8 Rovena
b1865	b1868	b1870	b1876

Sorrow also afflicted the busy doctor and his growing family – six girls and two boys were born between 1858 and 1876. In 1878, the same year that Charles Davis met his death in Melbourne harbour, eleven-year-old John Grenfell Moyle, his father's namesake, died in his St Mary's home from a painful kidney disease which no medical treatment could remedy.[268] Shortly afterwards John's only remaining son, Edwards Nance Vyvyan (who bore the Christian names of two of his Moyle uncles as well as his mother's maiden name) was apprenticed to the maritime service. According to his great-grandson, he spent some years as first mate on square-riggers engaged 'on the wool run' and did not escape the accidents so common on such voyages. He fell from the top mast and ruptured an ear drum, with the result that he was permanently deaf in one ear. This may explain his decision to abandon the sea and to return to the islands on which he would spend the rest of his life.[269]

Shortly before John died and Edwards went to sea there was an addition to the Moyle family – a little girl born in 1877 to seventeen-year-old Jessie, the doctor's second daughter. The baby was named Margaretta but not formally baptised until 1888 when no father was named on the certificate. An illegitimate birth was not uncommon in a busy sea port but it did not always happen that the child was brought up in the family home, especially if it was a respectable one like the doctor's. Margaretta, however, was recognised and listed in the 1881 Census as the granddaughter of John and Eliza Moyle, with no pretence that she was their daughter.

Even so, Margaretta's would not be an easy life. Illegitimacy, with which John was concerned professionally as well as personally, was normally seen as a disgrace in Victorian Britain. Several sympathetic contemporary novelists sought to erase the stain. Trollope's 'poor bastard' Mary Thorne is adopted by her uncle, the good Doctor Thorne, and manages to marry into the 'true blood' after unexpectedly inheriting a fortune. Dickens's equally virtuous Esther Summerson, who often feels that it would have been 'better and happier for many people' if she had died at birth, is lucky in her employment as housekeeper to the kind Mr Jarndyce of 'Bleak House'. It is he who facilitates her marriage to another kind doctor, the poor but handsome Allan Woodcourt. Both characters are saved from the usual sorry fate of fatherless children by the intervention of enlightened medical men – rather like John Moyle. But happy endings were rare. Historians find that children born out of wedlock at that time were 'likely to be handicapped materially, physically, mentally, socially and professionally'. The 'forlorn, friendless, lost' Anne Catherick of Wilkie Collins's *The Woman in White*, consigned to a lunatic asylum because 'there were certain advantages gained by shutting her up', reflects a common practice. It remained to be seen what Margaretta's destiny would be.[270]

A patrician contrast to Dr Moyle in the matter of illegitimacy is afforded by none other than Augustus Smith. Over Christmas 1865 the Proprietor actually read *The Woman in White*. He found it 'an awfully absurd story' and had no sympathy with the heroine, who was 'only fit to be shut up in an asylum'. It may be that the novel struck a painful chord, for Smith was himself the father of at least three illegitimate children, a son and two daughters born in the 1840s to Mary Pender, a Tresco shopkeeper. Smith never publicly acknowledged their offspring, Georgiana, Lawrence and Ellen, nor did he receive them into his opulent household. Instead, they were sent with their mother to live first in Plymouth and later in London. Census and probate records reveal that they all adopted Smith as their middle name, that Ellen died from tuberculosis at the age of seventeen in November 1865 (shortly before Smith read Collins's novel) and that the remaining brother and sister lived with each other for the rest of their lives. They were comfortably off, especially after the death of their father who left them £3,000 in his will. But they never married and seemed to have no place in conventional Victorian society. There was certainly no possibility of the Abbey or the Proprietorship being passed on to Lawrence.[271]

This side of Augustus Smith's life is still shrouded in mystery. It cannot be substantiated by private documents since Tresco Abbey's archive is closed until 2036 and it is not mentioned in the *Oxford Dictionary of National Biography*. Yet some of his contemporaries knew of it. His sister-in-law, for example, who was also the mother of his future successor Algernon Dorrien Smith, 'refused to visit Scilly, and discouraged her children from so doing, lest she or they somehow absorb Augustus's moral toxins'. This reputation may also account for Froude's mysterious comment at the end of his posthumous tribute to Smith's work in Scilly, that 'he was the wicked man of the islands'. John Moyle as 'a friend and sometimes confidant' of Smith, with whom he shared intellectual interests and social occasions and who witnessed one of the codicils of his will, must also have known about the three offspring. He was not, however, present at their births since Mary Pender was sent to the mainland for her confinements – one of which took place on Penzance Quay, perhaps prematurely 'after a lengthy rough crossing from Scilly'.[272]

Disasters and Misdemeanours

In the course of his work the doctor attended less protected unmarried mothers in Scilly, and he was much concerned with a woman who worked in the household of Smith's successor. In February 1887 a dead baby girl was found in the grounds of Tresco Abbey. The mother was identified as Alice Goddard, head laundry maid, who claimed that this had been a premature still birth. John's evidence at the inquest corroborated her story: 'He could not say that the child had existed independently of the mother. He attributed death to want of attention at birth.' Dorrien Smith testified that 'the circumstances of the birth left no stain upon her character.' Even so, Alice was sent to Bodmin Gaol to await trial at the Exeter Assizes for 'wilfully and unlawfully' concealing the child's birth. When her case came up in May the judge was satisfied 'that the prisoner had no reason whatever to think the child was born alive. She was in service in a most respectable family, and concealed the birth to hide her shame.' As Alice had already been in custody for some time, he 'sentenced her to one day's imprisonment, when she was immediately released.' Thus the testimony of the islands' doctor and proprietor enabled a 'kindly' judge to spare Alice the sentence of infanticide. Even if found guilty she would probably not have been executed because of a 'growing recognition of the impact of insanity, poverty and illegitimacy in shaping the actions of mothers who killed their new-born babies'– but she could well have been committed to a lunatic asylum. It's not known what became of Alice after she was released.[273]

Meanwhile single mothers throughout the country stood up in court to claim support for their illegitimate children from the fathers. It took courage to tell the story of their seduction, to give details of presents offered and promises of marriage made, and to call witnesses from the local community. If Cornwall is anything to go by, they met with more sympathy than condemnation: the crowd in one court room applauded when a father was ordered to pay two shillings a week; judges sent fathers who refused to support their illegitimate children to Bodmin Gaol; and the *Royal*

Cornwall Gazette campaigned against a new Bastardy Act which inflicted further 'hardship upon a number of young women who have already suffered a grievous wrong'.[274] But, of course, there were many young women who dared not take fathers to court and ended up in the workhouse or on the streets. In any case, the sums awarded were pitifully small. Life was still grindingly hard for single mothers who lacked the advantage, enjoyed by Jessie Moyle, of a family willing and able to support them.

John Moyle presided over several paternity cases in his capacity as a magistrate, a position he obtained in June 1871 on the recommendation of Augustus Smith. It was clearly not held against him that lengthy reports of his brother Vyvyan's forgeries and imprisonment appeared in national and West Country newspapers soon after his appointment.[275] As a popular family doctor he would presumably have attracted more compassion than blame.

Court records for the period of John's magistracy give the impression of a relatively peaceful society. He heard only one case of the wife-beating which was a regular occurrence in mainland Cornwall and one of indecent assault on a child in St Agnes; both defendants were found guilty but only ordered to pay fines of 17/6 and 10/- respectively. Two less serious attacks were reported as causing 'some amusement' in court. On St Agnes a 'cripple whose dog had inherited the canine propensity of barking at a cat' was beaten on the arms and legs 'in a most unmerciful manner' by the frightened feline's owner. The defendant in another case was accused of inflicting a black eye on a man who had unwittingly driven some sheep onto his land. He prompted laughter in the court room, which was apparently regarded as a scene of entertainment, by recounting his combat with the plaintiff: 'We both went down together and fought it out on the ground. There was no one near to interfere.' Both defendants were ordered to pay a five-shilling fine or spend a month in Bodmin Gaol. They opted for the former.[276]

Like much of John's medical work, court hearings were frequently connected with the sea. They involved sailors who refused to 'do their duty', ships which failed to complete voyages or the age-old Scillonian offence of smuggling. A particularly dramatic case occurred in November 1878. It concerned James Nance, 'a man of means [who] holds a good reputation as a pilot'. He had been discovered, after a chase over the cliffs of St Martin's, hiding under furze bushes 'in close proximity to certain goods belonging to the *Ely Rise*'. The proceedings attracted much attention: 'The court and street were crowded throughout the hearing, which lasted until late in the evening. ... More arrests were expected to be made in connection with the matter.' Nance was released on £200 bail and the charges were eventually dropped for lack of evidence. The coastguards continued to keep a close eye on him and in 1886 they caught him landing sacks containing tins of beef, which were 'not a natural production of the Scilly Islands [and] consequently part and parcel of some wreck'. He and another pilot appeared before the bench, consisting of Dorrien Smith, Moyle and two other magistrates. They were found guilty and each fined ten guineas. The magistrates expressed the hope that 'this would be a salutary lesson, not only to them but to others who attempted to do likewise'.[277] But the magistrates were not wholly occupied with crime and punishment. They held frequent sessions to judge how much salvage pilots should be paid for going to the aid of wrecked ships and saving sailors' lives, often endangering their own.

There was no reward, however, for St Agnes families who often assisted wrecked seamen cast ashore. Just six months after the *Schiller* went down the *Catherine Griffiths*, on a voyage to Rio de Janeiro, sank in thick fog, 'unhappily with all hands lost but one'. That one sailor managed to reach St Agnes, after being nine hours in the water. 'He was seen by a girl, who told her father,' reported the *Royal Cornwall Gazette*, 'and the poor fellow received prompt and kind attention.' Three years later the Welsh schooner *Integrity* drifted on to St Agnes after losing her mast and one of her crew off Bishop Rock. The islanders gave aid and comfort to the survivors, one of whom had a broken arm and ribs needing the attention of the doctor, who came over from St Mary's in the lifeboat even though 'it was blowing hard at that time'. Islanders acted without thought of payment, from the kindness of their hearts, but salvage sometimes came their way. Alexander Gibson's grandson Frank was told that after the *Schiller* disaster 'all these green notes were coming ashore, dollar bills, and one particular man paid kids a shilling a bucket for them'.[278]

Shipwrecks were often photographed by the young Alexander Gibson, who worked with his father John and brother Herbert from studios in Scilly and Penzance. It was a dangerous and laborious process, involving rough sea passages and cross-country treks loaded with a heavy field camera, which with 'and all its paraphernalia – a developing tent, a battery of three or four lenses and plates – together weighed substantially over thirty pounds'. The financial reward came from crew members who bought photographs as souvenirs and ship-owners who would pay half a crown a copy to use as evidence for insurance claims. But for Alexander Gibson, with his 'intuitive sense of pictorial form', photography was an art as well as a business. He took great care in posing and timing his shots. He liked to include people where possible and he sometimes employed an early form of photo-shopping, adding, say, clouds to a plain sky. He had no need for embellishment when the cargo steamer *Earl of Lonsdale* foundered off St Agnes in 1885, because it happened opposite the Troy Town maze. This ring of stones, which is said to

Alexander Gibson, Earl of Lonsdale, *1885*

have been put in place by Keeper Amor Clark in 1729 and was a popular spot with islanders, provided a graphic contrast to the sinking ship.[279] Scenes of wreckage, injury and death were part of everyday life for the current inhabitants of the Keeper's cottage.

Chapter 7

Leaving the Islands
1880-1911

The last Scillonian ship, the two-masted *Gleaner*, was launched on her maiden voyage from St Mary's in 1878. One of Alexander Gibson's earliest photographs captured that final moment of Scilly's shipbuilding industry, which had been in decline since the advent of large iron steamers requiring great quantities of imported materials. By 1882, reported 'An Old Salt' in the *Cornishman*, 'all the ship-building yards, save one, are turned into waste grounds, and scarcely the sound of a carpenter's tool is heard in the once busy hive of industry in these Isles'.

Alexander Gibson, Gleaner, *1878.*

With the closing of the yards investors lost money and the island's many shipwrights, sailmakers and carpenters lost their livelihoods. So did many of the seamstresses and milliners who had made fine clothing for yard owners and their wives and everyday dresses and shirts for lesser tradesmen and women. 'There is scarcely any work to do now', observed Richard Maybee in 1883, 'and you will see many people standing about ... who would willingly take any work they could get for low wages.'[280] The change to steam also decreased the number of ships coming into St Mary's harbour, where refuelling was difficult. In its turn this reduced the need for pilots and meant fewer opportunities to mariners, less custom for shopkeepers and a diminished supply of the foreign goods which had always brightened the Scillies. Augustus Smith's Tresco garden, for example, was home to three ostriches brought from Rio de Janeiro 'as a present by the master of a vessel'. And from German merchant ships taking shelter in the roadstead during the Franco-Prussian War in 1870 Smith purchased two tons of exotic shells which he used to decorate a new loggia, describing it as 'a most perfect boudoir' for a mermaid.[281] Similarly, Dr Moyle's drawing-room was adorned with a pair of handsome Dutch plaques given, I am told, by a grateful sea-captain. These have been handed down to me, two personal relics that have survived where many others have been lost. Island cottages, too, were often cheered with ornaments acquired from visiting ships – or from wrecks.

Delft plaques by Makkum Tichelaar c1860.

It was not long, however, before Cornish newspapers were reporting a more hopeful scene in 'the drama of the Scilly Isles': they were transformed into 'one vast Paradise of Flowers'. John Moyle pasted a more scientific account of this new source of income into his scrapbook: three long articles written by J. C. Tonkin in the *Cornishman* on the 'History of the Daffodil with Notes on its Culture in the Islands of Scilly'. After a learned botanical account of the flower's many different varieties Tonkin comes to the humble old English daffodil and the Scilly-white which grew wild on the islands:

> They were scattered about in hedge and ditch, almost unnoticed save by the children, who, on Saturday afternoons, amused themselves by picking 'lilies' (as they called them) and blue-bells. When a part of the waste land was brought into cultivation thousands of bulbs were thrown to the dung-heap to perish.

Scillonians only began to realise the potential value of these flowers during the 1870s. Credit is usually given to William Trevellick of Rocky Hill Farm who sent some of the flowers off to Covent Garden in a hat-box and received £1 for them. With every encouragement from Dorrien Smith, the new industry flourished. Vital advantages were soil and climate well suited to growing flowers and improved rail links, though cultivation has always been at the mercy of the elements. As more acres were devoted to bulb cultivation, more money invested and more new varieties introduced from abroad, daffodils came to replace potatoes as the main commercial crop. 'So universal is their culture,' wrote Tonkin, 'that there is scarcely a person with a square rod of ground but has his or her bed of narcissi.' By 1889 a multitude of hat-boxes would have been required to convey the blooms despatched from St Mary's, which weighed nearly 200 tons.[282]

Tilling the soil, planting, picking, bunching and packing the flowers, making boxes and preserving the bulbs are so labour-intensive that daffodil culture soon replaced ship-building as the main employer on Scilly. Instead of gathering posies children now had three weeks or a month's holiday from school during the busy season, boys picking flowers and girls tying them. Sometimes pupils simply stayed away and the school log book had to record 'many absent about flowers'. Inspectors regretted that 'even younger children are said to be sent to work'. The daffodil had saved the islands from another period of destitution.[283] It also provided picturesque subject matter both for illustrations in Jessie Mothersole's popular book on the Scillies and for picture postcards of island life produced by the Gibsons.[284]

Left:Jessie Mothersole, A Flower House on St Agnes.
Right: Alexander Gibson, William Trevellick and Edwards Moyle at Rocky Hill Farm.

The bulb industry has continued to flourish. As a young reporter on the *Morning Post* in the 1930s J.C. Trewin was sent to Scilly soon after one Christmas to 'see what the flowers are like'. He was entranced by what he found on the first of many visits to the Isles:

> My first flashing visit I spent on St Mary's with its cliffs of weathered granite, veronica-hedged flower-fields, dark velvet earth, shredded sand of almost lunar whiteness, palms and cacti, aloes and fuchsia, and swishing tamarisk. That night the circling sea looked like shot silk or frosted green glass. My path zig-zagged for two miles through glasshouses full of golden soleil d'or narcissi, past fields sown with green spears of budding bulbs, and by a spot where two arum lilies were blowing in the open four months before their time, the air was honey, the sun warm. Yet I had left London in a cotton-wool fog, and it was barely a fortnight since Christmas.[285]

Yet neither golden daffodils nor Elysian fields were enough to prevent many Scillonians, among them Davises and Moyles, from seeking their fortunes elsewhere in the last decades of Queen Victoria's reign.

Edwin Davis's offspring were scattered to the winds. Some of his daughters, whose lives will be followed in Chapter 9, accompanied their husbands to Australia or simply to busier mainland ports, while others took their dressmaking skills to more prosperous areas. Of the seven sons, two had died at sea, two were still sailing the oceans during the 1880s, and two were stationed at lighthouses. The youngest, Lewis Edwin, was the only one to be sent away to school and in the 1881 Census he was registered at Shebbear College in north Devon. Edwin and Martha probably had more money to spare now that most of their offspring had left home and no doubt hoped that their last son would follow a career on dry land. His devout mother may even have longed for Lewis to follow in her proselytising footsteps, since the college was originally founded by the Bible Christians to train boys for the ministry. However, its current headmaster, Thomas Ruddle, aimed rather to give a boy a liberal education 'fitting him for any position in life' and it is not clear which path Lewis took after leaving the school.[286] Indeed, his fate is something of a mystery – one of a kind that family historians often encounter.

According to family memory Lewis followed his brothers on to the waves and 'drowned on his first voyage' after leaving school. This account is supported by the Deaths at Sea register, which records the decease of a boy, Lewis Davis, on board the Brixham ship *Lyra* on 21 December 1881. The tragic tale could explain the observation of a pastor visiting Martha Davis at this time and finding that 'she was not able to attend to the means of grace regularly owing to personal and family afflictions'. Edwin's death on the *Lyra* would have brought the toll of marine losses to three out of seven Davis sons.[287]

There is strong evidence, however, for a different life story, which was compiled by the late Colin Mumford for the Isles of

Scilly Family History Group. According to this, seventeen-year-old L.E. Davis boarded the steamship *Aberdeen* at Plymouth and disembarked in Sydney harbour on 25 April 1884. Like most of the other steerage passengers he is listed as a 'shopman'.[288] Next he can be traced in Penrith, a commercial centre fifty miles west of Sydney, where he could have found work in a store. The main evidence for his presence in the town is that in July 1886 a Lewis E. Davis reported to the police the theft of a square gold locket containing three skeins of hair. There is no record of this precious memento of the young man's mother or sweetheart being retrieved before Lewis E. Davis was listed on the Penrith Death Register for 22 February 1887, with the names of his parents given as Edwin L. and Martha H. As there was no epidemic in New South Wales at this time it's impossible to establish the cause of Lewis's premature death. He was buried in the churchyard of St Stephen's Penrith the next day.[289] Whether by death at sea or by ill-fated emigration, Martha Davis was separated from her youngest son for the last few years of her life.

Headstone in St Agnes churchyard commemorating members of the Davis family: Thomas Lewis, Charles Royer, Martha and Alberta Sarah, 'Gone to be for ever with Jesus'.

Her own death occurred in September 1884, a few days after she suffered a stroke which did not respond to any treatment the doctor could offer. Martha was buried in St Agnes churchyard after a service in the Bible Christian chapel conducted by three circuit ministers. At that time the doctor would also have been treating the tuberculosis of her youngest daughter, Alberta, who died two months later aged twenty-one. She can be found commemorated with her mother and her sailor brothers Thomas and Charles on a weathered headstone, poignant emblem of the vanishing past.

Leaving the Islands

Edwin lived on by himself in the lighthouse cottage, no doubt with occasional help from his youngest remaining daughter Martha Mary, who had married Stephen Hicks, a St Agnes farm labourer. Trinity House records show that Edwin had much business to divert him from his lonely state. A signalling system between St Agnes and St Mary's was installed 'with a view to avoid so large an item of expenditure as was incurred in fetching medical aid on a recent occasion'; the lighting apparatus was improved so that it would flash every half minute; and the old cesspits in the cottages were converted to the recently invented 'inoffensive, safe and economical' dry earth closets. Edwin must also have been involved in plans for a new lighthouse and fog signal to be built on Round Island, a small granite islet on the dangerous northern shores of Scilly. This venture would complement rather than replace the St Agnes light but a further scheme, which Trinity House considered in 1885, would have made Edwin's lighthouse redundant: 'St Agnes Light to be removed to Giant's Castle Head', a promontory on St Mary's.

Alexander Gibson, Round Island Light, *1890s.*

This prospect may explain why Edwin applied that year for superannuation, which Trinity House granted at £59 per annum. In the event, Edwin delayed his retirement as the Giant's Castle idea receded.[290] Instead two costly and difficult projects went ahead: in 1887 Bishop Rock was heightened and protected with a new granite casing; and the new light was erected on Round Island. The Gibson brothers captured the public interest which these dramatic structures aroused. Many a 'jolly party', such as the one photographed, went on excursions to inspect the new lighthouse, receiving 'the greatest courtesy from the lightkeepers'.[291] Dr Moyle depicted it in one of his last Scillonian paintings, which is reproduced on the cover of this book.

The work of the islands' 'medical man' also attracted attention. The *Cornishman* regularly reported on Scillonian accidents and illnesses as well as unhealthy climatic conditions, such as a 'poisonous wind' which caused more sickness than the doctor had known 'for a very long time'. On a single day in October 1882 it catalogued a whole 'Chapter of Accidents': three men fell from a scaffold, a schoolboy 'received a severe blow in the eye' from a cricket-bat and a marine engineer tumbled into the water from St Mary's pier. All these patients survived after receiving the doctor's 'valued aid' but sometimes his labours were in vain. When, for example, a man drowned after diving into deep water even though he could not swim 'every effort was used, under the direction of Mr. J.G. Moyle, M,D, to restore animation, but to no avail.' John did not habitually paste stories of his exploits into his scrapbook but he did cut out an article which included a few lines about his frequent journeys 'over the mighty billows':

> Many a night when the lifeboat would have had a bad time has the doctor taken the helm at the call of duty, and, aided by a willing crew, perilled his life to cross the sea to some poor fisherman's wife in the hour of her travail, and is it small wonder after forty years of such service among the islanders that they speak of him with love and veneration?[292]

Similar stories of John's 'rough weather experiences' were recounted by his grandson, Trevellick Moyle, for the *Scillonian* magazine. A typical day in his later years involved going straight from a confinement in Bryer over a heavy sea to Porthlow on St Mary's Bay to attend Billy Prideaux's broken leg; after scrambling into a cart waiting on the beach, he was able to make Billy comfortable 'by setting his leg with the help of a jab of morphine'. Trevellick also recounts that his father, Edwards, was occasionally sent as a boy to Dorrien Smith's lime pit for a bucket of 'quenched lime', to be used as 'the foundation for all the cough and numerous other medicines' which John mixed for his patients. He was, like his own father Richard Moyle, a true surgeon-apothecary able to turn his hand to a great variety of tasks, 'an all-round man ... at home both with the pestle and the scalpel'.[293]

Sometimes the newspapers reported vandalism and street brawls with which John was concerned in his double capacity as doctor and magistrate. In September 1886, during a 'prolonged outbreak of rowdyism among St Mary's youths', an altercation erupted during a concert and dance held to raise money for the brass band fund. A hostile crowd followed two of the participants as they departed 'in company of two young women' and assaulted them 'with savage brutality' causing injuries to both men. The victims immediately presented themselves at John's house in the Parade, exhibiting faces which 'bore traces of a brutal attack'. The doctor used this as evidence in court where he and his fellow magistrates sentenced the two main assailants to a month in Bodmin Gaol with hard labour and fined the other young culprits ten shillings each plus court expenses. Thus, concluded the *Cornishman*, hooliganism in Scilly was checked and it could return to reporting lighter matters such as the 'nocturnal adventures' of the islands' cats.[294]

John also took part in less exacting activities. A 'rusticating journalist', visiting St Mary's on 'a red-letter day' to mark the opening of new public buildings erected for the Queen's jubilee, observed him at a ball held in the evening. The young scribe was patronising about the rustic crowd and 'rough and ready musicians', but he was clearly impressed by the seventy-year-old medical man from Penzance:

> Then there was the hale Old Doctor, who officiated as master-of-ceremonies, as young at heart as when he picked blackberries at Carn Galver, made mud-pies surreptitiously in the garden across the way at

Penzance, or toddled around in the shallow water at Marazion, without blushing for his nakedness. 'Partners for the polka!' he cried, and the floor was crowded with eager couples, for even an untamed elephant could go through the one, two, three movements of this dance, if he took the trouble to try.[295]

John continued to preside over waltzes, quadrilles, the Highland Fling and even a sailor's hornpipe until after two in the morning, by which time the temperature in the hall had increased 'until the festive crowd were treated to a Turkish bath'.

Such accounts give a good impression of a hard-working, popular and genial man, who took his duties seriously but did not stand on ceremony. Without a store of personal diaries or letters, it is harder to penetrate John Moyle's inner thoughts or to understand how he fared as one of the few well-educated men on the islands.

John obviously kept records and engaged in correspondence as part of his professional duties but the only such document to have survived is a letter written to a patient's niece, who happened to be one of Florence Nightingale's earliest trainee nurses. In it he gives a detailed account of how he is treating Mrs Hall's lumbar complaint and hopes that she will soon 'be able to walk out in the balmy air of a Spring in Scilly'. He also records the conversations he has had with her about the earlier visits to the islands of 'highly cultured folks' such as Mr and Mrs Lewes, Tennyson and Wilkie Collins.[296] Because of the recipient's connection with Florence Nightingale this letter has been preserved by the Wellcome Institute for the history of medicine. It gives a tantalising glimpse of a Victorian GP's everyday round – would that there were more.

I did possess, however, some examples of John's writing on non-medical topics. Interspersed among his scrapbook cuttings from the *Cornish Telegraph* and the *Cornishman* on largely Scillonian matters, are three long articles in his own hand. Two of them are acknowledged as copied from books he must have had in his library and one is evidently his own composition, but all reveal his preoccupations and thoughts during the last few years of his career. They deal with religious matters even though nothing in his previous life or background suggests that he was especially devout. Closer reading reveals that John was not finding solace in faith as old age approached but rather struggling to reconcile the scientific reasoning he applied to Natural History with a belief in God – as were many educated late Victorians.

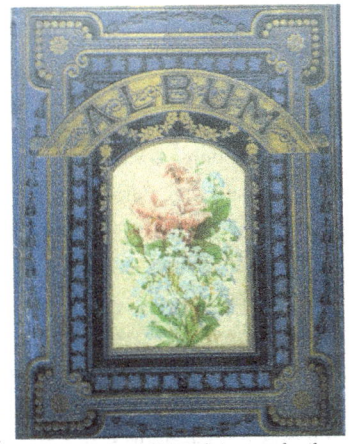

John Grenfell Moyle's scrapbook which he began on 27 August 1888.

The first piece comes from *Salvator Mundi*, a book of lectures by Baptist Minister Samuel Cox. It deals with the redeeming love of God and made me wonder whether John was thinking of his errant brother Vyvyan as he copied out sentences such as this: 'God permits those who have made an evil choice to do the evil they have chosen, and to suffer by and for it, to be corrected by it.' But even the impenitent, Cox argues, are not 'doomed, the very instant they die, to an endless and depraving torment', for a loving God could not allow his creatures to suffer in this way.[297] Clearly, neither he nor John believed in Hell.

Another concept often rejected in the wake of scientific discoveries was the creation story, which John tackles in the second article entitled 'The Bible'. Extracts taken, with some adaptation and underlining, from an address by the eminent neurologist, Dr James Ross, describe the first chapter of Genesis as 'a poetic history', rejecting the idea of 'special creation' in favour of Darwin's theory of 'assimilation and reproduction' throughout the 'struggle of existence'. But God is not denied. The extracts end with an affirmation of His 'superintending power' working in nature:

> God was within and around us. He was without us in the movements and affections of Matter and in the transformation of Energy. He might be found in the dust which we tread beneath our feet, as in the stars which shine on us from afar, and above all he is within us in our reverential feelings, in our instinctive longing after the Eternal and in the still small voice of our conscience.[298]

John clearly chose these sentences because they reflected his own ideas about religion. He also lived up to Ross's advice to the medical students he was addressing: to keep their medical knowledge 'afresh', to engage in 'wide culture' through literature, painting or music, to study 'the problems of knowing and being' and to allay doubts by following the precept 'Do the duty which lies nearest thee'.[299]

Inside John's scrapbook I found a home-made booklet containing the Hebrew alphabet and rules of grammar in his handwriting – he was obviously teaching himself the language in which most of the Old Testament was originally written. In the third essay, a very long one on 'The Devil', he uses this and his schoolboy knowledge of ancient Greek to analyse the Biblical use of the words 'Devil' and 'Satan'. He finds that they have often been mis-translated and that they really referred to a 'false accuser' or an 'adversary', to humans rather than to a demon. He goes on to argue that 'there cannot be two omnipotents, two omniscients', drawing the emphatic conclusion: 'If there is a God there cannot be a Devil.' As for why people go on believing in such a being, he claims plausibly that they simply 'cannot shake off received opinions ... tied up in the Bundle of Beliefs'. His real target is organised religion:

> The most powerful obstacle to the expulsion of the Devil is the paid Parsonry – they cannot afford to give up this invisible supernatural Friend. He is one of the best articles of their stock in trade and they don't intend to give him up.

Leaving the Islands

There is no evidence that John ever expressed such an anticlerical opinion in public, however rational it might have been. His views would hardly have been popular among Scillonians who still possessed, according to their native historian, 'all the essential characteristics of evangelism', among which were 'literal stress placed on the Bible and the certain belief in an after-life of rewards or punishments'.[300] Mid-century ecclesiastical returns reveal high attendance at all places of worship on the islands and this showed no sign of diminishing in later years. John himself, as a magistrate and well-known pillar of St Mary's society, no doubt attended the Anglican church when his medical duties allowed – but kept his opinions to himself. His quiet questioning was not, of course, unusual in the decades following Darwin's *Origin of Species* (1857) and *Descent of Man* (1871). The ecclesiastical historian, Owen Chadwick, finds that 'new views of the Bible became steadily commoner among Anglicans and nonconformists' during the 1870s and 1880s but that sceptics, like John, usually 'refrained from proclaiming these new opinions loudly'. Meanwhile, 'most preachers continued to assume that a real fish swallowed Jonah' – another indigestible concept for a man of science.[301]

The first of my great-great-grandfathers to retire from Scilly was Edwin Davis, who left St Agnes lighthouse in 1888 with no fanfares despite his having served forty-seven years as its Keeper. He didn't stay on the islands, as his own father had done, perhaps because there was no daughter willing and able to fulfil her traditional role by taking him in. Instead, he crossed the water to Penzance, where he took up

Edwin Lewis Davis in old age, photographed in the Gibsons' Penzance studio.

residence in 10 Union Terrace named after the nearby Union Workhouse. His widowed daughter Mary Jane Boulden came to act as helpmeet to the grizzled old man, who was not by all accounts an easy companion. Indeed, according to family legend he was 'a right old bugger'.

At the time of Edwin's move to Penzance his son John Hutchings Davis, whose wife had already died, lived nearby with his mother-in-law and three children. But he was at sea, engaged in the China trade aboard the screw steamer *Glencoe*. In February 1889 the family received the news that the ship had sunk with all hands lost after a collision with a sailing vessel during 'a blinding snowstorm, which at sea is worse than a fog'. First Officer J.H. Davis was among 'the names of those known to have left Liverpool on board the *Glencoe*'.[302] John's three orphans were brought up by their grandmother. Three (or four, if Lewis is counted) of the Keeper's seven sons had now perished at sea. When Edwin himself expired of senile decay in 1894 the death certificate was signed by his nephew William Legg, another master mariner and older son of his late sister Elizabeth, as none of his three remaining sons were in the vicinity.[303] Edwin is buried in Penzance Cemetery, where he shares a grave with his daughter Jemima who had predeceased him. The Trinity House pension ended with the Keeper's death, as did the tenancy in Union Terrace, so that Mary Jane was once again left without a home or means of support.

The Penzance grave of Edwin Lewis Davis and his daughter Jemima.

* * * *

Leaving the Islands

As there was no equivalent of Trinity House to pay John Moyle a pension, he 'worked well beyond sixty-five' like most doctors of that time.[304] After all, he had to support Jessie and Margaretta as well as his two youngest daughters, Janie and Rovena, who were still at school. There is no sign that the doctor was finding it difficult to cope with the peculiar difficulties of his practice but his decision to retire at seventy-three may have been hastened by his losing the 'stay and adornment' of his home. The death of 56-year-old Eliza on 6 January 1890 was as sudden and unexpected as that of Edwin's second wife, Martha, at about the same age. It was in November of the same year that John and his four female dependants left the islands.

The *Cornishman*, which had so often reported on John's medical work, gave a full account of the gathering held in St Mary's town hall to mark his departure. First, Algernon Dorrien Smith presented him with 'an annuity of £52 a year and a purse of gold containing £25', the proceeds of subscriptions varying 'from the 6d of the widow to pounds of those better able to afford such a sum. (Applause)'. Smith's tribute concluded:

> A doctor's work on these islands is in no sense light. He has often to cross stormy seas in open boats at all times and under all circumstances, but every one on these islands knows that since 'Our old doctor' came here forty-one years ago he has ever been ready to do this work. (Hear) Whether required by the wealthiest or the poorest amongst us he has never flinched at the call of Duty. (Loud applause) We are all of us liable, humanly speaking, to our failings, but he has always shown a good heart, in full sympathy with his patients, and with pluck and courage to carry out his work on the darkest night and the stormiest wintry seas. (Applause.)

Expressing his gratitude for the generous present, the doctor said that the annuity would render him 'altogether independent for the rest of a journey, which is now well nigh over. (No, no.)' In fact, it was lower than the lightkeeper's pension and, as a contemporary survey of working-class households in Lambeth found, it was very difficult to house, clothe, clean, warm, light and feed a family of four or five persons on 'round about a pound a week'.[305] If John was to live comfortably in his old age he would need to have money put by or help from his older offspring.

In his speech John paid graceful tribute to the stalwart character of Scillonians, unaffected by 'the fawning sycophancy of fulsome adulation'. Like the artist he was, he used visual imagery to make his point, comparing them to the coastline he had often painted:

> Take one of your grand headlands, say Peninnis! There it stands out – bold and steadfast on its ocean-bed! A storm comes on and the wind howls and the great waves clash over it – swirling, twirling, and seething with white foam! The gale is gone! And look at the majestic pile of granite! It is all the same – unaltered, unchanged, and undamaged. ... Now again regard this headland. It is summer-time and the granite is scintillating in the morning sun; and the headland is resting quietly on the calm water below. It is still unchanged!

He looked back to the shipbuilding, piloting and potato-growing which had flourished during his early years on St Mary's and welcomed the flower-culture which had taken their place. For the future he suggested that orchids might also be grown and that Scilly might now be developed as a health resort, concluding that 'there is no occasion for the inhabitants to lose heart'.

Five days after this presentation John and his daughters crossed over to the mainland, where a welcome party greeted him:

> A lady brought a beautiful bouquet to the railway terminus and her most affectionate greetings. The good old doctor had ushered her into the world and her children. The *Cornishman* cordially joins in the sincerest good wishes that the genial doctor's dignified ease may be prolonged and pleasant. Though he has dropped scalpel and discarded pestle, may the painter of the Queen's visit to Mount's Bay, which graces the Penzance town-council's room, give the public many a picture of the Sunny South Devon now to be his home.[306]

Leaving the Islands

In fact, John was not to settle in Devon. His journey to Dawlish was just to visit his daughter Annie, who was about to be married there. By the time of the 1891 Census, John and all his family had moved in with his oldest daughter Emma, who worked as a schoolmistress in Redhill, Surrey. Before leaving Penzance, however, John had his photograph taken at the Gibsons' studio, which displayed it in its window, prompting a further tribute from the *Cornishman*:

John Grenfell Moyle, 1890.

Before us, much as he has been for the last decades, is the doctor of the Scilly Isles – Mr J. G. Moyle. There is just a touch of the natty young man we saw when first we knew the doctor in the peeping handkerchief and horseshoe pin. Wonderfully well-preserved, too, is Mr Moyle ... considering his work, his exposure to weather, and his three score and ten (and a few years over). The worthy doctor looks at you, fair and square, but cheerily – just as he has done, thousands of times, as he entered the sick-chamber, to use his skill and, while he could, to employ those wondrous medicaments – the hopeful voice and cheerful countenance.[307]

John's last task had been to introduce his successor, Dr Francis Turnly Gage – 'a gentleman well versed in all the modern improvements of medical science, a skilful operator and a sound practitioner', who would 'rise, Phoenix-like, from the ashes – the dead ashes of the old bird'.[308] Unfortunately, scientific advances and sound skills were not sufficient to deal with the medical emergency which struck the islands soon after the new doctor's arrival. A pandemic known as 'Asiatic flu' had been advancing rapidly through Europe after its initial outbreak in the Russian Empire in May 1889, reaching Britain by the end of that year. It eased off in early 1890 but second and third waves arrived in 1891 and 1892, affecting large swathes of the country. Statistics are as uncertain as was diagnosis but it has been estimated that about a third of the population of England and Wales became ill and the official death toll was 110,000.[309]

The Isles of Scilly had escaped most earlier epidemics by means of the efficient quarantine system which John and his predecessors had enforced. But influenza, which many doctors attributed to 'miasma' or noxious vapours rather than to bacteria, was not a notifiable disease. Nor was it taken very seriously in most of the press. It's not surprising therefore that Scilly was stricken in late 1891 with 'fresh cases occurring hourly'. As in the country as a whole, where the Prime Minister was seriously ill and one of Queen Victoria's grandsons died, prominent Scillonians were not spared. The death was widely announced of the 'Queen of Scilly', Edith Dorrien Smith, and the new doctor was affected so badly that he could not attend patients.[310] Even if he had been fit, he could have offered no treatment except doses of quinine, whisky and brandy, or risky injections of sodium salicylate. These remedies did little to alleviate symptoms similar to those of the current coronavirus: runny nose, headache, fever, severe chest inflammation and impairment of the central nervous system. It was the deadliest influenza outbreak yet to hit Britain – though much worse was to follow in the twentieth and twenty-first centuries.

John must have been aware of the pandemic at his new home in Redhill and he might well have read in the *British Medical Journal* for August 1891 that the disease 'followed the steam train from London to rail hubs in the provinces'.[311] Meanwhile he carried on painting, using his Cornish memories as well as depicting his new environment – much as his brother Thomas had done in Australia. Two fine works bear the date 1892. A painting of Tooth Rock might even show himself and his late wife gazing at its sunlit surface, while a depiction of Redhill reveals his appreciation of a much less dramatic inland scene.[312]

John Grenfell Moyle, Tooth Rock, Peninnis Head.

John Grenfell Moyle, Redhill from the Common.

John did not have long to enjoy leisure with brush and easel. In April 1893 he suffered heart failure leading to 'oedema and moist gangrene of feet', from which painful conditions he died at the age of 76. The death certificate was signed by Emma, who was present and inherited a sum of £143 14s 6d and her father's effects. John's grave in Reigate cemetery has disappeared without trace and the inscription on his shared memorial in St Mary's is barely legible – but he is remembered in the islands to this day.

He had outlived all his siblings except the bank clerk William, who was still living in Islington, and the destitute Rev Vyvyan, whose further disgrace he did not witness. Later chapters will consider the lives of the women John left behind, as well as the many Davis daughters.

Back in Scilly change followed the departure of the two stalwarts of island life. The old lighthouse itself was improved with expensive new 'fountain lamps' installed soon after Edwin's retirement.[313] It survived until 1911 when it was superseded by a new structure on Peninnis Head, the southernmost point of St Mary's. When the St Agnes light went out for the last time the inhabitants of the island gathered around the tower to mourn the familiar old beacon. The building itself survives both as an ancient monument, a 'rare example of the early post-medieval coal-burning lighthouse towers', and as a day light which is always kept freshly painted. In 2022, however, it was illuminated for the first time in 111 years in honour of the Queen's Platinum Jubilee.[314]

St Agnes Lighthouse in 2022.

The medical and judicial practices previously followed by John Moyle were also subject to change. The flu epidemic so starkly revealed the danger of relying on one hard-pressed doctor to maintain the health of the islands that a Nursing Association was soon established. Two nurses on St Mary's and Tresco would now be on hand 'to supplement the doctor's work'. The islands also gained a Medical Officer of Health. His appointment followed on the Local Government Act of 1888, by which Scilly acquired its own freely-elected democratic Council to replace 'the autocratic beneficial rule' instituted by Augustus Smith. An Inspector of Nuisances and a School Attendance Officer would now keep islanders up to the mark.[315]

The restructuring also provided a new career for John's son, Edwards, who became Clerk to the Council and Registrar in 1894, acquiring so many administrative roles by 1914 that his entry in Kelly's Directory took up ten lines. He was so versatile and generous with his time that, as his obituary in the *Scillonian* put it, 'any good cause found in him an enthusiastic supporter'. 'One of the best-known men on the islands' was even a tourist attraction; the *Visitors' Companion* published by the Gibson brothers described him as 'the genial official ... always willing, if at leisure, to show any enthusiast' around the 'unique gardens' and 'Scillonian antiquities' at Rocky Hill, the flower farm and garden he took over from his uncle by marriage, William Trevellick.[316]

Edwards Nance Vyvyan Moyle in full wet weather gear.

The obituary of Edwards made proud reference to his father, remembering John as an 'unusually beloved' doctor and a 'clever amateur artist'.[317] But it made no mention of Edwards's own watercolours, which are now prized and collected by islanders.

His great-grandson, Peter Malec who lives in St Mary's, told me that Edwards would always have a supply of postcards with him, on which to paint when the mood took him. Every painting Peter showed me depicted the sea and ships which have always pervaded the life of Scillonians.

Characteristic seascape by Edwards Moyle.

The Davis name had already died out on the islands by the twentieth century but the bloodline has survived, as it has for the Moyles. When the last of the Keeper's seafaring sons, his namesake Edwin Lewis, was lost in a shipwreck in 1897 his widow and children left for the mainland. His sister Martha Mary was now the only sibling left on St Agnes, where her husband Stephen Hicks became the sub-postmaster. They had one son before Martha died in 1892, when the boy was only eight. Her death certificate indicates that she had been wasting away from tuberculosis for five years. The motherless family remained on the island and it was to be Martha Mary's grandson Lewis Hicks who converted the derelict Keepers' cottages to meet the growing demand for holiday homes. They were then inhabited by his son Francis Hicks, a bulb-grower and proud guardian of the sturdy old

Leaving the Islands

lighthouse. The nearby church, where many members of both the Davis and the Hicks families are buried, now contains beautiful memorials to the St Agnes lighthouse and to brave rescue boats – windows designed by the Scillonian glass artist Oriel Hicks, complete with Biblical texts.[318]

AND GOD SAID LET THERE BE LIGHT AND THERE WAS LIGHT.

WHEN YOU PASS THROUGH THE WATERS I WILL BE WITH YOU.

Chapter 8

Lighthouse Keepers and their Families

The Davis sons who complied with their father's wishes by leaving the merchant marine and entering the lighthouse service were his first-born William and the second youngest, Sam. By the time they posed in their uniforms for a Penzance studio photograph with the retired and rather shrunken Keeper of St Agnes, all their brothers had perished at sea except Edwin junior, who was also shipwrecked a few years later. William and Sam did not, like their brothers, turn their wives into widows. Even so, their family lives were far from easy since their work imposed demands for which their own lighthouse childhood had not prepared them.[319]

Edwin Davis with his sons, Samuel (left) and William (right.)

Lighthouse Keepers and their Families

Trinity House did not offer most keepers the chance to remain on the same land-station for the whole of their careers and it's not clear why an exception had been made for Edwin Davis. The usual practice was for a keeper to be rotated, according to the needs of the service, between lighthouses. These came in three types. As keepers interviewed by Tony Parker in the 1970s explained, there were shore lights where they lived with their families; rock lights which had some land around them, on which 'to 'stretch your legs, do a spot of fishing and get some fresh air'; and towers 'sticking straight out of the sea' where 'you can't get any exercise at all'.[320] Wherever he was stationed, the keeper's routine duties were much the same as those spelt out by Trinity House in 1839, but I suspect that as time went on they were more strictly enforced. Edwin had been taken by surprise when inspectors arrived by boat at 11.00pm in July 1861. According to their report:

> Mr Graves and Captain Ryder found the door of the lightroom was locked and the keeper absent. He came almost immediately and stated why he had left the house, and that he was not obliged to remain always in the lantern. He stated that during his experience of twenty-one years the chain of the revolving apparatus had only once broken, and was then replaced in a few minutes, during which the frame was kept moving by hand.

This example suggests that the constant presence of the keeper was indeed vital, but the inspectors were evidently satisfied with Edwin's explanation. His sons would probably have been dismissed for failing to maintain, as Trinity House instructed, 'perpetual watch ... throughout the night'.[321] But there is no evidence that they neglected their duties.

William Legg Davis m. Elizabeth Broom 1861
|
.. *1 Elizabeth b1864   2 Edwin b1872*

William Legg Davis entered the service in 1856 after a period as an apprentice mariner, which was thought to provide the best preparation for a lighthouse career. His brief training took place at Harwich and was designed, according to a twentieth-century keeper, to 'turn you into a good all-round handy-man so that you can put your hand to anything that crops up'.[322] As well as tending the lamps and keeping detailed logs, he needed to be able to cook, clean and generally look after himself during the two-month periods spent on rock or tower lights. William would need such skills for the next three years during which he was stationed on the new screw-pile tower at Gunfleet, which stood in the sandy seabed six miles off the Essex coast. Here he shared spells of duty and rudimentary accommodation with one other keeper.

It must have been during an interval of leave in Harwich that William met and married Elizabeth Broom, daughter of a Trinity House light-vessel mariner, well accustomed to the rigours of the service. Over the next thirty years William was given ten different postings to shore, rock and tower lights of varying degrees of comfort and convenience. During this time he and Elizabeth brought up a daughter and a son. She was obliged to pack the family's belongings into tea-chests, move to remote places where she had to make new friends and manage without her husband for months on end. Like the keepers' wives who spoke to Tony Parker, she had to be 'a self-contained person, ... not needing the company of other people all the time, ... able to do things for yourself'. On the other hand, Trinity House provided a keeper with the rare benefits of rent-free accommodation 'superior to that occupied by the same class in ordinary life', property maintenance, a safe job, a pension 'in case of age or infirmity', and provision for his widow or family in case of his death. Such benefits gave many of its employees 'a real sense of security and belonging'.[323]

The Davises were lucky in their third posting. After a spell at Portland Bill, William was appointed in 1866 as an Assistant Keeper of the new Dovercourt Lights built on the beach to guide vessels into Harwich harbour. The 1871 Census registered the couple with their seven-year-old daughter in the Lighthouse

Lighthouse Keepers and their Families

Cottages, which were rather similar to the one in which William had grown up, today billed as a feature of the historic maritime town. It was here that the family enjoyed ten years of normal domestic life, during which their son Edwin was born and their eight-year-old daughter baptised with the name of her mother.

On being promoted to the rank of Principal Keeper in 1876 William was sent to the Smalls Lighthouse, a move which his family could hardly have welcomed. It was the most remote of all Trinity House lights, built on a rock twenty miles off the Pembrokeshire coast in seas so storm-ridden that often the keepers could not be relieved for months. It's not clear where William's wife and children were housed during this three-year spell of duty but I'm sure that they heard fearful stories about earlier keepers. In 1801 one of a quarrelsome pair died and his colleague dared not commit the body to the waves in case he was suspected (like Thomas Kirby on St Agnes) of murder or incitement to suicide. He had to keep the light going in the company of his partner's decaying corpse for several more weeks, after which he was so worn and haggard that his friends and family did not recognise him. This tragedy inspired Robert Eggers to produce his film *The Lighthouse* (2016), a psychological thriller which took 'creative liberties' with the facts in an attempt 'to capture the lonely suffocating experience of being stranded on an ocean rock with no means of communication with the outside world'.[324] In the real world, Kirby's case prompted Trinity House to rule that there should always be three keepers on duty on a sea-based light. Subsequently

Victorian engraving of the Smalls Lighthouse.

the Smalls was the site of further disaster when a huge wave shattered the keepers' room causing severe injuries to all three, one of whom died. By the time William Davis took charge a new sturdier tower and landing-wharf had been built 'in the strongest manner possible, to resist the heavy seas'[325] – but Elizabeth must still have worried when the winds blew hard in the Irish Sea. The extra pay awarded to rock-keepers may have been some compensation.[326]

It was such a hazardous location that during William's time Trinity House further decreed that 'the Principal Keeper or the senior Assistant Keeper be always on the Rock' and relieved monthly (rather than two-monthly) and that 'a permanent extra keeper at Rock Pay be appointed'. Their work increased when they were supplied with 'gun-cotton rockets … to be fired every half-hour during foggy periods'. These proved so unreliable that they caused the death of one employee 'by an explosion in the detonator', after which new instructions on the handling of the devices were sent to the Keeper at Smalls.[327]

A brief and more comfortable spell looking after the two lights at Orfordness in Suffolk was followed by a four-year posting to Mucking, a screw-pile light on the mud-flats at the mouth of the Thames estuary. This sounds an unattractive setting for family life, especially as evoked by Dickens in his memorable description of Pip's desperate attempt to take Magwitch 'well down the river in a boat … and lie in some quiet spot' until they could escape to a foreign steamer:

> A little squat shoal-lighthouse on open piles, stood crippled in the mud on stilts and crutches; and slimy stakes stuck out of the mud, and slimy stones stuck out of the mud, and red landmarks and tide-marks stuck out of the mud, and an old landing-stage and an old roofless building slipped into the mud, and all about us was stagnation and mud.[328]

Mucking did at least boast a church, a pub and a school, as well as the 'solid-looking pair of white-painted cottages on the marshes', which I found displayed in a faded old photograph on a local history website.[329] It was in one of these substantial dwellings that William, Elizabeth, their seventeen-year-old daughter (known as Lizzie) and nine-year-old Edwin were registered in 1881, along with three boarders (a plumber, a seaman and a chalk quarryman) to supplement their income. There was enough land for a vegetable garden which enabled Elizabeth to provide wholesome meals for the household. Above all, the cottage was within reassuring sight of the lighthouse, which could be reached by means of a gantry. Even so, it must have been a solitary life, especially for a teenage girl like Lizzie, too old for the village school and with no occupation except helping her mother with the chores. Like another keeper's daughter, who recorded recollections of her life, she was often 'the only young girl on the station ... [and] never had a girl companion'.[330] She would also find it difficult to find a sweetheart.

The family's next destination was also quite remote, Great Castle Head Lighthouse on the jagged coast of Pembrokeshire at the entrance to Milford Haven. Erected in 1870, it had its own accommodation consisting of three adjoining houses complete, as a modern estate agent boasts, with flagstone floors and built-in Welsh dressers, in which Elizabeth could store the belongings transported by train from the Thames estuary. Edwin, now aged twelve, went to school in Milford Haven town, where he was probably 'regarded as something of an oddity, being English and living on a lighthouse'. This was the experience of Patricia Gumbrell in the 1950s, when she made the long and risky journey to school by bicycle and bus – until Trinity House provided a taxi for the lighthouse children.[331] In the 1880s Edwin had to walk the six miles or so to school – yet he gained enough education to qualify as an engineer.

It was not long before William was moved back to the Thames estuary, where he manned Maplin on Foulness Island for a year and Chapman on Canvey Island for three years. These were screw-pile lights perched on the sandbanks at the mouth of the Thames which had caused many a wreck. His wife, son and daughter decided not to follow him to these bleak locations but to settle near the East India Docks in Poplar, a busy area where Edwin could find engineering work. The 1891 Census named the eighteen-year-old lad as head of a household, living with his mother and sister at 16 Portree Street, a three-bedroomed bay-windowed terrace. Their proximity to the Thames meant that William could easily travel by Trinity House boat to join them during periods of leave. Moreover, this location was only a few streets away from Hackney, where some Davis kinsfolk were living. Family contact was obviously important for those moving from one remote station to another since, as Patricia Gumbrell observed, 'relations can seem very far away.'[332]

Before the end of 1891, however, Keeper Davis was sent back to south Wales. West Usk Light, at the mouth of the River Usk near Newport, was his final station, providing the family with accommodation in the rounded rooms below the lantern (which now serve as a picturesque wedding venue). William was still living there with his son and daughter when the next census was taken in 1901, but Elizabeth had died earlier that year. He retired in 1902, by which time he had served Trinity House for forty-three years and was entitled to an annual pension of £69 7s 3d. In addition, his travelling expenses 'first to Newport and subsequently to Penzance' were paid 'in accordance with the usual practice'.[333] Thanks to the opening of the Severn tunnel, then the Great Western Railway's greatest work of construction, he could make the journey from south Wales to far Cornwall on a single train.

The West Usk Lighthouse.

Lighthouse Keepers and their Families

It seems that William was intending to retire to Penzance, even though few members of his family still lived there. But his death in December 1904 was registered in Newport, where he was probably visiting his son and daughter who had moved into the town together. There was plenty of work for Edwin as a 'ship fitter' and it was here that forty-two-year-old Lizzie met Eugene Coquerel, a French lamplighter employed by Newport Gas Company, whom she married in 1906. The couple shared a small house (described in the 1911 Census as having three rooms including the kitchen) with Edwin but no offspring. Lizzie died in 1930 after fourteen years of married life and Edwin stayed on in Wales, but never married. Their hard-working lives had not brought this close-knit family much in the way of material reward.

Samuel (Sam) James Davis m. Mary Bowen 1884
|
1 Esther b1886 2 Alberta b1888 3 Thomas b1890 4 Samuel b1900

The lighthouse career of William's younger brother Sam was a little less demanding, with six different appointments as opposed to ten. After an apprenticeship as a mariner with his brother John and a three-year stint at Casquets in the Channel Islands, he became Assistant Keeper on Bardsey Island, two miles off the west coast of Wales. This was an awkward situation for English keepers, who were regarded with some suspicion by the 130 or so Welsh-speaking residents, but Sam's path was eased by the warmth of Principal Keeper Thomas Bowen and his family. The local minister's diary records that at Christmas 1882, the year of Sam's arrival, 'the Schoolhouse has been excellently made up for the occasion by Miss Mary Bowen', who played an active part in the celebrations and helped her mother serve tea and 'bara brith' (Welsh tea bread) to the children.[334] Two years later Sam married the amiable Mary – just as his sister Mary Jane had married Assistant Keeper Boulden – and they set up home in the cottage next door to his parents-in-law.

Three children were born to the couple before they left Bardsey in 1893. Such 'happenings caused a great deal of worry and excitement on the island', according to a keeper's daughter who was born there in 1903. There was no doctor on Bardsey and the crossing to the mainland hadn't improved since 1825, when a Trinity House inspector reported that 'the landing place is very confined and dangerous, being a small cove defended only by broken rocks, and gales of wind on the whole coast must be terrific.'[335] Even so, Esther and Alberta were safely delivered at Aberdaron on the Penrhyn peninsula and Thomas was born on the island itself. In 1892, however, the children lost the comforting presence of the grandparents after whom two of them had been named. Keeper Thomas Bowen died in office and his widow, Esther, left their cottage to live on the mainland with a Trinity House pension of £19 13s 4d.[336]

When the time came for Sam Davis to move, he was luckier than some keepers, transferring along the Welsh coast to Anglesey Island, where he served on two of its seven lighthouses over the next sixteen years. The first posting was to Skerries on an islet two miles offshore. Here his unfortunate colleague, Assistant Keeper Evans, suffered a mental breakdown and was sent to Denbigh Lunatic Asylum. His wages were at first paid to his wife but eventually Trinity House awarded a 'pension of £21 10s 8d to J.H. Evans who is insane'. Sam spent the rest of his time on Anglesey as Assistant and, after 1903, Principal Keeper of a lighthouse at the end of Holyhead's dog-legged breakwater, which is over a mile and a half long. Meanwhile Mary and their children moved into a rented terrace house in Mountain View, which was near the beach and within sight of the lighthouse.[337] It was, however, a sad period for the Davis family: in December 1893 eight-year-old Esther died of scarlet fever with Sam at her bedside. Trinity House made a payment of £5 towards the medical expenses incurred over the fourteen days of the child's illness.[338] Perhaps some consolation was afforded in 1900 by the birth of a late child, Samuel.

Lighthouse Keepers and their Families

Holyhead was a well-connected town, very different from the remote locations so often braved by keepers' families. It proved to be an excellent place to bring up the three children, who attended school and made friends; so when Sam was moved on in 1909, the couple decided to leave them there, living in the same house and cared for by Mary's widowed sister. Young Samuel was still at school, Thomas went to work as a clerk for Holyhead Water Company and Alberta helped her aunt at home.

Meanwhile Sam and Mary took up residence at Lynmouth Foreland, perched on the north Devon coast. Even though it was a newly built land light with substantial cottages, its inaccessible position on a steep north-facing cliff made it unpopular with keepers and their wives, as Tony Parker heard:

> It was one of those isolated ones ... three miles from the nearest main road. What's more it was built right on the edge of a cliff; and all the land behind it was up and down every few yards. ... The cottages were enclosed behind a great high wall you couldn't see over, it was exactly like living in a prison. ... It was lonely, bitterly cold in winter and usually wet and raining in summer, really it was a dreadful place.[339]

Keeper Davis at the Lynmouth Lighthouse.

The cottages have now been converted into a single National Trust holiday home boasting a sunset view, but it comes with the warning that 'the cliff falls immediately below the cottage to the sea and rises steeply behind the building', so that children must be 'supervised at all times'. No wonder Sam and Mary decided not to bring their family to this bleak outpost – but it must have been a wrench.

Their remote existence is captured in a contemporary postcard, in which I recognise Keeper Sam looking rather small and diffident as he poses on the lantern. But loneliness was not the only occupational hazard. Lynmouth's lenses worked on the latest system of high-speed rotation: clockwork was superseded by a mercury bath in a circular tray, which could be set in motion with a finger – or even by a small child. This produced a quicker flash and greater safety for seafarers; but not for the keepers, 'who breathed and touched the mercury on their daily cleaning rounds'. Even before this invention, mercury products had been used to clean and polish lenses but the fumes were now far more pervasive. As mercury poisoning can cause 'confusion, depression and hallucinations', some modern scholars have suggested that its use helped to account for the madness often associated with light keeping.[340] It may indeed explain several instances of erratic behaviour which appear in these pages.

In 1918 both Sam and Mary appear for the first time on an electoral register, after the Representation of the People Act gave all men the vote and enfranchised women over thirty if they were, or were married to, property occupiers. The property they occupied by that time was Happisburgh Lighthouse, one of a pair of lights erected in the 1790s to mark a safe passage around sands off the coast of Norfolk. The danger of coastal erosion, which still threatens

Happisburgh Lighthouse and cottages.

the village, had already prompted the demolition of the Low Lighthouse but the surviving one provided a comfortable setting for Sam and Mary's last years of lighthouse life. They were joined there by Alberta who features in the 1921 Census, performing 'home duties' alongside her mother but not qualifying for a vote even though she was over thirty. Sam seems, however, to have been pensioned off in 1922, for after that the couple's electoral address changed to 'Sand Dune', Happisburgh – an aptly named abode. Even if he had not retired Sam would soon have become redundant, for in 1929 Happisburgh was converted to a 'semi-watched oil light', which required simply an attendant paid £1 a week, and the cottages were sold off.

When the wartime population register was taken in 1939 Sam still inhabited 'Sand Dune'.[341] He is described as a 'Lightkeeper Retired' and a widower living with his daughter, Alberta, who was now the sole performer of 'unpaid domestic duties'. Mary had died the year before and now lay in St Mary's Churchyard at Happisburgh. Sam lived for another nine years to the age of 88. My grandparents knew him well and, despite his exposure to mercury, there was never any suggestion that his mental health was impaired.

Trinity House did not have to pay widows' pensions to either of the Davis keepers' wives since both died before their husbands. Their wifely role had been a particularly important one. They had to keep the cottages spruce enough to satisfy the Trinity inspectors who invariably arrived without notice; they often helped to clean the lighthouse equipment and keep records; they had to 'pay, pack and follow' like the wives of East India Company employees; they had to find accommodation if none was attached to the lighthouse; they brought up their children with only intermittent help; they were frequently obliged to take decisions without reference to their husbands; they had always to accept that their lives were dominated by the weather and by the sea. Above all, they were companions in their husbands' lonely task of keeping the lights which saved so many mariners. Rudyard Kipling poignantly evoked life in their 'vexed eyries':

> We bridge across the dark and bid the helmsman have a care,
> The flash that wheeling inland wakes his sleeping wife to prayer.[342]

Both these Davis wives relied on daughters once they grew old enough to assist. Unlike their brothers, neither Lizzie nor Alberta embarked on a career, even when they lived in places where work might be found. In due course they followed Victorian expectations by caring for their widower fathers. Unlike her cousin Lizzie, Alberta did not get married after her father's death. Instead, she established an independent life for herself, becoming known in the family as Auntie Bert. Probably subsisting on little income apart from the state pension, she was able to buy a cottage, 'The Crib' in Happisburgh. By the time she died in 1973 this was worth £9,567.[343]

Her brothers followed a different path from their father, Thomas as an insurance agent and Samuel as a schoolmaster. Both served in the First World War, married and settled in east London near their aunt Ambrosine and other relations. As neither couple produced children the line of Davis lightkeepers died out.

Within a generation the profession itself had also expired. New technology meant that all lighthouses could be controlled from Harwich: 'tidy impersonal rows of electronic aids now turn the lights on and off, measure the daylight, calculate the windspeed and battle the storms.' The last keepers left North Foreland lighthouse in 1998, 160 years after Edwin Lewis Davis had first lit up the oil-lamps of St Agnes. Most of the weather-beaten structures still stand, visited not only by technicians landing in helicopters to maintain and repair them but also by inquisitive tourists and by paying guests in search of a tranquil break. These lonesome sentinels remind us of their abiding function: to succour 'all who are beset upon the coasts of England.'[344] And they conjure up lost generations of custodians whose ceaseless task it was to keep the beacons bright.

Chapter 9

Davis Wives, Widows and Daughters

Little trace remains of Edwin Lewis Davis's first wife Jane (née Legg). As most of her short life (1816-47) was spent before the days of the ten-yearly census we don't know whether she worked for her living before marrying the lighthouse keeper. The births of her six children were, of course, registered and no doubt she lived on in their memories after her early death from tuberculosis. Otherwise, she is hidden from history, with no memorial except her name inscribed on one of many Legg family gravestones in the old churchyard on St Mary's.

Jane Davis reunited with her Legg family in death.

Her successor in the Keeper's cottage lived more in the public eye and appears in written records. Before her marriage to the needy widower, Martha Hutchings pursued a career as a woman preacher, so unusual that Samuel Johnson famously compared it to 'a dog's walking on his hind legs. It is not done well; but you are surprised to find it done at all.' He did not foresee the significant part that women would play in the Bible Christian movement which flourished in Devon and Cornwall during the early nineteenth century. Because it was a 'cottage religion', emphasising such homely practices as family prayer and Bible study, it seemed fitting for a young female convert like Martha to pursue her calling as an itinerant minister. The life was hard, involving frequent solitary journeys, uncertain places of rest and occasional hostility. Martha was paid £1.50 a quarter, as opposed to the £3 earned by men. She had to be 'always neat, plain, discreet, humble ... and diligent according to her sex' and to accept that though 'women may preach ...men must govern'.[345] Other Bible Christian women took up the call, though by the time Martha married Edwin in 1847 there were only four travelling the country. As the movement became more established it conformed increasingly to the general Victorian expectation that a woman's place was 'in the little island of home [where] she is the sun, the star'.[346] Male delegates to the Bible Christian Conference of 1869 cheered when the last woman itinerant preacher resigned.

After taking on her duties as the keeper's wife and stepmother of his six offspring Martha Davis bore eleven children of her own over the next twenty years. Even if assisted by one of the herbalist 'aunts' who often acted as midwives on the islands or by the doctor with obstetric forceps and chloroform at his disposal, Martha must have been exhausted and physically damaged by so many closely spaced pregnancies. Yet she kept her hand in as a preacher; on the frequent occasions 'when bad weather prevented the parson coming by boat from St Mary's' she would mount the pulpit at St Agnes parish church.[347] The Bible Christian chapel also demanded her support: she was expected to welcome itinerant preachers, provide refreshments at prayer and temperance gatherings, and make liberal donations of money. In October 1851, for example, the *Bible Christian Magazine* reported that several visiting brethren were accompanied on a walk to neighbouring Gugh island by 'Mr and Mrs Davis, who kindly went to show us the remains of an ancient building supposed to have been a druidical temple and some ancient sepulchres'. Edwin and Martha were surely present the same evening at a meeting where speakers urged the audience 'onward' in faith and made a collection for the Bible Christian Missionary Society which was generous considering 'the circumstances of the people'. The report expresses disappointment, however, at the islanders' reluctance to respond with sufficient amens to cheer 'the coldness of the winter and the stillness of death', blaming their lack of 'deep, ardent, zealous piety'. John Moyle regarded this emotional reticence more charitably, praising Scillonians' 'solid, upright dealings' and 'sterling worth of character'. No one exemplified these qualities better than Martha Davis.[348]

St Agnes Bible Christian Chapel, which now serves as the Island Hall.

Another project to which the Bible Christians of St Agnes contributed both cash and 'free labour' was the construction of a new chapel in 1874 at a cost of £156. As 'liberal supporters of the cause' the Davises were among the 300 people present at its opening to hear several addresses by male ministers interspersed with 'suitable melodies' from the choir and, of course, to partake of 'tea gratuitously provided by the friends'.[349]

A studio photograph of Martha with her two youngest daughters, Martha Mary and Alberta, seems to have been taken four or five years later, when both the teenage girls were still living at home.[350] The fine dresses indicate the pride they took in their appearance, no doubt aided by the family's dressmaking skills. The dark colours suggest that they were in mourning,

Martha Davis with her two youngest daughters, Martha Mary (left) and Alberta (right).

perhaps for one of the seafaring sons who predeceased Martha.

Scattered though the family was by the boys' maritime and lighthouse careers and the girls' need to seek work or follow their husbands away from Scilly, Martha's offspring felt warm 'filial affection' for her. The circumstances surrounding her death, described in an obituary by her son-in-law William Penrose, bear this out. On 11 September 1884 Martha 'was taking supper with one of her daughters who was home on a visit' to St Agnes when, 'in the midst of a conversation', she suffered a sudden fatal brain haemorrhage from which she died three days later. That night William's wife Eva, who lived with him in Weston-Super-Mare, apparently had a powerful sense of her mother's death:

> She woke suddenly in the night, roused her husband and said, 'Mother died.' He thought she had been dreaming and told her to go back to sleep. But she was right! When the letter containing the sad news arrived, they knew that she had awoken at the precise moment her mother died.

Certainly, Martha had been a model of courage and dedication. She resembled other indomitable Victorian women who, in the words of a modern historian, were remarkable for all that they achieved despite 'the restrictions within which they operated'.[351] From a remote island of barely two hundred souls, this overworked wife and mother transcended her humble origins and cast her influence far and wide.

The Daughters of Edwin Lewis Davis
Edwin Lewis m. 1 Jane Legg

1 Mary Jane	*2 Sarah*	*3 Jemima*
1840-?	*1845-1925*	*1846-91*

m. 2 Martha Hutchings

4 Thirza	*5 Eliza*	*6 Eva*	*7 Emma*	*8 Emma*	*9 Martha*	*10 Alberta*
1850-1936	*1853-?*	*1855-1936*	*1856 b&d*	*1858-1947*	*1860-92*	*1864-84*

Among the restraints imposed on women at that time was the convention that paid employment outside the home was only respectable if it resembled their domestic and maternal duties. After all, a career in such fields as politics, law or high finance would require 'prolonged education and mental effort', which contemporary psychologists thought to be 'dangerous to women's reproductive processes'. Without running this risk or facing the 'loss of gentility', they could sew, teach in an elementary school or, like Miss Matty of Cranford, sell tea to lady customers and 'comfits to children'.[352] All nine of Edwin Davis's adult daughters conformed to these expectations: five became dressmakers, three pursued brief school-teaching careers and one worked in a grocery shop. Needlework was the most natural choice for the Davis girls: not only had they been taught the skills at Augustus Smith's schools, but they could also be sure of a market for their wares among islanders with no easy access to shops. The 1861 Census lists about forty dressmakers on St Mary's, along with eleven tailoresses and four who described themselves more humbly as seamstresses, catering for a population of 1,500. Among them were Jane Davis's daughters Sarah and Jemima, aged sixteen and fifteen respectively, apprentice needlewomen living with their Legg relations on St Mary's.

Saving Lives in Scilly

By 1871 Jemima had managed to establish herself and two of her half-sisters, Eliza and Emma, in a terrace house in Church Street where the two older women worked as dressmakers and supported young Emma, who was still at school. Sarah continued to make clothes but she had moved to London, while sixteen-year-old Eva stitched at home on St Agnes. The 1870s saw further development in the five sisters' careers. Eva was now married to a Bible Christian minister. According to family records Eliza had 'married a Chudleigh' – all I could find out about her. Sarah was now living in Rochester with her widowed older sister Mary Jane Boulden but still worked in the trade. Jemima and Emma now lodged with Annie Sanderson, a former teacher of sewing at St Mary's school, and employed five apprentices in their dressmaking business.

I can't help admiring the way the sisters stuck together and supported each other. Historians continue to debate 'the functional and personal significance of the Victorian family' but I have constantly been struck by the mutual help and affection among both Davis and Moyle siblings.[353] Whether the needlewomen made a decent living is more in doubt. If nineteenth-century literature about 'slaves of the needle' is to be believed, this is unlikely. Newspaper articles, novels, plays and poems invariably showed them as exploited piece-workers, 'stitching away as if for very life' in garrets or back-rooms, earning starvation wages and frequently resorting to prostitution in order to put food on the table.[354] Thomas Hood's well-known poem 'The Song of the Shirt', written in 1843 about a poor widow and seamstress called Mrs Biddell, evokes the frequent fate of her kind:

> With fingers weary and worn,
> With eyelids heavy and red,
> A woman sat in unwomanly rags,
> Plying her needle and thread –
> Stitch! Stitch! Stitch!
> In poverty, hunger and dirt,
> And still with a voice of dolorous pitch
> She sang 'The Song of the Shirt!'

Davis Wives, Widows and Daughters

Frank Holl, Seamstresses, *c1875.*

The miserable conditions of 'slopworkers' (as they were often called) were also portrayed in *Punch* cartoons and in dozens of social realist paintings such as this one by Frank Holl.[355] The picture suggests something of the toil of Jemima Davis and her sisters in their Scillonian cottage where they certainly had much to endure. Customers could be demanding; needles, thread, candles and even perhaps an expensive sewing-machine had to be paid for out of what customers chose to pay them; their eyesight and posture might be ruined by many hours of close work; and the market for their wares was unreliable. There was no protection for such 'sweated' workers until well into the twentieth century, too late for any of the Davis sisters.[356] In any case, census records show a sharp fall in the number of dressmakers in St Mary's during the 1880s when the decline of shipbuilding reduced the islanders' spending power.

One who abandoned the trade was Emma Davis, who married Royal Navy seaman Southwell Mortimer Hicks in 1883 and moved to Portsmouth, where he was more likely to find work. It's not clear whether Jemima carried on without her or whether ill health forced her to retire, but records show that she died at her father's house in Penzance in February 1891. Her early death, at the age of 45, may indeed have been hastened by harsh working conditions; but it's equally likely that she had inherited the tuberculosis which killed her mother Jane. The fact that Jemima left effects worth £157 15s in her will suggests that she had not done badly from her twenty years of dressmaking. She bequeathed this sum to her sister and former business partner, Sarah, who may well have been in need of it; she had given up dressmaking and, at the advanced age of forty, married John Tuffee, a grocer from the East End of London. The legacy may have helped the couple to move to Lancashire, where John set up as a 'tea traveller'.[357]

It is impossible to weave the dress-making sisters' working lives into a finished tapestry because the evidence is so threadbare – ten-yearly census returns and a single probate record. I found no advertisements for their wares in the local press, no invoices or bills, no letters of thanks for the dresses, blouses, skirts, suits and shirts they fashioned for Scilly's more prosperous citizens. Time and chance have worn away the fabric of their lives. Yet the kind of artefacts they created can be seen in finery displayed by islanders as they posed for photographs in the Gibsons' studios. A patchwork of faded family portraits from my own collection, none of whom I can identify, gives some impression of the intricate adornment produced by the Davis sisters and their fellow needlewomen.

Collage of my Scillonian forebears, 'known unto God'.

The three Davis daughters who tried their hand at schoolteaching were the oldest, Mary Jane, and the two youngest,

Martha and Alberta. It was no easy option. After the death of her husband, Assistant Keeper George Boulden, in 1863, Mary Jane worked as the sole schoolmistress in the Cornish village of Landewednack. She must have qualified through the pupil-teacher scheme but, as she had not undertaken any further training, her pay would have been barely enough to support her daughter Loveday and three little boys. There are no surviving records of Landewednack school but it's clear that Mary Jane's teaching career was short-lived. The young widow's further efforts to sustain herself will appear later in this chapter.

I found more evidence of her younger sisters' classroom experiences. The logbook of St Agnes school reveals that fifteen-year-old Martha started teaching 'the little ones' there in May 1875, working alternately with another young islander as an assistant to the 'overtaxed' headmistress. There is no record that Martha had been trained for this role, which she clearly found too demanding; in June she 'asked leave to remain at home to assist her mother' and she did not return. The school struggled on with an insufficient supply of books and maps, inadequate ventilation, worn-out desks and lack of a 'tolerably capable Assistant', all noted in the inspector's report for 1876.[358] Three years later, in June 1879, Alberta reached the age of fifteen and 'commenced work at the school'. Sadly, the logbook goes on to record her prolonged absences 'through illness'. In January and February 1882, for example, she was barely present and there is no further mention of A. Davis after that. The tuberculosis which was to kill her in 1884 was already undermining her health.

Meanwhile the oldest of Martha's daughters, Thirza, had been working as an assistant in the shop owned by James Bluett of St Mary's, with whom she also boarded. Kelly's Directory describes Bluett as a grocer and draper, who no doubt sold his wares mostly to women.[359] This is all that is known of Thirza's life as a respectable single woman. In her case, as in many others, it is much easier to find out about her after she was married – through her husband's much more prominent career.

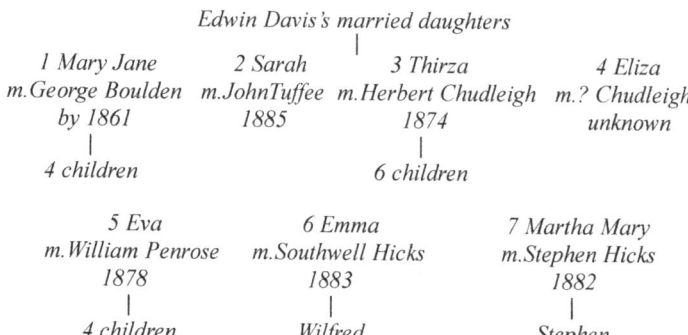

Only two Davis daughters married sailors, no doubt taking into account the dangers faced by their seafaring brothers. By a sad irony, though, the first of the wives to be widowed was Mary Jane, whose husband George Boulden worked as a lighthouse keeper to preserve nautical lives. Following his early death in 1863, Mary Jane led an unsettled existence. After working to support her four children as an uncertificated teacher in a Cornish village school, she moved to Rochester, where her sons were apprenticed as mariners and her daughter Loveday worked as a milliner. Loveday married an accountant's clerk in the town but there is no sign of Mary Jane going to live with her. Records show that all three sons emigrated, one to Australia and two to South Africa. Mary Jane's next move was to look after her widowed father in Penzance, as was expected of the oldest daughter, but she lost that home too when he died in 1894. This may explain why, like many indigent Victorian widows, she took on the role of 'lady help', performing domestic duties for a low wage but treated by her employer as a social equal. The 1901 and 1911 Census returns show that she acted in this capacity for the Scillonian Woodcock family on the Lizard peninsula. It's not known what became of Mary Jane once she became too old to earn her living.

Davis Wives, Widows and Daughters

Two Davis sisters did marry seafarers but both husbands found a safer option than sailing the seven seas. Emma's husband Southwell Hicks worked as a dock labourer after they moved to Portsmouth, where their only son, Wilfred, became a shipwright. Emma's adventurous older sister Thirza had already left her work as a shop assistant on St Mary's to travel alone to Melbourne, where she married her Scillonian sailor sweetheart Herbert Chudleigh. In the early 1880s the couple moved to Sydney where their six children were born. Thanks to Herbert's 'skill as a navigator and popularity as a captain', noted in the local press, he won promotion to become senior pilot of Sydney harbour and master of the pilot steamer *Captain Cook*. This service, so long familiar to Scillonians, had been guiding ships through the congested waters of Sydney Heads since an accident in 1857 resulting in 121 deaths. The post earned Herbert a good salary of £450 a year and made him an important figure in the bay. In due course he was appointed as an alderman and became a founder member of the League of Ancient Mariners of New South Wales, which survives to this day. When he died at 78 in 1925 the 'well-known skipper' was lauded in an obituary as a 'fine specimen of the old type of sailor'. He bequeathed over £4,000 to Thirza, who spent a comfortable old age with one of her sons and two of her daughters in Roseville, a leafy suburb of Sydney. She too left a substantial sum in her will.[360] Emigration had served her well.

Logo of the League of Ancient Mariners.

The only other Davis daughter to emigrate was Eva, who married the preacher William Penrose in 1878 and accompanied him eight years later to the area west of Adelaide known as 'Little Cornwall', such was 'the Cornishness of its population and culture'. Eva took with her a folding album containing many pictures of her large Davis family, which has passed down to her Australian descendants. The couple and their three children moved subsequently to Port Adelaide where the parishioners included sailors from the many ships at harbour, whom they hoped to guide along the channel of temperance and into the haven of the Bible Christian faith. Until his health broke down William Penrose was acknowledged in the local press as an 'able preacher and successful circuit minister', who was especially eloquent on 'the evils of intoxicating drink'. One tribute had to admit, however, that 'Mr Penrose has his faults', as are perhaps reflected in his stern countenance.[361]

Eva followed in her mother's footsteps by acting as organist and Sunday School superintendent, influencing 'many young people to join the church'. Her granddaughter, Marjorie Telfer, recounted that she also took services when her husband was too ill to get out of bed, driving a pony and trap to isolated chapels where 'some of the stiff and starchy old people didn't approve of a woman in the pulpit'. Even so, when William retired in 1903 she was presented with an elegant tea set as a tribute to the good she had done. Her granddaughter adds that Eva was 'a remarkably good-looking woman' who took pride in her appearance. The comment is borne out by a studio photograph of the couple, in which she is beautifully attired in an elaborate outfit, which was no doubt the product of the

Eva Penrose (née Davis) in Port Adelaide with her husband William.

dressmaking skills she had practised at home in Scilly. She nursed William 'kindly and tenderly' during 'a long and painful illness' from which he died in 1905. Devoted though she undoubtedly had been to him, Eva remarried less than two years later. Her new husband was Saunders Jelbart Penrose, who may well have been William's cousin. She survived him too and died at her daughter's Australian home in 1936.[362]

As a most 'careful and methodical' man, William Penrose had always made sure that the Adelaide newspapers announced the deaths of members of his wife's large family. On the occasion of his silver wedding in 1903 he paid tribute to four of Eva's deceased brothers, 'the late ship masters, Thomas L, Edwin L, John H, and Charles R Davis'.[363] But no mention was made of the elusive Lewis – or of the women married to these ill-fated mariners.

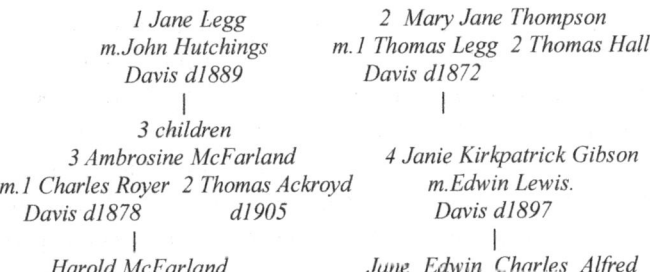

Edwin Davis's daughters-in-law

```
     1 Jane Legg              2 Mary Jane Thompson
  m.John Hutchings         m.1 Thomas Legg  2 Thomas Hall
     Davis d1889                 Davis d1872
          |                          |
      3 children
  3 Ambrosine McFarland       4 Janie Kirkpatrick Gibson
m.1 Charles Royer  2 Thomas Ackroyd   m.Edwin Lewis.
    Davis d1878       d1905           Davis d1897
          |                          |
   Harold McFarland          June  Edwin  Charles  Alfred
```

The only Davis nautical wife not to be widowed was Jane, married to Captain John Hutchings Davis. She died in Penzance four years before her husband was lost at sea in 1889 leaving three orphans to be brought up by their grandmother. The other three survived their husbands' deaths to pursue the precarious existence common to Victorian widows. They inherited no property or substantial investments and they did not receive pensions since very few professions offered one at this time – Trinity House was exceptional in this respect.[364] A Parliamentary Select Committee in 1861 found that men were hardly ever able to insure their lives for a worthwhile amount; master mariners, with their 'irregular employment and periods absent at sea', were no exception.[365] Nor was there any state pension until 1908, when men and women over seventy became entitled to five shillings a week. A nineteenth-century widow usually had to fend for herself.

She might find another husband even though Victorian society tended to regard a second marriage for a woman as 'a betrayal of her dead love'.[366] In any case, a widow with small children or an older relict with lines on her face was poor competition for a young single woman. Respectable employment was also hard to come by. Organisations such as the Civil Service and the Post Office began to accept female workers but preferred them to be under twenty and prepared to work for low pay. The nursing and teaching professions were seen as suitably feminine but these required periods of residential training which posed problems for mothers or older women. Work as a housekeeper or lady's companion provided a home as well as a small income, as it did for Mary Jane Boulden, but at the cost of losing autonomy. If no such prospects were available a widow was thrown upon the mercy of charitable bodies or of any relations willing and able to take her in. Survival, concludes one historian, demanded 'independence of thought and boldness of action' quite contrary to the familiar image of the feeble Victorian lady reclining on a chaise-longue.[367]

As this chapter illustrates, the Davis widows found various means of support. Mary Jane, the Welsh wife of Captain Thomas Legg Davis, ignored convention by remarrying less than a year after his death in 187. She and Thomas, along with their two young sons, had been living close to the docks in Liverpool, where she met the mariner who became her second husband. As Mary Jane was one of the most popular Victorian Christian names, and she took on the common surname of Hall, I have not been able to find out whether the children were absorbed into the new household or how long this seafarer survived his risky calling.

Ambrosine, the wife of Captain Charles Royer Davis who died in Melbourne in 1878, became a widow at the age of twenty-one. Just a year earlier the couple had married at the parish church in Hackney, where she was living with her parents, Francis and Eliza McFarland. They were migrants from Scilly to this fast-developing area which offered plenty of work for Francis, a ship and house joiner. To judge by the photograph of Ambrosine taken shortly before she married Charles, the family was doing pretty well. Little did the young wife imagine, as she and her baby son Harold saw Charles off from the South West India Dock in July 1878, that her prospects would soon become so uncertain.

Ambrosine McFarland, my great-grandmother, aged about 18.

When she was widowed the McFarland family rallied round, moving with Ambrosine and her infant into one of the bay-windowed terraced houses characteristic of respectable Victorian Hackney. The 1881 Census lists 32 Powerscroft Road as home to Ambrosine's parents in one unit headed by Francis, while the young widow was named as head of a separate ménage. This consisted of her three-year-old son Harold and her sister Eliza's family: mariner husband William Mumford and baby daughter Katie. Ambrosine was clearly charging the Mumfords rent as the census describes her as earning 'income by letting', a common occupation in an area inhabited by 'a succession of clerks, commercial travellers, merchants and master craftsmen'.[368]

In the mid-1880s Francis McFarland retired and returned to

Scilly with his wife, taking their young grandson Harold with them. There are two possible explanations for this arrangement. Ambrosine, who was now in her thirties, might have stood more chance of finding a husband if she had no son to look after. And Harold was a delicate child for whom sea air could be beneficial. There was also good reason to hope that St Mary's would provide him with a sound education. So it turned out; and Harold, who was my grandfather, acquired a love of learning which he passed on to me.

He first attended the boys' elementary school and then went on to Carn Thomas School for older boys, together with his cousins Edwin, Charles and Alfred, sons of Edwin Lewis Davis junior.[369] The Diocesan Inspectors' Report regularly commended all four cousins for their knowledge and repetition of the Bible and Prayer Book, passages of which remained with Harold to the end of his life. In one of his last letters he advised me to read Solomon's prayer in the second Book of Chronicles, which has 'a refrain or cadence somewhat similar in shape to the gentle undulations of the Downs or the immense rollers of the Pacific'. Not all the curriculum was of such interest to him. He told me that 'we boys sang in unison a great deal' and remembered the 'bitter protest' with which he sang the 'ridiculously untrue' if not 'deliberately misleading' lines: 'If I work, then, with a will, It will be but playing still.' Nevertheless, he got through his regular exams in Arithmetic, Writing, Spelling, Reading and Grammar, passing Standard VI with credit in 1895. His Davis cousins were just as studious and Edwin became a pupil-teacher at Carn Thomas, gaining a first-class certificate in

Carn Thomas School, St Mary's, Scilly.

the Queen's Examination. The school logbooks show, however, that many of their fellow pupils were absent for weeks on end, picking blackberries or flowers, or simply playing truant. Inspectors' reports lamented the boys' lack of 'intellectual vigour' and the frequency of their being 'sent to work'. Despite Augustus Smith's efforts, compulsory education was still not popular on the islands.[370]

Meanwhile Ambrosine made a fresh start by moving into the area of 'enormous immigration' around the new Clapton railway station, together with her sister's family which now included baby Frank.[371] Ambrosine also took a job as a Post Office telegraph clerk, one of the first communications-technology occupations open to women – a demanding role for which they certainly did not receive 'equal pay for equal work'. She gave up this job when in 1893, at the age of 35, she married Thomas Ackroyd, a schoolmaster, and moved further north into Leyton. The relocation may have been prompted by Hackney's becoming, as Charles Booth noted in his landmark survey *Life and Labour of the People in London*, poorer and much more crowded. 'Leafy Leyton' in the meantime had been transformed, after the opening of railway extensions, from a rural village 'into a suburban dormitory for clerks and workmen mostly employed outside the area'. Ambrosine and Thomas Ackroyd were probably attracted by its proximity to the 'trees, ponds, glades, and open spaces' of Epping Forest, preserved for public use by an Act of Parliament.[372]

They must have been among the first tenants of 65 Waterloo Road, a three-bedroomed terraced house. Among their neighbours, as the 1901 Census reveals, were clerks, schoolmasters, engineers, tradesmen, a gasfitter, a piano teacher and a pew opener, some of whom took in boarders or employed a young housemaid. There was no living-in servant in the Ackroyd household, which included Ambrosine's 23-year-old son Harold, now returned from Scilly to become an accountant's clerk, and her niece Katie, who had qualified as a schoolteacher.[373] Harold was also studying for his articles at evening classes run by London University and in 1902 he gained a distinction in 'The Economics of Exchange, Finance and Taxation'. He was an energetic young man: every day he would walk to and from his office in Holborn and at weekends he would quite often hike fifty miles to Cambridge 'turning over his studies in his mind'.[374] Also in his head were the extended passages of poetry which I so often heard him recite in later years, Longfellow and Kipling being his favourites. His Scillonian education had clearly given him both a head for figures and a love of literature.

The Ackroyds had no children and the marriage lasted only twelve years before Thomas died in 1905 aged 41. But Ambrosine could still rely on a strong family network. By 1911 she had moved from 65 to 62 Waterloo Road, sharing it with Harold, now a fully-fledged accountant and head of the household, her widowed sister Eliza and her niece Katie, who was still teaching. Thus, there were two incomes to help support the widows, who in the absence of a housemaid did the necessary cooking, shopping and cleaning. This regime continued until Harold's marriage to Gladys Hall in 1914 and Eliza's death in 1919. By this time Ambrosine was entitled to an old age pension, on the strength of which she was able to carry on living in Waterloo Road, in the company of Katie and her new husband, Thomas Edwin Bowen Davis. Related families often intermarried at that time and Tom, as he was called, was the older son of lighthouse keeper Sam Davis, Ambrosine's brother-in-law. Tom (now named as head of the household) was employed as an accountant's clerk for a car hire firm in Brixton and Katie was an elementary school teacher in Clapton. Ambrosine has no listed occupation but I'm sure that she looked after the house and prepared meals for Katie, whose job involved hours of preparation in the evening, and Tom, who had to commute to south London.

During the 1920s Ambrosine continued to live in Waterloo Road, where she posed in her back garden, surrounded by her nephew Frank Mumford with his wife Annie and their son

William, Katie and Tom, and a dog called Regath. Frank was obviously visiting London with his family since he had by this time set up as a butcher on St Mary's; I believe Harold used to travel to Scilly every year to help his cousin with his accounts. It looks as though there was a close relationship between Ambrosine and her niece and nephew, both of whom she had known from infancy, and she seems fond of young William too.

Ambrosine surrounded by her family.

At some point during the 1930s Ambrosine moved into one of the five bedrooms of Harold and Gladys's newly built house in Hampstead Garden Suburb. Their youngest son Tony remembered her as 'an invalid, perhaps a recluse', who never went out and was 'quite remote from us'.[375] I suspect that her health had failed by this time and that she needed the care of her daughter-in-law.

Ambrosine's headstone.

Ambrosine died in 1937 aged 81 and she is buried in Walthamstow cemetery with her second husband, who was resting well, like Duncan in *Macbeth*, 'after life's fitful fever'. Subsequently they were joined in death by Tom, commemorated as 'One of God's good men', and his 'beloved wife' Katie, who had continued to live as a devoted childless couple in Leyton. Ambrosine's two long widowhoods had been cheered and sustained by her family, whom she had in turn nurtured for as long as she was able. Her own epitaph echoes

Jesus's words about Mary of Bethany: 'She hath done what she could.'

The last Davis sea-widow was Janie, née Gibson, the Scillonian wife of Captain Edwin Lewis Davis. She had already demonstrated her intrepid spirit while Edwin was away at sea: 'whenever Capt Davis was in a getatable European port, she joined him there, generally taking one of the children.'[376] These adventures carried on until 1897 when Edwin was lost in a shipwreck off the coast of Brazil while on a voyage to Rio Grande, bequeathing effects worth £173. The couple's three sons had distinguished themselves at Carn Thomas school (alongside their cousin Harold) – and also in Band of Hope entertainments where 'Master Edwin' was judged a 'good old Santa Claus' and Charlie 'a jewel of a boy'.[377] By the turn of the century they were ready to leave Scilly to pursue careers in teaching and journalism on the mainland. Janie had launched her offspring in life but she was now in her fifties, too old to seek employment and unlikely to remarry. Like most widows, she had to give up the family home and sell its contents to realise the value of her inheritance. Her first recourse after that was to move in with her brother's family on St Mary's to act as their housekeeper. Her daughter, confusingly also called Janie, tried to help with the finances by teaching Art at Carn Thomas. But 'Miss Janie Davis' was frequently 'absent with a bad cold' and she had to leave after two years because of ill health. She went on to qualify as a music teacher.[378]

By 1911 daughter Janie was married to a customs officer in Tetbury, Gloucestershire where the census registered her mother as a visitor. But after reaching the age of 70 in 1913 Janie Davis had her old-age pension and was able at some point to move into a separate house in the same town. This is where she was registered as a voter from 1929 to 1932, staying on in Tetbury even after her daughter died in 1930. Janie had clearly established an independent life for herself. Her death in 1933 at the age of 90 was registered in Woolwich, where she must have been visiting her son, Edwin, who was now headmaster of All Saints

Elementary School near the Barracks. Janie had had the 'energy and ingenuity' as well as the 'boldness of action' she needed to overcome the challenge of Victorian widowhood. She had also lived long enough to benefit from the welfare measures and female parliamentary franchise introduced in the early twentieth century. Government was beginning to ease the burden for low-paid female workers, mothers looking after families and elderly widows with nowhere to turn

Chapter 10

Moyle Wives and Daughters

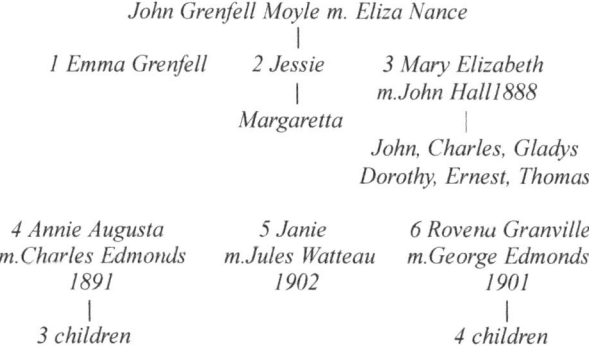

In a passage at the end of his retirement speech John Moyle paid tribute to the ladies who 'graced and honoured' the occasion. 'What is the world without lovely woman?' he asked, expressing his gratitude for the nursing, nurturing, charm, good cheer and adornment they provided. More unusually, he also celebrated the way 'woman is now coming more to the fore and giving up something of her hitherto back seat'. He mentioned in particular women's hard-won achievements in his own fields of science and medicine and named the American surgeon Susan Dimock, whom he had special cause to remember. Refused entry at Harvard Medical School on the grounds of her gender, Susan qualified as a doctor in Zurich before returning to the United States in 1872 to work in the New England Hospital for Women and Children. Here, as John Moyle recounted, she became 'one of the most skilful and successful operators known in the annals of surgery' before 'she lost her life in that terrible disaster, the wreck of the *Schiller* in May 1875', when she was only 28.[379] John must have attended the inquest on her body, which was among those washed up on St Mary's, before it was taken back across the Atlantic for burial in the Forest Hills Cemetery, Boston.

I'm sure that John also admired Elizabeth Garrett Anderson, the first English female doctor, whose career was remarkably similar to Susan Dimock's. After gaining a licence from the Society of Apothecaries through a loophole in the regulations (which they were quick to remove), she, too, gained a medical degree on the Continent and went on to practise in a hospital for women and children. Against sustained opposition Elizabeth gained entry to the British Medical Association and was still working in the profession at the time of John's retirement. She was also active in the campaign for women's suffrage alongside her sister Millicent Garrett Fawcett. This was a female aspiration which John's speech did not mention but he was clearly referring to Millicent's daughter, Philippa, when he praised the woman who had 'attained the highest honours in mathematics at Cambridge' that very year. 'The tripos has been reached', he exclaimed to applause, though he failed to point out that Philippa was not awarded the title of Senior Wrangler which was open only to men. John's final point met with laughter as well as applause: 'And now the parsons must look out for their pulpits as she is preparing to invade them also.' It would actually be another hundred years before women were ordained in the Church of England – but perhaps John had in mind nonconformist women like Martha Davis and Eva Penrose who had regularly invaded pulpits or mounted soapboxes.

John Moyle's tribute to 'woman' reflects his gratitude to his late wife Eliza, whose hard-working life had followed the path taken by many Victorian women. After an impoverished childhood and a basic elementary education, she earned her own living as a seamstress before getting married to a considerably older man; her career ended with her marriage; she was an essential helpmeet in her husband's work; she bore numerous children and had the sorrow of losing a son at a tender age; she had no living-in servant to help with the cooking, cleaning and childcare; and she died of a stroke in her fifties, before her younger offspring had left home. Unlike Martha Davis, Eliza had no public role which would cause her to be mentioned in newspapers or official reports but clues exist to give us an idea of life as she experienced it.

Census records show that the household was very busy: eight children were born in quick succession, including Jessie who was later categorised as 'imbecile from birth'. The couple also took in Jessie's illegitimate daughter Margaretta with no pretence that she was their own child. Of course, the house included the doctor's surgery, with equipment to be maintained, visiting patients to be accommodated, records to be kept and finances to be managed. Eliza Moyle was not one to behave like the wife of Dr Gibson in Elizabeth Gaskell's *Wives and Daughters*, who ignores her husband's 'dirty work' and 'sits in the drawing-room like a lady' engaging in 'pretty babble'. When medical practices were 'rooted in the household', writes one historian, 'the doctor's wife was centrally important as a guiding hand.'[380]

Eliza Moyle (second from left) with her daughters: Emma, Jessie, Mary, Annie, Janie and Rovena.

A charming photograph reveals that the Moyles' family life was not 'all work and no play'. It shows them at a picnic and must have been taken in about 1880, after the death of young John Grenfell and Edwards's departure and before

Moyle Wives and Daughters

any of the older girls left home for good. Margaretta does not feature. Eliza appears as a pretty woman dressed informally, seated on a log behind all her daughters ranged in order of age. I have found no studio portrait of Eliza and suspect that she preferred being pictured in this more natural fashion.[381]

Another possible image of Eliza is to be found in John Moyle's home-made Hebrew grammar booklet, which contains a sketch drawn across its sewn pages. It's little more than the doodle of an idle moment depicting a woman picking fruit, which look like the blackberries that flourish on the islands. It's tempting to imagine that she was his wife.

Dr Moyle's doodle.

The last glimpse of Eliza is contained in her death certificate, signed, of course, by her husband. The medical terms, paralysis and hemiplegia, clearly indicate that the doctor's wife died of a stroke. So did Martha Davis, the wife of the St Agnes lighthouse keeper, as recorded in layman's language by her son-in-law: 'She suddenly ceased speaking, put her hand to her head, and never moved or spoke again [before] her spirit quietly took its flight.' Both wives died at about the same age. It seems that for them, as for many other women of their time, multiple pregnancies and years of heavy housework had taken 'a tremendous toll'.[382] With greater access to birth control, the married Moyle daughters (like the Davis girls) chose to bear fewer children.

The two oldest Moyle daughters, Emma and Jessie, remained single all their lives. Jessie, who appears in the 1861 Census simply as a one-year-old baby and in 1871 as an eleven-year-old 'scholar', was to be categorised as 'imbecile' or 'feeble-minded' in all future census returns. The description would originally have been supplied by John Moyle as head of the household and, as a doctor, he would have used the term in its contemporary clinical sense to denote someone 'whose intelligence does not exceed that of a normal child of about seven years'.[383] Thus Jessie's mental infirmity might not have been apparent in her early years when she seems to have attended elementary school along with her siblings. But by the time she was seduced (or raped) and made pregnant in 1877 she was clearly a vulnerable teenager. I suspect that the man who took advantage of her was not a Scillonian. The islands' small population would have made it easy, especially for the doctor/magistrate, to identify him as father of the child and force him to pay maintenance. It is much more likely that Margaretta's absent father was one of the many sailors passing through St Mary's port. The rest of Jessie's forty-two years were spent in her parents' household and later in those of the two sisters closest to her in age, Emma in Surrey and Mary in Cornwall. I have found no record of any other relationships or of employment outside the home where, I imagine, she helped to look after her daughter.

Emma Grenfell Moyle, on the other hand, pursued a long career as a schoolteacher. Life for such lone women could be hard and 'old maids' tended to be objects of pity, disapproval, suspicion or ridicule in a society which idealised marriage. But sometimes, like George Gissing's spirited 'odd women', they could achieve a measure of independence which their wedded sisters lacked. The intertwined lives of Emma and her younger sister Mary, who became my great-grandmother, shed light on the relative benefits and drawbacks of Victorian marriage.

Emma was the doctor's oldest child, born in 1858. Like her siblings she attended the elementary school on St Mary's, where no secondary education was available. But a clever child could be selected at the age of thirteen as a pupil-teacher, a role which Emma Moyle performed from April 1875 in St Mary's Infants' School (regularly visited by her father in his capacity as doctor). Her duties included taking charge of about forty children, whom

Scillonian logbooks sometimes describe as restless and noisy, as well as preparing lessons and attending weekly tutorials with the school mistress. As a female apprentice Emma would also be expected 'to do all the household work of the school premises, except scrubbing the larger and rougher floors'. Altogether these tasks took up around nine hours a day, for which as a girl she received a third less than boy pupil-teachers, who were paid £10 per annum, rising to £20 in the last year. According to the Newcastle Commission of 1861, 'The strain upon pupil-teachers, the younger ones in particular, was heavy.' One training college principal concluded that their five-year apprenticeship 'made many young people grow old too soon'.[384]

Emma's experience bore out this judgement. The headmistress, Caroline Wheeler, was a strict disciplinarian. She punished eight truant boys, for example, by giving them only dry bread for dinner and making them stand apart from the class for a week with the word 'Truant' written on their backs. She was also severe with her young apprentice, who found the first two years very testing. Emma's lesson on the 'offering up of Isaac' was described as a 'complete failure'; she was chided for having an 'obstinate spirit' and a 'sulky temper'; she was rebuked for 'not complying immediately with the wishes' of the headmistress; she and her fellow apprentice were 'kept in because they had not done their home lessons'; and, not surprisingly, she was often 'very unwell'. After eighteen months it looked as though Emma might be judged 'unfit for the office of teacher' and the inspector's report directed that she 'must improve in every subject'.[385]

The third year of her apprenticeship was better. Miss Wheeler had resigned her post and Emma was now fifteen, more able to conform to rigid school routines. She became 'less playful' in the classroom and most of her lessons on such topics as 'The Cat' or 'Sugar' were judged 'satisfactory' – though one on 'Coal' was 'very imperfectly said'. By the summer of 1874 she had clearly learned the ropes. Her pupils were 'interested and orderly', sang 'very nicely indeed' and had improved in their reading. Emma survived her tough apprenticeship and was able to travel to Truro in June 1876 to take the Queen's Scholarship exam. This tested her knowledge of scripture and syntax. She also had to write an essay and give a demonstration lesson, but as a girl she was not questioned about algebra or geography. These subjects were reserved for boys whereas she had to display 'a special proficiency in sewing'.[386] Having passed, she was entitled to attend a residential teacher training college with an annual grant of £20 (rather than the £25 issued to male students) or to go straight into a school as an uncertificated teacher.

For the time being Emma adopted the second option, living at home and working as an assistant teacher at St Mary's Girls' School, which took pupils aged from eight to thirteen. The logbook for September 1876 praised her as 'energetic and industrious' and recognised the good progress made by her pupils. 'E. Moyle's class does her credit', wrote the headmistress in November and in January 1877 she was happy to leave the school in Emma's charge when she herself was absent through illness.[387] That is the last reference to her presence at the school and it must be assumed that she went off to college. As most admissions registers have not survived it cannot be definitely established which one of the few women's training colleges Emma attended but it's almost certain that she opted for the one most accessible from her island home, the new college in Truro. Even this involved a difficult and expensive journey, by means of the notoriously rough passage to Penzance and the West Cornwall Railway with its recently installed broad gauge.

Evidence that Emma went to Truro College is provided by a report in the *Royal Cornwall Gazette*: at a concert performed by second-year leavers on 6 December 1878 'Miss Moyle' sang two solos, 'Angels of the Hearth' and 'The Lost Sheep Brought Home'.[388] It's true that there were other Miss Moyles living in Cornwall but none, as far as I know, trained as teachers at this time. Emma was twenty in 1878, just the age at which she would have graduated after two years at college. Both songs were

Victorian Christmas favourites. The title of the first suggests that it exalted the feminine domestic role, which would hardly have been appropriate for young women just beginning their teaching careers.[389] In fact, the lyric by Helen Burnside, the popular writer of Christmas card verses, expresses regret for 'dear long vanish'd faces' which no longer haunt the fireside.

The song may well have resonated with homesick students inhabiting premises described by a later Principal as 'grey, bare and comfortless'. The description was certainly apt: the college's bare floorboards, undecorated stone walls and dormitory cubicles matched Spartan conditions in boarding schools of that time. Equally characteristic of school were the japes recalled by one Truro graduate, such as covering fellow students' pillows with flour. Like most training colleges of that time, Truro imposed a strenuous regime designed to 'form such habits and impart such sentiments ... as may best befit those whose calling it is to instruct and educate the children of the working man.' They followed a strict timetable of study, lectures, military drill, household work and afternoon walks in groups of four. This routine was interspersed with periods of teaching practice at St Paul's School, where a student had to give a lesson which was 'criticised by all the students in her presence', and observe others given by a mistress.[390] Their only leisure was on Saturday afternoons, but, even then, students were not free to go into the town without giving a strict account of their time. Former students remembered buying such treats as 'fancy lunch biscuits, jam or small sausages without skins' to relieve the monotonous college diet. Sundays involved compulsory attendance at St Paul's Church, wearing bonnets which must not be trimmed with

Diocesan Female Training College, Truro.

frivolous flowers or feathers. But some alumnae had fond memories of cosy afternoons 'making toast for Sunday tea'.[391]

By the time of the leavers' concert students had taken and passed all the compulsory subjects in the certificate examination: Religious Knowledge, Arithmetic, Grammar and English Language, School Management, Domestic Economy and Needlework, Reading, Spelling and Penmanship. They had also had to give three 'criticism lessons' in front of the Principal, Head Governess, church dignitaries and fellow students on such topics as 'A Railway Station', 'How to Dust a Room', 'Winter and Summer Coats of Animals' and 'King John and Magna Carta'.[392] It sounds a frightening ordeal, after which the students were qualified, as the Chancellor reminded them at a special service in St Paul's church, to take on 'the great responsibility of their work'. All the leavers were apparently 'provided with schools': the board schools set up by the 1870 Education Act, together with the existing church schools, provided plenty of work for teachers.

Scilly, however, was not affected by the act since Augustus Smith 'had long anticipated its requirements of education for all'. And it was in one of his schools that Emma took up the post in which she is listed by the 1881 Census: 'Certified School Mistress of Mixed School'.[393] I could find no evidence in any surviving Scillonian logbook for Emma's presence at this time and conclude that she must have been teaching at one of the off-island schools, the logbooks of which are missing. Her return was no doubt prompted both by a longing to return to her Scillonian home and by the expense of setting up house for herself elsewhere.

Now absent from the Moyle household was eighteen-year-old Mary Elizabeth Alexandra, who had followed her sister's example by embarking on a teaching career. The 1881 Census identifies her as a pupil-teacher at St Michael's School in Cadbury, Devon, living in the school house with its young headmistress Kate Tiley. Away from her parents and without the strict discipline imposed on Emma at Truro, Mary could live more freely. There may not have been many temptations in this small farming village, but she was not far from more stimulating scenes of provincial life in Tiverton or Exeter.

Once her apprenticeship was over Mary applied for teaching jobs in Cornwall rather than for training college. A newspaper report shows that in January 1883 she was one of eight candidates for the post of schoolmistress at Helston but that she was unsuccessful. On 3 June 1884, however, she wrote in the logbook of Chacewater school: 'I, Mary E.A. Moyle, commenced duties today, having been appointed to take charge of this school until further notice. This is a temporary arrangement.'[394] Whether the rather surprising employment of an uncertificated and inexperienced twenty-year-old in such a senior position had anything to do with local family connections, I don't know. It's true that one of the managers who visited the school and checked the registers was a Mr A. Moyle but I have not been able to link him to Mary's late great-uncle, Doctor Matthew Moyle of Chacewater. Anyway, she was given a demanding role. Attendance fluctuated wildly. Children stayed away in bad weather or to attend such events as a circus, a menagerie or the Kenwyn feast. At least one boy was absent because he had no boots and others did not appear when they couldn't 'bring their school fees with them', as demanded by the School Board. On half a dozen occasions during her year at Chacewater Mary recorded that there were 'so few children present, they were sent home again'. By January 1885 the average number registered had gone down from 71.8 to 35.1 and it was no wonder that the Attendance Officer called so often. Even so, the infant school received a good report for Religious Knowledge, which recognised the children's 'spirit and intelligence' and the pains taken in their instruction. But in March of the same year H M Inspector L King Esq delivered a less favourable general report:

The order is certainly better than it was, but the instruction is still unequal. ... The Infants are tolerably advanced for their age but more might be done to vary their employment and render it more interesting. Considering the number of Infants it appears to be very desirable that they should be taught as a separate department by a Certificated Teacher who would be confined to their instruction.

By this time Miss Moyle's 'temporary arrangement' was coming to an end. When she resigned in June her pupils and colleagues showed more appreciation of her efforts than the inspector had done by presenting her with *Poems by Lord Byron* in an edition fit to be 'welcomed in every family'; from 'Don Juan', which the poet himself acknowledged as bawdy, it included only 'carefully selected beautiful passages'.

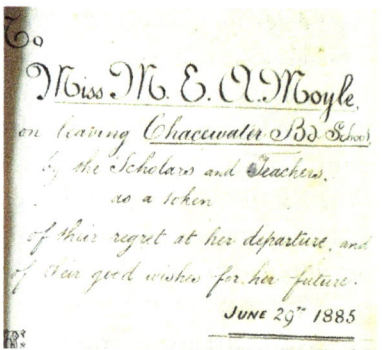
Book inscription on Miss Moyle's departure.

There is no evidence that Mary continued teaching after this somewhat discouraging year. She may have resembled Baptista Trewthen, the Scillonian heroine of Thomas Hardy's *A Mere Interlude*, who found her pupils 'troublesome', dreaded visits from the inspector and was confused by the Education Committee which was 'always changing the Code, so that you don't know what to teach, and what to leave untaught'.[395] In any case, Mary seems to have stayed near Chacewater, where she had found her own Byronic hero in the shape of John Hall, a local carpenter. This relationship clearly flourished and the couple were married in Scilly on 10 March 1888. Seven months later they were still in St Mary's, probably at the Moyles' house in the Parade, when their first child was born and baptised with the names of his grandfather and deceased young uncle, John Grenfell. It looks as though the pregnancy predated the wedding, a circumstance which would not have unduly shocked the liberal-minded doctor.

Moyle Wives and Daughters

* * * *

It is unlikely, however, that Emma Moyle was present at the wedding or the baptism, close though the sisters were. Like so many young Scillonians she had been obliged to leave the islands in order to gain promotion. In September 1887 she had made the long journey to Redhill in Surrey to take up an appointment as 'mistress at Battle Bridge School'. A year later she was appointed to a new post in the same town, writing proudly in the logbook of St Matthew's Girls' School on 24 September: 'I, Emma Grenfell Moyle took charge of this school.' At the age of thirty she had become headmistress of a publicly-funded church school of over 200 pupils on a salary of around £100 a year.[396] It was a challenging job in which she would impose discipline, frame courses of study, work out timetables, supervise pupil-teachers and teach in the 'upper standards'. The notorious 'payment by results' system made the task even more onerous, for grants awarded to schools depended on the satisfactory attendance and performance of their pupils. Head teachers had to keep detailed logbooks and inspectors arrived at frequent intervals to check on attendance and test every child over the age of six in reading, writing and arithmetic as well as optional subjects 'taught according to a graduated scheme'. The system had many critics, one of whom claimed that it made children resemble 'specimens on a board with a pin stuck through them like beetles' and provided no 'equipment for the battle of life'.[397] It was to be modified during Emma's career at St Matthew's, partly as a result of pressure from the National Union of Elementary Teachers, but its constricting effects were long felt in the classroom.

It must have required all Emma's attention that year to cope with these demands, which were compounded by frequent visits from local and diocesan clergy to check on the children's grasp of the Bible and Prayer Book. Her main problem was that many children were irregular in their attendance, since Redhill parents were as reluctant as those of Chacewater and Scilly to accept the need for compulsory education. Girls were especially likely to be kept at home – to mind the baby, run errands and help with the chores. In addition, there were epidemics of mumps, whooping cough and measles, the last of which caused the school to be closed for a month in the spring. Summer events distracted the children even more from the three Rs. After their annual excursion to Eastbourne attendance was 'very poor'. As luck would have it Her Majesty's Inspectors visited immediately afterwards, returning to test the pupils a few days later when Emma recorded 'very small attendance owing to the Foresters' Fete'. The Inspectors' perfunctory Report for 1889 found fault with the children's performance in reading, arithmetic, spelling and grammar while acknowledging that their discipline, sewing and singing were 'very good'. The result must have been disappointing for Emma: the grant was reduced from the £154 awarded under 'the able charge of Miss Vile', her predecessor, to £136. Out of this sum the managers had to pay the teachers and maintain the school over the next year. Such was the arbitrary power exercised by HMIs – just as it is by Ofsted inspectors today.[398]

The next eighteen months brought dramatic changes to both the sisters' family lives. On their mother's death in January 1890 Emma was granted a week's leave of absence to attend the funeral and comfort her father. On his retirement later that year he went to stay initially in Dawlish, where he gave his fourth daughter Annie in marriage to widower Charles Edmonds, a baker and shopkeeper of that town who already had two sons. After that Emma accommodated her father, together with her three unmarried sisters and Jessie's daughter Margaretta, in a bay-windowed semi-detached house in Grove Hill Road, Redhill. They all lived on her salary plus the proceeds of the pension fund which the islanders had given the doctor and such money as twenty-year-old Janie earned as a dressmaker. Jessie was now thirty and still described in the 1891 census as 'imbecile from childhood', while fifteen-year-old Rovena was a 'scholar', as was Margaretta, now listed as just another sister – doubtless to preserve the respectability of Emma's ménage. The busy household was officially headed by Dr Moyle but Emma clearly paid the rates for she now appears on the electoral role for municipal, county and school board elections, a right given to unmarried women ratepayers in 1867. Meanwhile, some of her young sisters became part of the local community; they sang solos, for example, with St Matthew's Temperance Choir and at a Soldiers' Entertainment.[399]

Mary Hall must also have travelled to Scilly for her mother's funeral in 1890, taking one-year-old John and her second son, Charles, born a month earlier. Sadly for her, the village in which she was raising her brood had fallen on hard times, caused by the decline of its copper industry. Over the ten years before 1891 the population of Chacewater fell from 3,558 to 2,053 as the mines closed and there was less work for the craftsmen sustained by them.[400] Among those who left was Mary's husband John whom the 1891 Census noted to be 'in the USA'. He may or may not be identified as the John Hall, joiner, listed among those arriving in Boston in May 1890 – but he is certainly the pickaxe-wielding man whose photograph has passed down through the generations. The tool suggests that he was working as a miner but there is no further record of his American venture or of any money sent back to support Mary, their two sons and baby daughter, Gladys, born in December 1890. Thus both sisters were now in charge of households which had to be run on a tight budget.

John Hall of Chacewater, probably when digging for gold in America.

There must have been frequent correspondence between Emma and Mary as their circumstances changed during the 1890s.

During the Easter holidays in 1893 Emma nursed their father through his last painful illness and signed his death certificate on 6 April. Four days later she reopened the school but 'owing to ill health from overstrain' she could not resume her duties for another week. There is no record of Mary and her three children attending Dr Moyle's funeral but it is clear that she and Emma exchanged news over the next few years about John Hall's return from America, the births of Dorothy, Ernest and Thomas Hall in Chacewater and Emma's move to a smaller house in Redhill. At some point they agreed to share out their domestic responsibilities, a common arrangement among hard-pressed families at the time. In 1897 six-year-old Gladys went to live with 'Auntie Em', who became both her guardian and her headmistress for the next seven years, with Dorothy joining her sporadically between 1900 and 1907. Jessie, now classed as 'feeble-minded', was sent into Mary's charge in Chacewater, leaving her daughter Margaretta behind with Emma. Meanwhile the younger Moyle sisters left Emma's nest to get married, Janie to Jules Watteau of Paris and Rovena to her sister Annie's stepson George Edmonds. If only we still had the letters in which the emotional and financial motives for these complicated arrangements were no doubt discussed.

The Edwardian period, so often evoked as a sunlit leisured age, brought change in the tough working lives of both sisters. As Emma grew in experience, government inspectors found less fault with St Matthew's and awarded higher annual grants, reaching over £200 by 1902. But the reports also reveal mounting pressures. With the growth of Redhill's population, the school became 'overcrowded and insufficiently staffed' and the head teacher 'much overweighted', often having to take charge of two standards herself. No solution was found to the problem of four classes occupying the same room, which made teaching 'difficult and trying'.[401] Even so, Emma found time to challenge the attendance officers who constantly took down the names of persistent absentees but did nothing to make them come to school. She instituted her own inquiries, discovering that some children were being sent out to work, to beg, to accompany their parents on the Kentish hop-picking fields or 'to fetch soup between the hours of ten and twelve', presumably from a charity kitchen. More frivolously, some attended Sanger's Circus when it came to town or went to 'watch a woman walking on a ball'.[402] It's not clear that Emma managed to prevent such truancy but there was certainly nothing she could do about the outbreaks of scarlet fever, diphtheria, mumps, measles, influenza and German measles which regularly caused the school to be closed for a month or more. Regular medical inspections introduced by the Liberal government helped to improve the children's hygiene and to record physical defects, while the introduction of swimming and other sports improved their physique, but not until the discovery of more vaccines were these epidemic scourges brought to an end.

The reform which most affected Emma's world was the Education Act of 1902. Children were now entitled to free secondary education if they passed a scholarship exam, for which St Matthew's girls were prepared, often successfully. The Act also created an Education Committee in Reigate, of which Emma became a member 'representing various interests in pursuance of the scheme'. By 1914 she also belonged to the Children's Care Association, which was charged with improving 'the general fitness of the growing generation'.[403] These were welcome new opportunities for a woman to exert some influence in public life, even if the frequent evening meetings were hard to fit into Emma's busy schedule at school and at home. Her house in Redhill remained a hub for the scattered family. Rovena's second child,

Emma Moyle in studious mode.

for example, was born there and baptised at St Matthew's church, even though she was then living in Bude with her husband, a ship's cook. In addition, Emma had her nieces Gladys and Margaretta to care for.

It's true that Gladys was by this time more of a companion than a charge. On her thirteenth birthday, 23 December 1903, she had been appointed as a monitress, a prelude to her entering the pupil-teacher scheme which had been Emma's own route into teaching. But Gladys had an opportunity her aunt had not enjoyed. From September 1905 she was able to complete her apprenticeship by alternating her teaching work at St Matthew's with attendance at the new Redhill Girls' Secondary School. Of the fifty-seven girls on the first register, pupil-teachers outnumbered scholarship holders and there was only one fee-paying pupil. Of particular interest are the occupations of the parents, most of whom were tradesmen or artisans rather than professionals and only one had 'private means'. Among them were three gardeners, three schoolteachers, three timberyard foremen, two carpenters, two grocers, two policemen, two butlers, two porters, as well as a single baker, plasterer, dressmaker, nurse, stationer, groom, coachman, tailor, organist, teahouse manager, coal merchant, attendance officer and engine driver. The new school really was leading girls from modest backgrounds 'In Lucem', as its motto claimed from the start.[404]

The young Gladys Hall, my grandmother.

Gladys did well at Reigate County School for Girls (as it was soon renamed), taking part in plays, contributing thoughtful pieces to the early school magazines, winning the English prize and matriculating in 1909 with particularly high marks in English and French. I think she also enjoyed the chance to enjoy the 'merry schoolgirl' life extolled by the headmistress.[405] In October 1909 Emma proudly recorded in her logbook that her niece had been awarded a County Council scholarship worth £50 a year for a Home Science and Economics course at King's College for Women, London. The household moved to Station Road in Redhill, no doubt to facilitate Gladys's rail journey to the city.

I have always understood that Gladys was a suffragette and it is the case that Redhill had an active branch of Emmeline Pankhurst's Women's Social and Political Union, of which a 'Miss Hall' was listed as a member. I like to picture her as part of the large contingent which travelled by special train to attend a 'magnificent and inspiring' demonstration in London in June 1911 – but there is no proof of her presence. She graduated from King's in 1912, with a good reference from the Warden who commended her 'unusual thoughtfulness', 'interesting and cultivated mind' and 'capacity for independent consideration'.[406]

Margaretta's capacities, however, are shrouded in mystery. The only surviving record of her receiving any education is that in 1897, aged nearly twenty, she was awarded a certificate for being 'never absent, never late' at St Matthew's Sunday School.[407] In the 1911 Census she was listed for the first time as 'feeble-minded', a category first adopted in the 1901 Census to denote a minor degree of 'imbecility'. I can only speculate about the behavioural problems which led Emma to label Margaretta in this way or about her reasons for sending her niece to join the 950 inmates of Netherne Lunatic Asylum on 23 December 1912.[408] But one clue is Emma's involvement with the campaign to improve juvenile fitness, which suggests that she shared Edwardian concerns about social degeneration.

Britain's declining industrial position in the world and reverses suffered during the Boer War raised fears that the nation was in a state of decay. Social reformers, educational psychologists and scientists recommended 'eugenic' solutions such as the segregation, sterilisation or even elimination of 'unfit' members of society. As the Regius Professor of Physic at Cambridge pronounced, 'Feeble-minded persons are prolific; the thing can only be bred out.' This opinion was cited in the 1908 Royal Commission Report on the Care of the Feeble-Minded, whom it defined as those incapable 'of competing on equal terms with their normal fellows or of managing their affairs with ordinary prudence'. It noted that such 'mentally deficient persons' had 'a very marked degree of fertility and survival to old age, especially among those of the higher grades who are termed feeble-minded.' The Commission thus recommended that, for their own good and to prevent them from passing on their inherited condition, such people should be placed in 'large and controlled institutions where they will be ... kept under effectual supervision so long as may be necessary'. But it did not advocate the 'simple surgical operation' of sterilisation which, in the view of Liberal cabinet minister Winston Churchill, would allow 'the inferior' to circulate 'freely in the world without causing too much inconvenience to others'. The subsequent Mental Deficiency Act of 1913 simply required County Councils to make 'suitable and sufficient provision for the care of defective persons'.[409]

Margaretta was in her mid-thirties by this time and, as 'a spinster of no occupation', was usually alone in the house while Emma and Gladys pursued their busy lives. It seems likely that it was the lack of 'effectual supervision' which led Emma to comply with a 'great new principle of right-doing' by consigning her niece to Netherne Asylum in nearby Coulsdon, opened by Surrey County Council in 1909. As a 'feeble-minded' woman of child-bearing age and the daughter of an acknowledged 'imbecile', Margaretta was segregated as a means of 'bettering the general condition of our people'.[410] Thanks to the valiant efforts of archivists like Julian Pooley of Surrey History Centre, many patients' casebooks have been salvaged from the wreckage after such hospitals were closed in the 1990s. Unfortunately, Margaretta's records were not retrieved. It is therefore impossible to be certain of her diagnosis or of her treatment in this 'world unto itself, high on a leafy hill, with its own water tower, farm, workshops, laundry and church'.[411] She was probably deemed 'incurable' and would not therefore have been given contemporary therapies such as ice-baths, cranial surgery and opiate drugs. Nor is it likely that she incurred the injuries noted in the asylum's Female Medical Journal resulting from fits, fights or self-harm. There is no record of her complaining to the County Council Visiting Committee which toured the hospital regularly and listened to 'the usual troubles' ventilated by some inmates. It is not clear whether she was also visited by Emma or Gladys. I suspect that Margaretta quietly followed Netherne's structured regime of essential work in the garden, laundry or kitchen interspersed with sports, dances and fancy-dress parties. The only certain fact is that she became institutionalised under the strict custody of Netherne's locked and gender-segregated wards until her death in 1930.[412]

Postcard of Netherne Asylum, 1919.

Long before Margaretta entered Netherne she had lost the company of her mother when Jessie moved to Chacewater to live with her sister Mary until her death in 1902. That household was subject to many strains, as Mary struggled to bring up her four sons and her daughter Dorothy (who was sometimes sent to stay with Emma), in an area where work was still scarce. Mary's husband may have found employment during the 1890s on the many local buildings financed by the Cornish philanthropist, John Passmore Edwards, to provide 'sources of sweetness and light to the people of their respective neighbourhoods'. The Chacewater Literary Institute, Bodmin Free Library, Helston Science and Arts Schools and Liskeard Cottage Hospital are among the handsome edifices which required the skills of joiners such as John Hall.

Meanwhile, the oldest son, John Grenfell, moved to Penzance to work as a gardener at Trengwainton House, where he was accommodated in a 'lock up dwelling room', before emigrating to Australia.[413] When John Hall senior died in September 1910, at the age of forty-six, Mary also set out to make a new life.

With her three youngest sons and Dorothy, Mary travelled north to the thriving industrial town of Bradford. The census of March 1911 reveals that she had set up home in a five-room terrace house in the Manningham district, taken in a female lodger and sent twelve-year-old Thomas to school. All her other offspring had found work in the mills, Charles as a wool sorter, Dorothy as a silk winder and fourteen-year-old Ernest as a jobbing boy. There was more money coming in now but it must have been hard for the Hall family, fresh from Cornwall, to adjust to the 'taste and smell of smoke', 'long, straight, hopeless streets', 'great oblong many-windowed' factories and thronged footpaths, all evoked in Mrs Gaskell's novel *North and South*.[414] But the boys would doubtless have cheered with the rest when, during an exciting replay match in April 1911, Bradford City won the FA cup.

The first half of 1914 saw several changes in the lives of both sisters. Emma returned to school on 5 January after an unspecified operation in October 1913. She clearly hoped that this would bring an end to the ill health which had caused her to be absent from her duties for long periods over the previous two years and which may well have prompted her decision to send Margaretta to Netherne. Sure enough, the logbook records no absence for Emma during the winter and summer terms, despite the usual outbreaks of illness among the girls. Thus she was able to organise the mandatory Empire Day celebrations in May, with appropriate lessons, patriotic songs and an address on 'the duties of citizenship and upholding the Empire'.

An occasion which gave Emma more joy, I suspect, was Gladys's wedding at St Matthew's church on 18 July 1914. The bridegroom was none other than thirty-six-year-old Harold McFarland Davis, son of Ambrosine and Charles Royer Davis, and grandson of the St Agnes lighthouse keeper. It's likely that they met in London where both were working and that it happened through Harold's cousin and schoolfellow, Edwin Gibson Davis, headmaster of Plumstead Elementary School, for it was he who acted as witness to their marriage. As the other witness was Emma Moyle, the register represents the uniting of the Moyle and Davis families from which I spring. The reception was probably held in the four-bedroom detached house into which Emma and Gladys had moved, 33 Lynwood Road, which they named St Mary's in recognition of their Scillonian roots.

It's unlikely that there was any talk among the wedding guests about the assassination of the Austrian archduke, Franz Ferdinand, in Serbia which had occurred in June, for few suspected that this would lead to a global conflict. Yet by the time Emma closed the school for the summer holidays on 29 July, Austria had declared war on Serbia with the backing of Germany and opposed by France and Russia. After German troops entered Belgium on 3 August as part of the Schlieffen Plan for the conquest of France, Britain declared war on Germany to defend Belgian neutrality. When school resumed at the end of August, a British Expeditionary Force of 160,000 men was already engaged in heavy fighting in Belgium and northern France.

It seems that Mary Hall and her other offspring did not travel from Bradford to attend Gladys's wedding, perhaps because they could not afford the time or the expense. In any case, by then Charles and Ernest had recently joined the West Yorkshire Regiment, a unit in the Territorial Force created in 1908 for home defence rather than overseas service. In return for payment of about five shillings a week, recruits would take part in regular training exercises and summer camps. No sooner had they set off for their first fortnight of such training when war was declared and the regiment was quickly incorporated into the Regular Army. On 8 September both brothers voluntarily signed overseas service papers and began to train for action. Fifteen-year-old Thomas was still too young to enlist.

Nearly all areas of life were affected by the war during the next four years and St Matthew's School was no exception. Emma records that she had to close early on winter afternoons because of 'the scarcity of lighted lamps and the darkened globes of those that are alight'. Over the Christmas holiday 'soldiers billeted in the town used the school for feeding rooms' and their return in February caused the school to be closed for a few days. Soon she was being told to 'curtail expenses by ordering only what is absolutely necessary' and to have dark blinds fitted 'to conform to new lighting regulations'. More positively Emma writes of taking in Belgian girls, of pupils giving a concert to wounded soldiers, of a War Savings Association being formed and of the children being let off afternoon school to 'see an aeroplane display in connection with the War Savings week'. A further half-day's holiday was granted when St Matthew's raised £1,000 in war savings. During the last months of the war in 1918 the school was repeatedly 'closed by the Medical Officer for influenza' but no pupils or staff seem to have lost their lives during the deadly pandemic.[415] Nor does the school logbook mention any instance of a girl losing an older brother or a father in the war. Yet the memorial plaque in St Matthew's Church suggests that this must have happened as it contains 106 names of parishioners 'who gave their lives for their country and its cause in the Great War 1914-1918'.[416]

Even Margaretta's segregated life changed as a result of the war. Netherne received inmates from the neighbouring Brookwood Asylum, which was taken over for military casualties, and it lost half its staff to conscription. The resulting 'underfeeding, overcrowding and inefficient nursing' was blamed by the Medical Superintendent for the wave of deaths from tuberculosis in 1917. Margaretta would not have been allowed to mix with the convalescing soldiers, who came in to help the market garden provide the country with vital food supplies, or with seventy-five service patients suffering from brain injuries or shell shock. But their presence brought the hospital into public view and this led to improvements in the 1920s. The asylum became known as a hospital while inmates (renamed as patients) could buy food in a newly-opened canteen, wear their own clothes, enjoy weekly cinema shows and listen to radio sets in the wards. I hope Margaretta was able to benefit from some of these changes before she died of complications arising from gallstones and was buried in the hospital grounds in March 1930.[417]

The Hall family in Bradford also endured hardships during the war years: shortages of food and other commodities which eventually necessitated rationing, the fear of Zeppelin raids causing dark streets and blacked-out houses, and the billeting of soldiers in homes and public buildings. At least Dorothy's job was not at risk, women's labour being in great demand as so many young men were in the trenches. Their numbers eventually included all four Hall boys. Charles and Ernest left for Belgium in April 1915 when their regiment joined the British Expeditionary Force; John joined an Australian Infantry battalion at the end of that year and arrived in France in May 1916; and on reaching seventeen in February 1916, Thomas enlisted with the Worcestershire Regiment. As battle raged all along the Western Front their mother and sisters anxiously scoured the casualty lists in newspapers and dreaded the postman's knock. Gladys was fortunate in not having to worry about her new husband, even though the conscription introduced in 1916 applied to all men between the ages of eighteen and forty-one. Harold's chronic asthma rendered him unfit for military service, though he was probably drafted into other war work.

The first Hall casualty was Ernest, who was concussed and shell-shocked on 4 September 1915 during routine trench warfare around the Belgian town of Ypres.[418] He was shipped home and spent a fortnight in King George Hospital in north London. Ernest was allowed five months of recuperation and he probably visited his mother in Bradford before rejoining his unit in February 1916. He took part in the huge British offensive launched in July of that year on the Somme, as did Charles and John. John became one of its 650,000 British casualties when he was wounded at Pozières in August. At the end of the year he was consigned to hospital for a fortnight with trench foot. During 1917 the West Yorkshires took part in another costly engagement, the third battle of Ypres, in which Ernest was again reported 'wounded in action'.

All four brothers took part in resisting a last desperate German offensive along the Western Front in the spring of 1918. It was during this action that Charles was wounded for the first time, captured by the Germans and taken to Niederzwehren prison camp. Here he died of his wounds on 26 May and was buried in the camp cemetery, where he has a marked grave. A day later his youngest brother Thomas was killed during the battle of the Aisne; he has no grave but his name is inscribed on the war memorial in Soissons.[419]

Private Ernest Granville Hall during the First World War.

Privates John Grenfell Hall and Thomas Gerald Hall.

The two remaining brothers survived the last bloody months of the war, although John was wounded again and Ernest became seriously ill with Spanish flu. By the time peace was declared on 11 November both had been promoted to the rank of Lance-Corporal. Ernest was demobilised in February 1919, returning to England with an 'exemplary' service record, and John returned to

Moyle Wives and Daughters

Australia, where he was entitled to nineteen acres of land as a 'soldier-settler' and set up as a horticulturist. The handsome Ernest was the only son left to comfort his bereaved mother in July when Bradford held its victory celebration, described in the local press as 'earnest, but restrained, and free from any boisterous blatancy which might have grated those in whom the collective joy was dimmed by personal grief'.[420] Five thousand of the city's men were mourned that day, including hundreds of 'Bradford Pals' mown down by German machine guns as their battalion went over the top on the first day of the battle of the Somme.

As the sisters obviously knew, their brother and his family in Scilly, the only Moyles still there, were also involved in the war. Edwards Moyle served in the Defence Volunteers, which guarded the garrison, quay and new wireless station, while both his sons were conscripted. The Scillies occupied a strategic position in the western approaches to Britain and as German U-boats attacked shipping close to their shores, the islands came to play a vital part in the war at sea. The historian Richard Larn explains;

Edwards Moyle on Home Guard duty.

> The Royal Navy Auxiliary Patrol Service on St Mary's and the Royal Navy Air Service on Tresco worked at full stretch, answering radio signals, sending out trawlers, drifters, rescue tugs and floatplanes to assist, attacking U-boats, deterring others, and maintaining their aircraft and trawlers which were bringing in countless injured seamen.[421]

A seaplane from Tresco which bombed and sank a German U-boat in May 1917 was the only one of these new aircraft to achieve such a feat during the whole war.

Islanders who were not on active service, mainly women such as Edwards's wife Eva and daughter Lily, contributed by providing over 1,000 servicemen with billets, assisting at signal stations, growing vegetables instead of flowers, and helping in the overstretched hospitals housed in various halls and hotels. Sometimes, too, they benefited in age-old fashion from cargo washed up on their shores – even hard ship's biscuit or tins of dried meat were welcome additions to a lean wartime diet. Meanwhile Edwards Moyle's sons were sent further afield. Trevellick's war record shows his progression from the signals service at Land's End to the RNVR land base at Portsmouth. John joined the Devonshire Regiment and fought, like his Hall cousins, at Ypres and the Somme. Both returned safely in 1918 – unlike the fifty-four servicemen whose names are carved on Scillonian war memorials.[422]

Like most British families, the Moyle sisters experienced a mixture of relief, joy, hardship and grief in the aftermath of the war. Even though a dearth of young men doomed many women of that generation to spinsterhood, Mary was able to celebrate the marriage of her daughter Dorothy to Harry Scott, a packing-case worker, in St Luke's Church Manningham in October 1919. Delight at the birth of Dorothy's son a year later was mixed with Mary's continuing sorrow for the two sons who were honoured on the war memorial in their native Chacewater.

Chasewater war memorial.

Her enduring pain is reflected both in the sad eyes of her post-war photograph and in poems she wrote at this time. 'A Mother's Lament for her Son Killed Somewhere in France' asks:

> Was he sore dismayed,
> When Death sprang upon him
> Or passed he unafraid?

She portrays herself weeping beside the chest which contains the boy's books, toys and infant clothes. Many of the poems are addressed to 'dear Tommy-lad', who fills her 'Mother-heart', perhaps because Thomas was so young when he went off to war that the memory of his childhood was closest to her. The most optimistic of the poems is 'Mother Dear' which ends with this verse:

> But the seeds of good we sow
> Both in shine and shade will flow.
> And will keep our hearts aglow
> While the days are going by.

In one of her poems Mary sought solace from 'a gracious God', though unlike many mothers, sweethearts and friends bereaved by the First World War, she did not dabble in spiritualism.[423]

Mary's family clearly provided some comfort in her distress. Her sister Annie Edmonds, whose husband was still working as a baker in Dawlish, visited Mary in 1918 after the loss of Charles and Thomas. Tragically, Annie herself died while she was in Bradford, her death being registered in October. This was the month in which a second wave of the Spanish flu pandemic swept through the city and possibly caused or aggravated the cerebral haemorrhage noted on the certificate. At the time of the 1921 census Mary was visiting Gladys and Harold Davis in Finchley and getting to know her two grandsons, five-year-old John Grenfell Royer (named after his

Mary Hall after the First World War.

Saving Lives in Scilly

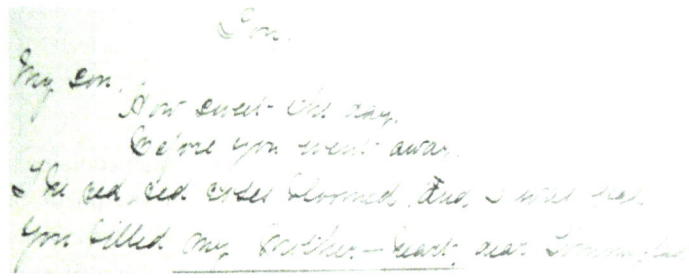
Extract of a poem in which Mary Hall laments the death of her son Tommy.

Moyle and Davis grandfathers) and Michael aged two. Back in Bradford Mary also saw something of her sister Rovena Edmonds, who moved to the city at some point after the war and helped her husband George employ the skills he had learnt as a ship's cook to set up as a 'journeyman cake baker and confectioner'. They seem to have made a go of it and stayed on in Bradford for the rest of their lives.[424]

But Mary clearly felt unsettled and embarked on a peripatetic existence not uncommon among widows. I tracked her down next on the 1929 voting register for Hounslow, where she was a joint householder with her son Ernest. She then lived for a time with her daughter Gladys at the comfortable residence newly designed for Harold in Hampstead Garden Suburb. Here her youngest grandson, Tony Davis, remembered Mary as 'a very kind lady'. But by 1939 she had returned to her native Cornwall, where she shared a house in Camelford with her twice-widowed sister-in-law, Caroline Broad (née Hall). Her final move was to Bournemouth, perhaps to be near her daughter Dorothy who lived there with her unemployed husband.[425]

The post-war years had also been difficult for Emma Moyle. The strain of keeping a school going through the long conflict and the worst flu epidemic ever recorded took its toll on all teachers. For much of 1919 one member of St Matthew's staff was 'unable to perform her duties' because of 'severe nervous debilitation', while for most of the winter term Emma herself was incapacitated by laryngitis and other illnesses. She would return to school but then suffer a relapse or she would be unable to attend 'owing to inclement weather'. By this time she was sixty and had perhaps begun to lose what a Parliamentary Committee on teachers' pensions called 'the vivacity needful for success'. Her comments in the school logbook became more scrawled and perfunctory. She decided to resign that Christmas even though she would not receive a pension for another four years. She was clearly worn out after the 'long and faithful service as a head teacher in the borough during the past thirty-two years', for which the Education Committee recorded its 'appreciation'.[426]

After her retirement, Emma carried on living in 33 Lynwood Road, sharing the house, now that both Gladys and Margaretta had left, with a succession of independent single women. Four post-war electoral registers list her first with Sarah Rose and then with Ermyntrude Griffen, all now qualified to vote in parliamentary as well as local elections. At the time of the 1921 Census, however, she was recorded, along with her sister Mary, as a visitor to the Davis household in Hampstead Garden Suburb and described as a temporary elementary school teacher. Affectionately known as Auntie Em, she was no doubt a welcome guest – but she did not have the autonomy she had enjoyed for so long. Another woman's name replaced hers alongside Miss Griffen's among the voters in Lynwood Road and for seven years Emma's name is missing from all electoral registers. I can only assume that she stayed on in her niece's house, thus losing the qualification required for a woman voter of being a householder in her own right. No doubt she paid her way by means of supply teaching and the pension she received after she turned 65, 'utterly inadequate' though it was said to be.[427]

It was 1928 before Emma regained her right to vote. In that year all conditions were removed and women were at last qualified on the same terms as men. In any case, Emma had by that time moved to Poole where she shared a house near the harbour with Miss Ellen Maude Marshallsay, a retired music teacher who had recently 'come Home' from India.[428] This sounds like a comfortable seaside retirement but it didn't last long, for Emma died in June 1930 aged 72. She was buried, as she was baptised, in a church within sight and sound of the sea – but it's not clear that any of her siblings, nieces or nephews attended the funeral at St Mary's, Longfleet.

Among the effects, worth £233, which Emma left to my grandmother Gladys Davis were her father's scrapbook and the red exercise book containing her own genealogical notes, both of which have been so useful in my research. The most puzzling item is a poem pinned to the inside cover of the exercise book. It is written not in Emma's plain cursive style but in a Victorian copperplate hand which looks rather feminine. The author is clearly a friend who loved Emma and mourns her death which came quickly and 'in peace'; she weeps beside the grave 'with nought but the murmuring wave/To break the stillness, Friend'; 'faint and weary' she longs to be 'swallow'd up' in Death herself. I suggest that the poet was Miss Marshallsay who lived on in Poole and would have been able to pay frequent visits to her dear friend's grave.

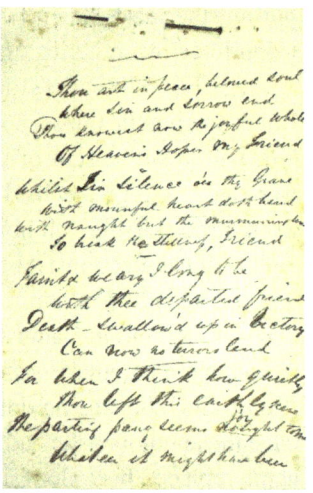

Three of five verses grieving for Emma Moyle.

As the poem suggests, Emma was not the loveless spinster often mocked or pitied in Victorian and Edwardian cartoons – Max Beerbohm unkindly referred to such women as 'the unenjoyed'. She was, as the oldest daughter, the centre of family life after the death of her parents; she spent her whole working life among children; she engaged in public life; she cared for her young protégé, Gladys; and she had close friendships with other women. I feel sure that her life was no less fulfilled than Mary Hall's or that of the other married Moyle or Davis sisters.

Epilogue

The Davis Family at War
1939-1945

Gladys Mary Hall 1890-1980 m. *Harold McFarland Davis 1878-1968*

1 John Grenfell Royer Davis m. *Gladys Mabel Boulton 1939*

Vyvyen   Rodney

2 Michael McFarland Davis m. *Aline Butler 1942*

Alison   Ruth   Diana

3 Anthony Charles Davis m. *Moira Duncan*

Christopher   Duncan

Only twenty-one years after Mary Hall's sons, Charles and Thomas, were killed in what H.G. Wells described as the 'war that will end war', their sister Gladys's two oldest boys volunteered to fight in the Second World War.[429] My father, John Grenfell Royer (always known as Gren), and his younger brother, Michael McFarland, enlisted respectively in the Royal Navy Volunteer Reserve and Royal Air Force. As Mary Hall's grandsons in their turn 'travelled West' to 'storm and wrack', she understood all too well the anxiety their parents and their new wives would feel.[430]

My father, a journalist on the Exeter newspaper *Express and Echo*, was prompted to choose the Navy by his Scillonian ancestry

John Grenfell Royer Davis in training with HMS Drake.

Gunner Davis aboard SS Rangitiki, *1940.*

and the seafaring spirit it had bred in him. In later years he rarely spoke about his war experience but the photographs he sent back to Gladys, his 'dark and petite' bride of April 1939, help me to trace his progress.[431] After training at Devonport naval barracks (known as HMS *Drake*), he was dispatched to SS *Rangitiki* to man the First World War anti-submarine gun with which, like all merchant ships engaged in transporting vital supplies, she was equipped. By November 1940 Gunner Davis was in mid-Atlantic, aboard the *Rangitiki*, the largest ship in a convoy of thirty-seven merchantmen escorted from Bermuda to Liverpool by a single armed cruiser, HMS *Jervis Bay*.

This did not prove sufficient protection when the convoy encountered the powerful German battleship, *Admiral Scheer*. Hopelessly outgunned, *Jervis Bay* engaged the enemy, one seaman comparing it to a bulldog attacking a bear. This action gave the convoy time to scatter before *Jervis Bay* was overwhelmed by *Scheer*'s 'shells coming in thick and fast, like a shower of flaming meteorites'. After resisting this onslaught for over twenty minutes, *Jervis Bay* was reduced to 'a burning wreck manned by the dead and the dying'. The Germans' next target in the scattered convoy was the 'floating leviathan', *Rangitiki*, which they mistook for a troopship. She managed to escape by creating a smoke screen and resisting the temptation to return fire, so as not to reveal her position. Even so, as her captain recorded, 'it was nothing short of a miracle' that she had suffered no casualties.[432]

Frank Mason, Self Sacrifice: H.M.S. 'Jervis Bay' in action with S.M.S. 'Admiral Scheer', 1940.

Once it was all over, the press extolled the convoy's 'thrilling voyage'. West Country newspapers also printed a photograph of Gunner J.G.R. Davis telling a small boy 'the epic story of the *Jervis Bay*'. In reality, five of the convoy's merchant ships were sunk, with heavy loss of life. My father never forgot the ordeal or the heroic self-sacrifice of *Jervis Bay* and for as long as I can remember a copy of this painting of the ship hung in our house.[433]

After a period of leave Gren rejoined *Rangatiki* on a mission to transport troops and weaponry to north Africa. This time the convoy had a heavy escort, which served it well during an engagement with the *Admiral Hipper* on 'a thoroughly miserable' Christmas Day. Gunner Davis must have been glad to arrive safely in Suez.[434] In April 1941 he was appointed sub-lieutenant by HMS *President III*, the 'stone frigate' (ie shore base) tasked with drafting men to serve on defensively equipped merchant ships, known as DEMS. It was in that uniform that he was photographed with his brother Michael, both looking very sober before departing on hazardous assignments.

Michael and Gren Davis, 1941.

Saving Lives in Scilly

Promoted to the rank of lieutenant, Gren would now serve on the 'Murmansk Run'. Between August 1941 and May 1945 seventy-eight Allied convoys of merchant ships transported vast quantities of munitions and other supplies – blankets, flour, lard and dried eggs as well as trucks, tanks, aircraft, ammunition and barbed wire – across the Arctic Ocean to Russia. After the German invasion in June 1941, Stalin's Soviet Union was in dire need of such material and Churchill was determined to render assistance to Britain's new ally in this 'unique and terrible theatre of war'. Despite being escorted by as many armed vessels as the Royal Navy could spare, the twice-monthly convoys subjected sailors to a ghastly ordeal. Not only did they have to run the gauntlet of submarine-launched torpedoes, aerial bombing and the guns of surface ships, but they were also at the mercy of natural forces. Winter brought almost continual darkness and such acute cold that hypothermia quickly set in on lifeboats and any sailor falling overboard could only survive for a matter of seconds. Ships were smothered in ice, rolled excessively in stormy seas and were blanketed in thick fogs – though there were occasional displays of the *aurora borealis*, a magical apparition which delighted Gren. Summer meant that the convoys could venture further north and opened up the White Sea port of Archangel but also brought incessant daylight, which exposed ships to the constant risk of attack.[435]

Nor was there much comfort to be found in the Russian ports of Murmansk and Archangel. Reports came back that there were 'no amusements and no shops', no fresh provisions except 'yak meat and rather poor vegetables' and no decent medical arrangements. Hospitals, for example, were often 'crude and dirty', lacking antiseptics and anaesthetics – as Gren may have found when he suffered a serious bout of pneumonia.[436] Men made the best of such entertainment as there was on offer – dances and film shows at the Navy and International Clubs, performances by the Red Army choir, inter-ship sports contests, ice-skating and the ready supply of cheap vodka.

Epilogue: The Davis Family at War

Any contact with Russians was fraught with difficulty, since they often behaved more like enemies than allies. Under Stalin's harsh Communist regime fraternisation with westerners could lead to a charge of high treason, espionage or propagation of bourgeois lifestyles. It has now come to light that this was the fate of many Russian women who formed relationships with, and sometimes even married, British and American seamen they met through their work as interpreters or customs officers. After the war they were sent to labour camps and any 'foreign' offspring were deprived of state support and denied the chance of higher education.[437] I suspect that Gren, a romantic young man who was now a proud father, sought his own consolation in exploring the Russian countryside. Photography was forbidden but he did manage to acquire (probably through bartering chocolate and cigarettes) an oil painting of a peaceful rustic scene, which he sent back to his wife. It hangs in my house today, as war rages again in Europe following Russia's invasion of Ukraine in February 2022. This time, Britain and other countries are sending military supplies to be used against rather than by Russia.

The sole memento of my father's service in Russia.

Because of my father's reticence, the elusiveness of merchant ship records and the secrecy still shrouding the Arctic operation, which was not given its own medal until 2012 (long after Gren's death), I don't know which of the convoys he served on. Fortunately, his was not among the eighty-seven merchant ships which were sunk; nor was he among the nearly 3,000 sailors who lost their lives; and he was not maimed by gunfire or frostbite, as thousands were. I know, however, that the experience left 'ineradicable scars' on him as on so many others. The radio play he wrote in 1948 may well have sprung from memories of men dying in wintry waters. *Strange Danger* tells the story of Sir Cloudesley Shovell's battle fleet being wrecked on Scilly's Western Rocks in 1707, incorporating some of the 'fanciful legends associated with this incident'.[438]

In his post-war job as West Country correspondent for the *News Chronicle* Gren often had to report on a 'drama at sea', such as that of the *Flying Enterprise*. On Christmas night 1951 the American freighter was so badly damaged by a storm in the English Channel that her crew and passengers had to be rescued, only Captain Carlsen remaining on board. By 4 January the ship was listing so badly that the tugboat *Turmoil* was sent out to tow her into Falmouth. To help fasten the tow line Mate Kenneth Dancy 'took a long step across the gap as the vessels reeled apart and Captain Carlsen was not on his own any more'. After five days, however, the tow failed amid new storms and the two sailors had no choice but to 'make a jump for it'. Then, Dancy recounted in an 'exclusive report to the *News Chronicle*', 'we just lay there floating hand in hand until the *Turmoil* came and hauled us on board'. I know from what my father told me afterwards that it was he who interviewed Dancy and gained his autograph for the album I kept at the time. My father took a special interest in this brave young man whose war service in the Merchant Navy had 'earned him every war ribbon except a Russian one' – which, as Gren well knew, had not been awarded.[439]

Soon after this he was transferred to the London desk of the *News Chronicle* and began to write under his third forename. Royer Davis reported on many different stories but gained a particular reputation as the newspaper's amateur meteorologist. Like his grandfather and great-uncles on the oceans and two great-grandfathers in sea-girt Scilly, he always paid close attention to the weather. He would write an annual forecast based, he explained, on his memory of weather patterns over many years: 'By applying this knowledge in the old-fashioned method of looking at the higher sky I can often form an accurate opinion of

Epilogue: The Davis Family at War

forthcoming tendencies'. Never really happy behind a desk, Gren retained the roving spirit of his forebears.

The middle Davis brother Michael had, like Gren, left school at sixteen when their father's accountancy business was badly affected by the 1930s depression and he never had the chance of higher education. Despite his longing to go on to Cambridge, Michael entered the Air Ministry as a junior clerk and when war broke out three years later he naturally gravitated towards the RAF, serving in Bomber Command. He was a little more communicative than Gren about his wartime experience; although not talking much about it to his wife and three daughters, he did open up to one of his sons-in-law, Graham Vickery. He also wrote down some of his memories.

Observer Michael Davis (third from left) with his bomber crew, 1941.

In a wry, self-deprecating tone, typical of him (and of many in his generation), he tells of his role as an Observer: 'What a name', he comments, 'for doing navigation and bomb aiming!' He passes quickly from his participation in bombing sorties, which included 'a disastrous navigation failure followed with an outstanding navigation success', to his triumphs at shove-halfpenny, which meant that he never had to buy his lunchtime beer. Laconically he recounts an accident at an airfield near Cambridge with an H2S, a new airborne ground scanning system:

> I picked up my gear and disconnected the H2S which promptly blew up in my face. I had been on leave when the H2S indoctrination had taken place and knew nothing of its internal destruction device designed to fool German investigators but in practice achieved my only visit to Addenbrooke's hospital.

Soon after this, writes Michael, 'it was *Tirpitz* time again'. By January 1942 that mighty German battleship was anchored in a Norwegian fjord, striking dread into the hearts of Arctic seamen like his brother and keeping a Royal Navy patrol constantly on duty in its vicinity. Michael's crew was given the job of dropping a 'minebomb', a device which exploded when its fuse was triggered in deep water, close to the *Tirpitz*:

> I pressed the button and announced grandly over the intercom 'Bombs Gone'. But unfortunately the bomb had not gone and nothing we could do would make it go. Our return flight was somewhat overshadowed. We knew whose stupidity would be the first to be questioned. We touched down nicely and started to relax a bit. Not for long. 'It's coming after us', shouted the tail gunner. Our wretched minebomb had at last left the bomb rack and was now bouncing down the runway after us. I explained to the crew that it could not explode as it had a pressure fuse but the general feeling was that the sooner we were off the runway and on the taxi track the better.

With such tales Michael conveys both the gallows humour and the unforeseen hazards characteristic of wartime.

In 1942 he was made a flight-lieutenant and it was in that uniform that he married Aline Butler in July. The couple were not destined to spend much time as newly-weds. Later that year, before he could achieve the thirty missions which would have earned him a Distinguished Service Cross and a spell on ground duties, Michael's bomber plane narrowly avoided a mid-air collision when flying over the Black Forest.

> The strain needed to avoid this was more than the aircraft could take and the engines caught fire. Luck gave me a fault-free parachute descent but the next morning (I know nothing of the rest of the night) I met a fellow with a rifle and held up my arms ('Hande Hoch'). This was followed by two and a half years of boredom with some unpleasant interludes.

Epilogue: The Davis Family at War

That is all that Michael wrote about his crash and capture. But he later told his daughter Ruth that the widow of the rear gunner had got in touch with him to find out 'what had really happened to her husband'. Michael explained to her that 'there was a strict evacuation procedure for aircraft in trouble, based on the man nearest the escape hatch going first.' The rear gunner, who had to crawl out of his turret, was, as so often happened, trapped in the plane. Michael jumped after being told to do so by the skipper but only one other member of the crew survived. The rest were among over 57,000 Bomber Command crewmen (46 per cent) killed during the course of the war.

Michael was taken to the officers' compound in Stalag Luft 3, a camp at Sagan in Silesia reserved for captured air force personnel. His youngest daughter, Diana, heard him talk of the journey to the camp in a train with small wooden upright seats, on which the prisoners slept 'very crammed together'. He felt an insect moving up his back and biting him but was 'told not to fidget'. On his arrival at the camp he was, like all new arrivals, questioned by the senior British officer about his capture, transit journey and interrogation by the Germans. There followed the closely guarded years of 'intense boredom' in barracks described by escapee Eric Williams as so 'thick with the sour smell of overcrowded living' that they resembled 'a squalid prolific slum'. Prisoners 'forced themselves to live in harmony, to make their unpleasant surroundings as bearable a possible', observing house rules such as those recalled by Michael: 'only using light pencil to complete crosswords and endless use of tea leaves until clear water was poured'.[440] To relieve the tedium there were fortnightly performances in the prisoner-built theatre, education in well-attended classes supervised by academics, and a great variety of sports. The standard of fitness at this stalag was said to be high and not too much damaged by the woefully inadequate food supply, supplemented as it was by Red Cross parcels from home, the contents of which were shared out 'for the common good'. Even so the inmates were always hungry, though they apparently fared better than some of their German captors, whom Michael once witnessed squabbling over swede and other vegetable peelings.

Michael doesn't look too under-nourished in a photograph of him with three fellow-prisoners, though this was taken early on to be sent as a reassuring postcard to his family. Letters home, despatched via neutral Switzerland, were allowed; but they had, of course, to be censored and were sometimes very delayed. Prisoners could also receive parcels of fresh clothes (but only uniform), cigarettes, games and anything else to help fill the time. Such communication was clearly very important for morale, as was a well-hidden improvised wireless. The camp's radio operators received daily BBC news bulletins and communicated them by semaphore to selected officers around the compound, who took them down in shorthand; they were then read out to prisoners in their barracks, before being destroyed.[441]

Front and back of postcard from Flight-Lieutenant Michael Davis to his parents, 1942.

All new POWs heard a talk about the 'ceaseless war against the enemy', which involved non-cooperation with their captors and a well-developed escape organisation. Men were invited to give their names to barracks representatives if they wanted to help and the escape committees came to know 'who were the leading spirits, the experts, the keen escapers, the self-effacing but thoroughly co-operative men, and the "not-interested" class'.[442] At

Epilogue: The Davis Family at War

around the time of Michael's arrival, digging had started on about seventy tunnels, most of which were discovered before they were complete. But in October 1943 Eric Williams and two other men did manage to gain their freedom through the famous 'Wooden Horse' tunnel.

Stalag Luft 3 is most renowned for the 'Great Escape'. This took place in March 1944, after long preparations involving many inmates. Michael was one of the 'penguins', who shuffled around the boundary fences getting rid of excavated sand from specially adapted socks, while other prisoners diverted attention by playing noisy games of football. And all but three of his wooden bunk slats were used to prop up the tunnels or to make a railway on which trolleys could convey the escapees. Seventy-nine prisoners eventually managed to get through 'Harry' tunnel but the scheme was discovered before the remaining 120 of the selected escapees could enter. Michael's bunk mate was among those who had to abandon his bid for freedom and slip back to his hut, where he was consoled with precious items such as biscuits, tea and an unused crossword puzzle. Nearly all the fugitives were either arrested as they emerged from the tunnel or recaptured beyond the wire, despite having been provided with laboriously prepared civilian clothes, forged documents, food, maps and compasses. Only a Dutchman and two Norwegians made it to Britain.

The normal punishment for runaways was a period of solitary confinement, part of which might be spent without heating, food or washing facilities. On this occasion, however, the Nazis were so alarmed by the ingenuity, daring and determination of the attempt that, on Hitler's direct orders, they took savage reprisals. Fifty of the escapees were taken to another prison and shot. This may be one of the 'unpleasant interludes' to which Michael referred as he doubtless shared in the 'general feeling of depression' disguised by 'a stiff front' which pervaded the camp when the deaths were announced. It was after this that a coded message told inmates that 'it was no longer their duty to escape'.[443]

Christmas 1944 brought a little cheer with a performance of Handel's *Messiah* and the arrival of long-delayed parcels containing such festive items as canned turkey, plum pudding, cigarettes and candles. Best of all was the radio news that the German offensive in the Ardennes had stalled and that Russian troops were advancing from the east. At the same time rumours spread through the camp that Hitler had ordered the execution of all POWs or that they would simply be abandoned without food and water. Michael's own memory was that in January 1945 'the Red Army was nearby and the camp guards disappeared' so that 'evacuation was everyone for himself'. What actually happened is that on 27 January the guards ordered the 11,000 prisoners to leave the camp, a process which took eight hours. Michael built a small sledge out of bed slats to carry supplies. He then marched westwards, part of a fifteen-mile column ordered to stay in line on pain of being shot. In practice, freezing temperatures, hunger, exhaustion and outbreaks of dysentery caused many prisoners (as well as guards) to fall by the wayside during a five-day march. There is no record of how many died. The conclusion of a recent history account echoes Michael's own words: 'Each man's struggle was his own, a unique battle to survive ... to get through the ordeal as best you could.'[444] Michael did get through, commenting only on the abandonment of his sledge, which was 'fine when snowy, no good when wet'.

At the railway junction of Spremberg, prisoners were given a hot meal of horsemeat stew before being herded into windowless wagons for a three-day journey to Stalag VII-A at Moosburg, during which the filth and stench became overpowering. Postal arrangements broke down at the time and subsequently Michael told his family nothing about the three months he spent at this camp. It had been built for 10,000 but now housed 130,000 men, who slept in tents or air-raid trenches, shared overflowing latrines, waded through seas of mud and consumed such scarce German fare as sauerkraut from large wooden barrels. Again, it was 'every man for himself'.[445] The camp was liberated by General Patton's army on 29 April, the day before the fall of Berlin and Hitler's suicide.

After arriving home in May, Michael returned to the Air Ministry to work in the office of the Chief of Air Staff, Charles Portal. It is difficult to know whether he experienced the deep bitterness resulting from the 'sterility, deprivation and enforced passivity of Stalag life', a response predicted by an Army report of February 1944.[446] Michael was a man of few words but some of his remarks did betray feelings of resentment. He remembered, for example, that his uniform was riddled with lice when he came home but was not changed. He noted furthermore that he was only given ten days' leave (seven of which were spent in Scilly) before starting work again, commenting that it would be 'a bit different in similar circumstances nowadays'. He insisted too that, while half his salary was paid to his wife during his imprisonment, he never received the other half, a grievance common to many POWs. Most significantly, he refused many years later to take part in a *Timewatch* programme about Bomber Command. Michael feared that people who had not witnessed events so 'vital to the continuation of the life of the nation' might adopt 'latter-day revisionist theories' repugnant to those who 'took a direct part in it all'.

Poets of both world wars expressed the unspoken regrets of stoical servicemen like Gren and Michael. In 'Strange Meeting', for example, Wilfred Owen wrote of a soldier's mourning for 'the undone years, the hopelessness', fearing that his experiences will remain a 'truth untold' and that the suffering has been in vain:

> Now men will go content with what we spoiled,
> Or discontent, boil bloody, and be spilled.[447]

At least, unlike Owen who wrote these words shortly before his death in the last weeks of the First World War, the Davis brothers were able to return to their families.

The war had brought 'frightful disruption' to the Davises, as is shown in a memoir which Tony, the youngest brother, wrote for his own sons. He was just settling into his first year at Haberdashers' Aske's, his brothers' old school in West Hampstead, getting to know his classmates and achieving good marks, when 'all this was shattered by the outbreak of war'. His experience illustrates the hasty and improvised arrangements which were made for children, who were expected to do as they were told without asking questions:

> It was decided that I should join a party of pupils being evacuated to the south Midlands. ... It was a mixture of north London schools making up a big party. I remember being part of a horde of kids on station platforms, all with a gas mask tied on. I was billeted with a family in Kettering, but for reasons unknown to me I was shifted almost at once to Wellingborough. My foster-parents were very kind, and I wish I had not been such a snooty grammar-school type of kid, and had realised what good people they were – and patient. I don't think there were any from Haberdashers' at the Wellingborough school, where I was rather lonely.

By summer 1940 'there had been no real war at all', as far as civilians were concerned, and Tony was brought back to London. No sooner had he started the autumn term at Haberdashers' than the Germans launched their bombing campaign on British industrial centres, among which the London docks were a prime target.

The Blitz induced the Davis family to split up. Harold stayed in London, while Gladys took Tony to Barnstaple in north Devon, 'a calm and civilised place' where they lived in a small rented house. This was a much pleasanter experience for Tony than his first evacuation. Although always 'anxious about whether he could keep up with the lessons', he did well at the local grammar school

Epilogue: The Davis Family at War

and enjoyed bicycle rides in the hilly countryside. The highlight of his time there was when 'Michael got a lift one day in a Dakota to the RAF field at Braunton, a few miles away (I saw his plane pass over the house) and came to see us.' Tony much admired Michael's aerial exploits and, according to his sister-in-law Aline, he 'minded dreadfully' that he was too young to fight, a feeling which didn't fade after the war. But, like other youngsters, he did his bit. In Barnstaple he spent his holidays working in a munitions factory or potato-picking and, after returning to London in 1942, he was on the rota for night-time fire-watching at Haberdashers'.

It was during one of these night watches that Tony saw one of the first V1s, 'a dark aircraft silhouette travelling across the clouds, with a curious orange flame exhaust behind it'. He never forgot the sight of these flying bombs, and the V2 rockets which succeeded them, or the damage that they wrought. On one occasion a V2 landed a few miles away and totally destroyed the house of someone he knew. Tony also witnessed the flight of American heavy bombers over London: 'Since there were so many, I counted them … I reached a count of about three hundred and still they were coming. From that time, I really believed that the allies could win the war.'

Tony Davis as a wartime schoolboy.

As a result of the conflict Tony had endured a rather anxious and lonely adolescence. His return to Haberdashers' had not been a happy one, even though he did well on the scientific A-level course he had chosen. The 'long interruption' of his London schooldays left him without any friends and he 'did not form any real acquaintanceships' during his two years in the sixth form. Like the recent pandemic, the Second World War had unforeseen and often unrecognised effects on the young.

Tony's infant nephew and niece, my brother and I, conceived during Gren's periods of leave, were less affected by such tribulations. Unconscious of the 'Make Do and Mend' measures necessitated by wartime shortages, I wore for my christening in December 1941 a gown made by my mother from parachute silk. But I can still hear in my head the rising and falling wail of air-raid sirens as bombs fell on Exeter in April and May 1942 during the 'Baedeker raids', in which targets were chosen for their cultural rather than their strategic or military value. My mother later told me that she used to take me into bed with her so that, if we were hit, we would both die together. Hundreds of civilians were killed or injured in these attacks on the city and many historic buildings destroyed, causing my mother to seek a place of greater safety.

Making do in wartime: the author's christening dress.

We moved ten miles away, to a gardener's cottage on the Bicton estate where my mother's parents worked as chauffeur and head cook. We fared well, our household being augmented by the arrival of my brother Rodney in 1943 and my mother's sister with her baby boy. Here the women were able to carry out further government injunctions – to 'Dig for Victory' and to 'Save Kitchen Scraps to Feed the Hens!' I don't suppose my brother and I did much digging but a blurred and damaged old photo suggests that I enjoyed feeding Grandma's chickens. Our rations were now

Helping out on the Home Front.

Epilogue: The Davis Family at War

supplemented with fresh eggs as well as home-grown vegetables and, I am told, by rabbits caught by the cat. Unlike older children, we had never tasted sweets, ice-cream or bananas and didn't miss what we had never known. As for toys, I expect that they were improvised or passed down, as happened in most wartime families. Further photographs reveal a rattle (which may be home-made) and a single doll I treasured for many years. I don't think we suffered much from the absence of a father we didn't know and we were too young to understand the anxiety our mother and aunt felt for their husbands in the front line.

The two older Davis brothers resumed their married lives after being demobbed. Gren had to get used to the presence of two young children; he had already met me but now there was a two-year-old son he had never seen. Like many war babies, Rodney found it hard to accept this stranger in the house and I'm not sure that their relationship ever really recovered. Michael's three daughters were all born in the post-war years, during which he pursued a successful career in the Air Ministry.

Meanwhile Tony took up the opportunity, denied to his brothers and all his forebears (except his disreputable great-uncle Vyvyan Moyle), of a university education. At Imperial College, London, where he took a degree and a doctorate in Chemistry, he was able at last to make good friends. He found them in the Mountaineering Club and took part with them in Welsh hill walking and in 'Alpine climbs which had been inaccessible during the war'. Companions describe him as 'fearless' but 'a safe pair of hands on a mountain'. Even so, these were dangerous expeditions, during which avalanches and falls were always possible and one fellow climber suffered severe frost bite. I can't help wondering whether his adoption of such an adventurous pursuit was an unconscious attempt to emulate his brothers' military experiences – and I suspect that it caused almost as much worry to his parents and later to his wife Moira.[448]

Gladys and Harold had no such concerns about their grandchildren. None of the wars of the later twentieth century called us to arms; nor did we go to sea, fly aeroplanes or climb mountains. Born though we were during a global conflict and growing up in its austere aftermath, we were blessed with the welfare state, National Health Service and free secondary education established in its wake. We have benefited, too, from the medical advances of post-war decades: treatments for the tuberculosis which caused the early deaths of my great-grandfather and several of his siblings and vaccines to prevent the scourges of polio, measles, diphtheria and whooping cough which swept through Emma Moyle's school. We may have more cause to fear for our own grandchildren in the face of modern dangers, such as the erosion of public services, the emergence of new diseases and the approach of irreversible global warming. We can only trust that they have inherited the resourcefulness, courage and resilience of their Scillonian ancestors, for whom life was never easy. Nor will it be for the islanders in the future despite the boon of tourism, facilitated by more stable vessels, small planes and helicopters. This provides much seasonal employment but puts a severe strain on the limited supply of housing and water. The low-lying archipelago will be among the most vulnerable places in the United Kingdom, as rising levels and changing weather patterns pose a threat to homes, roads and marine life. Young climate champions at the Five Islands Academy worry that future generations won't be able to have the same experiences they have had, because it might already be too late.

It was Grandpa Harold's stories which first introduced me to the islands of his own childhood. As Tony recalled:

> Scilly was often present in his thoughts. He told me once that in any quiet moment he might imagine himself back in the Islands, perhaps on the grassy bank at the back of Porth Cressa, and feel as though he were there in body – hear the waves striking on the beach, feel the sea wind.

Epilogue: The Davis Family at War

He gave voice to these recollections in a blank-verse poem he sometimes read to me: 'Winter Vision of the Cassiterides' – an ancient Greek name meaning 'tin islands', which have sometimes been identified as the Scillies. Through the eyes of an exile, he conjures up a vision of his childhood home at different times of day, comparing it to the fleeting sights revealed by the beam of a lighthouse:

>Then let us now – from prison-on-the-Thames,
>From dark industrial cities of the north,
>Or happy homes in distant hemispheres
>Founded by sons and daughters of the Isles
>Or their descendants; valiant pioneers
>Who shaped their course to every compass-point –
>In thought arise, go forth, and by the aid
>Of that true magic carpet of the mind,
>Imagination, change our place and time,
>Dwelling awhile on those far distant shores
>Where erst our age of innocence was passed.
>
>For grey days now have vanished; in their stead,
>Through morning, noontide, evening and still night
>Again to morning, change the wondrous hues
>Of sky, and sea, and rock-encircled isles.
>
>Let us in fancy walk beside the sea,
>Along the cliffs, and by the mighty rocks –
>Steadfast defenders of the fertile fields –
>That well have borne the buffet and the blast
>And stern assault of winter's fiercest storms;
>And now, like sentinels, their vigil keep,
>Marking the codal, wheeling lighthouse beams
>That greet, but warn, the passing mariner
>Through the short watches of the summer night
>That lie between the twilight and the dawn.

Saving Lives in Scilly

We may not long sustain sweet fancy's flight.
So, like the changing, waning lighthouse beams,
Our vision fades, the inspiration dies,
Our dreams dissolve into the vanished past.

A vintage postcard of the 'rock-encircled isles' and the 'wheeling lighthouse.beams'.

Harold's lines summon up not only the dramatic Scillonian scenery but also characters who inhabited his own mind and whose stories are told in this family memoir: Davis sisters and Moyle brothers travelling as 'valiant pioneers' to 'distant hemispheres'; Doctor Moyle using his brush to portray 'wondrous hues of sky, and sea'; Keeper Edwin Davis guarding mariners from the 'mighty rocks' around the islands; Charles Royer Davis and his sailor brothers racked by 'the buffet and the blast' of the oceans; Mary Hall and her offspring seeking a new life in 'dark industrial cities of the north'; his own 'age of innocence' spent with his cousins on those 'distant shores'; and his sons Gren and Michael visiting or writing of Scilly soon after returning from war.

I have tried also to revive lives and times blanked out in family memory: Rev Vyvyan Moyle convicted of fraud and confined in prisons and workhouses before being buried in an unnamed pauper grave; Edward Moyle reduced to destitution and ending his days in a New Zealand penitentiary; and Margaretta Moyle, her

Epilogue: The Davis Family at War

true origins disguised after she left Scilly and her last twenty years spent shut away from the world in a County lunatic asylum. How keenly they might have longed for Cornish shores.

There are also those whose fates are lost to history for lack of evidence. I have not been able to establish whether the lighthouse keeper's youngest son, Lewis Edwin Davis, died as a sailor or as a shop assistant in Australia; why Granville Moyle died so suddenly in Canada; or how near to death my father came during his time on the Arctic convoys. The fabric of other lives, like those of the Davis dressmakers in Scilly, the homeless widow, Mary Jane Boulden, or the 'imbecile' Jessie Moyle, remains threadbare. But I hope that this collage of Davis and Moyle histories illuminates the people themselves, the times through which they lived and the rock-encircled isles which nurtured them.

Notes

The references in these notes can be used in lieu of a bibliography for further consultation.

The place of publication for books is London unless otherwise stated.

The source used for British newspapers:
https://www.britishnewspaperarchive.co.uk

The source used for Australian newspapers:
https://trove.nla.gov.au/newspapers

The main sources used for census, birth, marriage, residence, death & probate records: www.ancestry.co.uk and https://www.findmypast.co.uk
I consulted Trinty House records at London Metropolitan Archives (LMA), which has since been renamed The London Archives.

Introduction

[1] Wilkie Collins, *Rambles Beyond Railways or Notes in Cornwall taken A-foot* (Cornish Library, 1982), 41 & 67.

[2] Mine is thus a 'family history as a public history', similar in its aims to Alison Light's excellent account of her own ancestors, *Common People: The History of an English Family* (2014), 255.

[3] I have donated this scrapbook to the Isles of Scilly Museum, where it can be viewed close to where it was compiled. Catalogue number: RN8908

[4] King James Bible, *Ecclesiasticus*, 44.

Chapter 1

[5] Family records state that William came to Scilly 'under jury rig after having his ship dismasted in the Atlantic and just stayed on'. Unfoliated Guildhall papers show that William Slater Davis did his apprenticeship as a tinsmith in Long Lane, Bermondsey.

[6] Graeme Spence, *A Geographical and Nautical Description of Scilly* (1790-92), Introduction, 7; Geoffrey Grigson, *The Scilly Isles* (1977), 16.

[7] William and Mary married in 1806 and their children, Mary Anne and William Slater, were born and baptised in Southwark in 1807 and 1809 respectively. There is no mention of William junior in Scillonian records but census returns show that Mary Anne went to live in Scilly as a young married woman.

[8] Glynis Cooper, *Agnes, The Last Outpost* (no date), 25.

[9] Spence, *Description of Scilly*, Introduction, 3.

[10] https://archive.org, *Life, Journals and Letters of Henry Alford, Dean of Canterbury* (1873), 415-6; https:// play.google.com, Sophia Tower, 'Description of the Isles of Scilly' in *In Memoriam: Scilly and its Emperor* (Uxbridge, 1878), 121-2; photograph by Pilgrim of Brixham.

[11] This was the opinion of Robert Heath, an officer at St Mary's garrison in https://archive.org, *A Natural and Historical Account of the Islands of Scilly* (1750), 83.

[12] R.L. Bowley, *The Fortunate Islands: The Story of the Isles of Scilly* (St Mary's, 2004), 76.

[13] Heath, *Natural and Historical Account*, ii, iii, 49, 68, 82, 86 & 99.

[14] https://archive.org, William Borlase, *Observations on the Ancient and Present State of the Islands of Scilly, and their Importance to the Trade of Great Britain* (Oxford, 1756), 36, 66, 124 & 133. Borlase was a Cornish clergyman, antiquarian and naturalist who visited the islands in the 1750s. See also G. Forrester Matthews, *The Isles of Scilly; A Constitutional, Economic and Social Survey of the Development of an Island People from Early Times to 1900* (1960), 58-9.

[15] Spence, *Description of Scilly*, 8 & 10.

[16] https://archive.org, John Troutbeck, *A Survey of the Ancient and Present State of the Scilly Islands* (1794), 19, 22-7, 33-6, 58-60, 106 & 170.

[17] https://freepages.rootsweb.com, Acorn Archive, *Hearts of Oak, Letters from Pellew to Earl Spencer, First Lord of the Admiralty*, 28 December 1797 & 25 April 1798.

[18] Mark Bowden & Allan Brodie, *Defending Scilly* (Liverpool, 2011), 53; https://archive.org, Isaac William North, *A Week in the Isles of Scilly* (Penzance, 1850), 108.

[19] I am grateful to Richard Larn for providing me with the story of Emidy's visit to Star Castle which he originally published in *The Scillonian*.

[20] Emidy's history is told in Vyvyen Brendon, *Children at Sea: Lives Shaped by the Waves* (2020), 28-51 & Richard McGrady, *Music and Musicians in Early Nineteenth Century Cornwall* (Exeter, 1991).

[21] https://archive.org, James Silk Buckingham, *Autobiography* (1855), 163 & 174-7.

Notes

²² Spence, *Description of Scilly*, 7.

²³ https://play.google.com, George Charles Smith, *Report Detailing the Extreme Miseries of the Off-Islands of Scilly* (1818), 39, 25-6, 30, 14 & 49 and *The Scilly Islands and the Famine occasioned by the Legal Prevention of Smuggling with France* (1828), 10; Bowley, *Fortunate Islands*, 81.

²⁴ Robert Maybee in *Sixty-Eight Years' Experience of the Scilly Isles* (1883) quoted in Bowley, *Fortunate Islands*, 86 & 88.

²⁵ See Matthews, *Isles of Scilly*, 142-4.

²⁶ https://www.scilly.gov.uk, Charles Johns, *Isles of Scilly Historic Environment Research Framework: Resource Assessment and Research Agenda* (2021), 158 & 190.

²⁷ Heath, *Natural and Historical Account*, 89. Lighthouses and other navigational aids were and still are run by the 16th century maritime charity, Trinity House, which is ruled by a court of thirty-one Elder Brethren.

²⁸ https://www.researchgate.net, Cathryn Pearce, 'Neglectful or Worse: A Lurid Tale of a Lighthouse Keeper and Wrecking in the Isles of Scilly' in *Troze*, September 2008.

²⁹ Captain W. Chaplin, 'The Story of the St Agnes Lighthouse on the Isles of Scilly', unpublished and undated manuscript in Trinity House, London, 19.

³⁰ https://www.gutenberg.org, *The Autobiography of Benjamin Franklin*, ed Charles Eliot (New York, 1909), chap xix.

³¹ Borlase, *Observations*, 37 & 42.

³² Troutbeck, Survey, 146-7; Spence, *Description of Scilly*, Introduction, 1 & 5.

³³ Heath, *Natural and Historical Account*, 87-8; Buckingham, *Autobiography*, 175; Chaplin, 'Story of St Agnes Lighthouse', 76-8, 92, 114-5, 117 & 133.

³⁴ Chaplin, 'Story of St Agnes Lighthouse', 60-1 & 166-9; London Metropolitan Archives (LMA), Trinty House Archives, CLC/526/MS30025/012, 12 February 1839 & 013, 21 April 1840 & 08, 4 December 1832. Census records of 1841, 1851 and 1861 show that after his retirement William moved to St Mary's, where he lived at different times with his two daughters, Elizabeth and Mary Anne, both of whom married Scillonian mariners named Legg. Elizabeth's husband was Tobias and Mary Anne's was John.

³⁵ Peter Mandler, 'Augustus Smith' in *ODNB*, ed. H. C. G. Matthew & Brian Harrison (Oxford, 2004).

³⁶ Elisabeth Inglis-Jones, *Augustus Smith of Scilly* (1969), 69.

³⁷ North, *Week in Isles of Scilly*, 73 & 18.

³⁸ Moyle's retirement speech quoted in *Cornishman*, 27 November 1890. Hugh Town is the main residential and business area of St Mary's in the narrow strip of land beside the quay and below Star Castle. It took over from 'Old Town' as the main centre when the Castle was built.

39 The Census of 1861, for example, lists seven inmates who were natives of Scilly. In 1878 it was decreed that 'paupers from the Isles of Scilly will no longer be received by Penzance Union', *Cornishman*, 14 November, 1878.

40 https://www.google.co.uk/books, Augustus Smith, *Thirteen Years' Stewardship of the Islands of Scilly from 1834 to 1847* (1848), v-vi & Mandler, *ODNB*.

41 Inglis-Jones, *Augustus Smith of Scilly*, 79.

42 *Hampshire/Portsmouth Telegraph*, 15 August 1846, *North Devon Journal*, 10 September 1846 & http:// www.queenvictoriasjournals.org, *Queen Victoria's Journals*, 8 September 1846.

43 Smith, *Thirteen Years' Stewardship*, x, xvii & 40.

44 *Standard*, 17 August; Queen *Victoria's Journals*, 13 August 1847; Tower, *Scilly and its Emperor*, 118.

45 *Queen Victoria's Journals*, 14 August 1847.

46 *Standard*, 17 August 1847.

47 Tower, *Scilly and its Emperor*, 117.

48 Thus Barclay Fox notes his presence in September 1840 in his *Journal*, 1832-1854, ed. R.L. Brett (Fowey, 2008), 208. Barclay was a member of the wealthy Quaker Fox family who lived in and around Falmouth. He was a son of Robert Were Fox, an industrialist and a scientist of some distinction, with mining and shipping interests in Cornwall.

49 Tower, *Scilly and its Emperor*, Augustus Smith to Lady Tower, 20 April 1857.

50 North, *Week in Scilly*, 141 & ii; Tower, *Scilly and its Emperor*, Smith to Lady Tower, 19 December 1850.

51 Tower, *Scilly & its Emperor*, Smith to Lady Tower, 1 January & 4 February 1866; Francis Hicks quoted in *Country Life*, 17 January 2008.

Chapter 2

52 Advertisements and news items quoted in *Hearts of Oak*.

53 By kind permission of Penlee House, Accession Number PEZPH: 2002.91.

54 I owe this information to Zelonie Moyle, another great-great-granddaughter, who consulted the 1844 tithe map of Penzance, showing that the property was leased from Mr Scobell, a solicitor.

55 Mary Abbott, Family Ties (1993), 97; Stephen Gillam, *Of Patient Bearing: A History of General Practice in Eight Generations* (Norfolk, 2021), 34. Dr Gillam's medical forebears occupied the same social standing in Holt as Dr Moyle did in Penzance.

56 https://west-penwith.org.uk, Pigot's Directory of Cornwall, 1844; description of Penzance in https://www.british-history.ac.uk, *A Topographical Dictionary of England* (1848); Barclay Fox, *Journal*, 13 January 1850.

Notes

⁵⁷ By kind permission of Penlee House, Gibsons of Scilly, 'Children with a toy wheelbarrow in Cornwall'.

⁵⁸ *Royal Cornwall Gazette*, 7 July 1810; https://www.penwithlocal-historygroup.co.uk, George Clark, *Report to the General Board of Health on a preliminary inquiry into the sewerage, drainage, and supply of water, and the sanitary condition of the inhabitants, of the borough of Penzance* (1850), 6-7; https://newlynarchive.org.uk, William Williams diary and *Lancet* 1832.

⁵⁹ *Royal Cornwall Gazette*, 29 September 1832.

⁶⁰ The Cornish covid death rate soared from 281 in March 2021 to 40,923 by September, out of a population of about 600,000.

⁶¹ Barclay Fox, *Journal*, 30 September 1849.

⁶² Minutes of Proceedings upon Preliminary Inquiry relating to Penzance Corporation Waterworks Bill, February 1948, 137-9; Clark, *Report to General Board of Health*, 7.

⁶³ Roy Porter, *Blood and Guts: A Short History of Medicine* (2003), 37.

⁶⁴ Barclay Fox, *Journal*, 1 & 27 October 1833 and other entries.

⁶⁵ Porter, *Blood and Guts*, 78; *Royal Cornwall Gazette*, 12 August 1820 & 29 March 1850.

⁶⁶ Anne Digby, *Making a Medical Living: Doctors and Patients in the English Market for Medicine, 1720-1911* (Cambridge, 1996), 7 & 144-6; Elizabeth Gaskell, Cranford (first published 1853, Penguin, 1976), 167.

⁶⁷ Numerous references in *The Cornishman* and *Royal Cornwall Gazette*; letter to Lord John Russell, March 1839 quoted in Dorothy Thompson (ed.), *The Early Chartists* (1971), 188.

⁶⁸ Quoted in Digby, *Medical Living*, 136; Anthony Trollope, *Doctor Thorne* (first published 1858, Penguin, 1991), 95.

⁶⁹ The pocket book is now in the Morrab Library, Penzance. Established in 1818, it is the only surviving independent library in Cornwall and houses a large collection of rare books and periodicals.

⁷⁰ George Clement Boase, 'Reminiscences of Penzance' published in *The Cornishman*, 1883-4, ed. P.A.S. Pool (Penzance, 1976), 24 & 94. Other details come from a family genealogy compiled in a red exercise book by Emma Grenfell Moyle, John Grenfell Moyle's oldest daughter. It is known in the family as 'Aunty Em's little red book' and is in my possession.

⁷¹ I have used the spelling of Mary Anne Moyle's name as it is recorded in her father's pocket-book and in the will signed by her brother William, even though census records often use the more common spelling, Ann.

⁷² Boase, *Reminiscences*, 31-4 & https://archive.org, John Davy, *Memoirs of the Life of Sir Humphry Davy* (1836), vol 1, 13-14.

[73] Boase, *Reminiscences*, 28, 31 & 34; https://wp.lancs.ac.uk, John Davy, 'Some Notices of My Life' ed. Andrew Lacey (2018), 5-7; Davy, *Memoirs of Humphry Davy*, 18. In *Common People*, 214-5 Alison Light gives a similar account of 'thrills for the young' in Portsmouth where she and her forebears grew up.

[74] https://archive.org, *Annual Report of the Cornwall Polytechnic Society* (1833-3), 21.

[75] By kind permission of Penlee Gallery, PEZPH.

[76] Trollope, *Doctor Thorne*, 309.

[77] Arthur Penrhyn Stanley, *The Life and Correspondence of Thomas Arnold* (1846), 365-6.

[78] Wellcome Library, London.

[79] This information comes from an article by Zelonie Moyle in *My Cornwall*, 2010 and on https:// www.artcornwall.org.

[80] Packet Surgeon's Journals in https://www.maritimeviews.co.uk; Barclay Fox, *Journal*, 98 &100; https://repository.falmouth.ac.uk, Megan Oldcorn, PhD thesis, 'Falmouth and the British Maritime Empire', 128.

[81] *Royal Cornwall Gazette*, 15 September 1843.

[82] Charles Dickens, *Bleak House* (first published 1853, US edition 1964), 250, 252 & 630.

[83] *Cornishman*, 20 April 1893.

[84] See William Barlow in Brendon, *Children at Sea*, 122 & 125-6.

[85] Boase, *Reminiscences*, 94.

[86] The medal has now been donated to Penlee House and the programme to the Morrab Library.

[87] I am grateful to Peter Judge of Praeds & Company Archive for finding this record.

[88] The 1851 Census shows Vyvyan living as a 17-year-old scholar at Glebe House, St Allen, with George Morris, his wife and two daughters.

[89] By kind permission of Penlee House, PEZPH: 1989.75. Both this painting and the earlier one of St Michael's Mount were exhibited at the Penzance School of Art in 1854. This one was bought by the Corporation and given a place of honour in the Council-chamber; obituary of Dr Moyle in *Cornishman*, 20 April 1893.

[90] *Royal Cornwall Gazette*, 25 July & 3 August 1849.

[91] By kind permission of Penlee House, PEZPH: 1989.64.

[92] Census record 1851.

[93] Collins, *Rambles Beyond Railways*, 2.

[94] Ibid, 81-91.

[95] Ibid, 106-12 & 31; engraving by William Miller in public domain.

Notes

96 Collins, *Rambles Beyond Railways*, 115-7.
97 Ibid, 41-4.
98 Ibid, 44, 55-6 & 69.
99 *Royal Cornwall Gazette*, 8 February 1850.
100 *Royal Cornwall Gazette*, 20 & 27 April 1855 & Collins, *Rambles Beyond Railways*, 42.
101 *Cornish Telegraph*, 30 May & 6 June 1855.
102 *Royal Cornwall Gazette*, 1 March 1823.

Chapter 3

103 National Probate Calendar 1858-1995, Letters of Administration of the Personal Estate and Effects of Elizabeth Moyle late of Penzance.
104 George Gissing, *The Odd Women* (first published 1893, 1980 edn.), 5-6.
105 Edith C. Rickards, *Zoe Thomson of Bishopthorpe and her Friends* (1916), 87, 140 &142.
106 https://en.wikipedia.org, 'Wandesford House'; Rickards, *Zoe Thomson*, 143.
107 https://www.pure.ed.ac.uk, Ingrid Jeacle, 'The Bank Clerk in Victorian Society' in *Journal of Management History*, vol 16, 312-26.
108 [bid, 312-26; Anthony Trollope, *The Small House at Allington* (first published 1864, Penguin, 2005), 44 & 504.
109 Now donated to the Morrab Library.
110 A.J.P. Taylor, *English History*, 1914-1945 (Oxford, 1967), 1; Piers Brendon, *Thomas Cook: 150 Years of Popular Tourism* (1991), 85.
111 Collins, *Rambles Beyond Railways*, 38.
112 A.L. Rowse, *A Cornish Childhood* (first published 1942, Truro, 1998), 34.
113 See Philip Payton, *The Cornish Overseas* (Fowey, 1999), 87-8 & 181.
114 Portrait posted on *Ancestry* by descendant Judy DeCourcey.
115 In 1837 British forces chased off the crew of the steamboat *Caroline* before setting fire to her and casting her adrift over the Niagara Falls.
116 These volumes have been donated to the Morrab Library.
117 Engraving by George Vertue from a portrait of Walter Moyle by an unknown artist in *The Works of Walter Moyle Esq; None of which were ever before Publish'd* (1726). The only other member of Richard Moyle's family to show any interest in the crest was his nephew, Granville Borlase Moyle, whose Australian obituary referred to his 'family crest with a Latin motto'.
118 Letters in *The Whole Works of Walter Moyle, Esq* (1727), 213 & 225; 'Mr Moyle's Charge to the Grand Jury at Liskeard, April 1707' in *Works of Walter Moyle Esq*, 157-8.

119 'Some Account of Mr Moyle', & 'Argument against Standing Army' in *Whole Works of Walter Moyle*, 30-1, 51-2, 59 &181.
120 https://www.nla.gov.au, Records of Royal Marine Museum, M2636-7, 11-13, Diary of Lt Gerrard Montague, 15 March 1842, 1 January, 27 July & 30 September 1843, 20 September 1844.
121 Ibid, 24 May & 23 November 1842, 3 March 1843; Letter in *Works of Walter Moyle*, 402-5.
122 Caird Library, HRD/2/1, C.W. Hereford, Midshipman's Log HMS *Trafalgar*, 10-13 August & 17 October 1854; *Times*, 18 October 1854.
123 Drawing posted on *Ancestry* by Judy DeCourcy.
124 *Cornish Telegraph & Morning Chronicle*, 9 & 12 February 1859. The term 'died suddenly' can refer to death from a stroke or heart attack but is sometimes used as a euphemism for suicide.
125 1851 Census. The couple seem to have had no children but lived with Jane's sixteen-year-old brother, an apprentice mariner.
126 https://www.slv.vic.gov.au, VPRS: 947, PRO Unassisted Passenger Lists 1852-1923.
127 The 'epidemic of abandonment' is a phrase used by a character in Rose Tremain's novel about the gold rush, *The Colour*, (Vintage, 2020), 228, where a Melbourne warehouse clerk says that the very mention of gold will make men 'desert their dearest things'; Granville's decision to emigrate was explained in his obituary, *Kilmore Free Press*, 17 December 1914; arrival of the *Emigrant* reported in *Melbourne Argus*, 2 May 1853.
128 PRO Unassisted Passenger Lists, Jun - Jul 1853; *Times*, 28 February 1853 & *Illustrated London News*, 5 March 1853, 180.
129 PRO Unassisted Passenger Lists, May - Aug 1861; *The Ballarat Star*, 16 May 1861 & 30 July 1860.
130 See Payton, *Cornish Overseas*, 237-42.
131 'The Penal Department' in *The Age* (Melbourne), 25 November 1856, 4.
132 *Melbourne Argus*, 2 March 1857; 1861 census; *Royal Cornwall Gazette*, 4 April 1862.
133 Electoral roll for Moliagul, Loddon district, 1856.
134 Photograph in State Library of Victoria; *Kilmore Free Press*, 6 March 1884.
135 Obituary in *Kilmore Free Press*, 17 December 1914.
136 https://archive.org, *The Australian Encyclopaedia*, vol 1 (Sydney, 1979).
137 The original of this painting is in private ownership. A reproduction is held at the State Library of Queensland, https://www.slq.qld.gov.au.
138 This painting was sold by the Bridget McDonnell Gallery, Australia in 1998.
139 https://www.nla.gov.au, PIC Drawer 6152 R8420, digitised item.
140 Ibid, PIC Drawer 2126 PIC/8767, digitised item.

Notes

[141] *Western Star and Roma Advertiser*, 11 January 1885 & 27 March 1886.
[142] Tremain, *Colour*, 128 & 164; Cambridge University Library, RCMS 304, letters from Thornhill family in New Zealand.
[143] https://paperspast.natlib.govt.nz, *Daily Southern Cross*, 4 November 1872.
[144] Auckland Libraries Collection 1-WO236.
[145] https://paperspast.natlib.govt.nz, *Daily Southern Cross*, 2 July. 1873.
[146] Ibid, *Auckland Star*, 2 July 1873.

Chapter 4

[147] 'By kind permission of Penlee Gallery. I owe this information and the image to Katie Herbert (Curator and Deputy Director) and Sally Francis (Citizen Curator) of Penlee House and to Zelonie Moyle who told me about their discovery.
[148] John Arlott, *Island Camera: The Isles of Scilly in the Photography of the Gibson Family* (Newton Abbot, 1972), 9.
[149] *Yorkshire Gazette*, 1 December 1860, 30 April & 18 July 1863, 5 January 1867; *Newcastle Journal*, 20 January 1863 & 18 October 1864; *Western Daily Press*, 26 March 1873; *Leeds Mercury*, 1 January & 24 March 1873.
[150] Trial reports in *Birmingham Daily Post*, 4 January, *Northern Echo*, 6 & 7 January & *Aberdeen Journal*, 8 January 1871.
[151] *Pall Mall Gazette* 22 December 1866 quoted in H. Kirk-Smith, *William Thomson, Archbishop of York: His Life and Times*, 1819-90 (SPCK, 1958), 133 & E.I. Carlyle & H.C.G. Matthew in ODNB (Oxford, 2004), vol 54, 566.
[152] Borthwick Institute for Archives, Visitation Returns, Inst. AB, 89; Kirk-Smith, *William Thomson*, 113.
[153] Anthony Trollope, *Framley Parsonage* (first published 1861, Penguin, 1986), 495. Trollope's plot bears uncanny similarities to the story of Vyvyan Moyle.
[154] www.discoveryourancestors.co.uk, *Bulmer's North Yorkshire Directory*, 1890 cited in Nick Thorne, 'For the love of money is the root of all kinds of evil'.
[155] https://creativecommons.org, photograph by Simon Armstrong.
[156] Basil Thomson, *The Criminal* (1925), 69; Borthwick Archives, V.1871.
[157] https://www.google.co.uk, Robert Henry Mair, *The School Boards, Our Educational Parliaments* (1872), 161; *Morning Post*, 29 March 1869; *Middlesbrough Daily Gazette*, 19 June 1872; *Leeds Mercury* 24 December 1872 & 1 January 1873.
[158] *Leeds Times*, 18 January 1873; Borthwick Archive, Resignation Files, RES 1873; Basil Thomson, *The Criminal*, 69.
[159] *Northern Echo*, 15 & 22 January 1873.

Saving Lives in Scilly

[160] Margot Finn, Michael Lobban & Jenny Bourne Taylor, *Legitimacy and Illegitimacy in Nineteenth Century Law, Literature and History* (2010), 101.

[161] *Middlesbrough Daily Gazette*, 30 December 1872. A copy of this article is housed with the archbishop's papers. *Northampton Mercury*, 4 January 1873.

[162] *Birmingham Daily Post*, 4 & 7 January, *Northern Echo*, 6 January, *Leeds Mercury*, 1 & 9 January, *Bradford Observer*, 11 January & *Stamford Mercury*, 17 January 1873; Trollope, *Framley Parsonage*, 34.

[163] https://www.normanbyhistorygroup.co.uk, St Helen's Church records researched by Sylvia Fairbrass, 2013; *Northern Echo*, 3 February & *North Country News*, 4 February 1873; *Birmingham Daily Post*, 24 March 1873; *Morning Post*, 5 March, 1873.

[164] *Birmingham Daily Post*, 24 March 1873; Patrick M. Geoghegan, *Dictionary of Irish Biography* (2009). Seymour was well able to understand his client's situation as he had himself been censored by his seniors for dubious business dealings in the 1850s.

[165] *Leeds Mercury*, 24 March 1873.

[166] *Bradford Observer*, 25 March 1873.

[167] Finn, Lobban & Bourne Taylor, *Legitimacy and Illegitimacy*, 94.

[168] https://discovery.nationalarchives.gov.uk, HO24/19, Pentonville Prison Registers, vol 4.

[169] Letter from the Earl of Chichester, one of the superintending commissioners of Pentonville, to the Home Secretary, 1856, quoted in Vyvyen Brendon, *The Age of Reform* (1994), 57.

[170] https://warwick.ac.uk/fac/arts/history, C. Lytton, 'Suicide and insanity in nineteenth-century prisons: The effect of the separate system of discipline on convict mental health', 12.

[171] https://eprints.bbk.ac.uk, Ben Bethell, 'The Star Class in English Convict Prisons 1863-1914', PHD for Birkbeck, University of London, 2020, 42-3; https://www.crimeandjustice.org.uk, 'An exception too far: gentleman convicts and the 1878-9 Penal Servitude Commission' in *Prison Service Journal*, July 2017, 174.

[172] Pentonville Prison Registers, vol 4. Rev George Wilkinson can be identified as the vicar of St Peter's, Eaton Square, who later became Bishop of Truro. He was a near contemporary of Vyvyan's and they may have known each other at Oxford.

[173] https://www.crimeandjustice.org.uk, Helen Johnston & Joanne Turner, 'Disability and the Victorian prison' in *Prison Service Journal*, July 2017, 13.

[174] Pentonville Prison Registers, vol 4; *Daily Gazette*, 10 April 1878.

[175] Basil Thomson, *The Criminal*, 69; *Truth*, Vol XLV, January to June 1899, 144; Census 1881.

Notes

[176] Census 1891 & Thorne, 'For the love of money is the root of all kinds of evil'.

[177] *Bristol Mercury*, 10 November 1894 and V. H. Moyle, *Notes on the Ecclesiastical History of Ashampstead* (1895),7-9.

[178] *Truth*, January 1899, 143-5; Robin Quinn, *The Man Who broke the Bank at Monte Carlo* (Gloucester, 2016), 151.

[179] Report in *Western Mail*, 6 February 1899; Moyle, *Ecclesiastical History of Ashampstead*, 8-9.

[180] Anthony Trollope, *The Last Chronicle of Barset* (first published 1867, Penguin, 2002), 362 & 61.

[181] Census 1901. William died in 1907.

[182] Letter from Rev V. H. Moyle to a potential investor, *Financial News* and *Daily Mirror* quoted in *Truth*, 9 November 1905, 1148; advertisement posted in https://robin-quinn.co.uk/partners-in-crime-4.

[183] The leaflet and the letters were later produced in court and are quoted in https://www.oldbaileyonline.org, 5 February 1906, Case 242, as well as in contemporary newspapers and periodicals, eg *Truth*, 9 November 1905 & *Daily Mirror*, 13 November 1905.

[184] Amy Elizabeth Elliott quoted in Old Bailey Proceedings, 5 February 1906, Case 242.

[185] *Truth*, 9 November 1905.

[186] *Gloucester Citizen*, 11 November & *Dundee Gazette*, 13 November 1905.

[187] Drawing (which may not accurately record Vyvyan's appearance) from *The Constitution, Atlanta*, 10 December 1905.

[188] These words were widely reported, eg *Manchester Courier and Lancashire General Advertiser*, 10 February 1906.

[189] Basil Thomson, *The Criminal*, 70 & 73.

[190] W.D. Morrison's evidence to a report on 'English Prisons Today' quoted in Victor Bailey, 'English Prisons, Penal Culture and the Abatement of Imprisonment, 1895-1922', *Journal of British Studies,* vol 36 (Cambridge, 1997).

[191] *Evening Telegraph*, Charters Towers, Queensland, 12 December 1907.

[192] LMA, Christ Church Workhouse Index to Porter's Register, 1907-8.

[193] Research by Maria Brownsea of Brookwood Cemetery Limited, September 2021.

[194] Crockford's Clerical Directory, 1932; https://archive.org, *Hong Kong Telegraph*, 18 May 1912, *Hong Kong Daily Press*, 22 & 30 December 1927.

[195] *Royal Cornwall Gazette*, 29 March & *Western Daily Press*, 26 March 1873.

Chapter 5

[196] LMA, Trinity House Archives, CLC/526/MS30025/012, 12 December 1839 & /015, 25 April 1843.

[197] Chaplin, 'Story of St Agnes Lighthouse',164; https://archive.org, *Report of the Royal Commissioners on Lights, Buoys and Beacons*, 1861, vol 1, 13.

[198] https://archive.org, Rev George Woodley, *A View of the Present State of the Scilly Islands* (1822), 317.

[199] https://www.google.co.uk/books, Rev George Woodley, *Narrative of the Loss of the Steamer 'Thames' on the Rocks of Scilly, on the 4th of January 1841*, 10, 11 & 16.

[200] https://scillypedia.co.uk, *Leeds Times*, 6 January 1841 & Letter from Stewardess Mary Meyler, 5 January 1841; https://creativecommons.org, Andrewrabbott.

[201] https://www.trinityhouse.co.uk, 'Instructions for Lighthouse Keepers', 1839.

[202] *Report of the Royal Commissioners on Lights*, vol 2, 91.

[203] htts://www.gutenberg.org, Jessie Mothersole, *The Isles of Scilly, Their Story, their Folk & their Flowers* (The Religious Tract Society, 1910), 159.

[204] Chaplin, 'Story of St Agnes Lighthouse', 27; LMA, Trinity House Archives, CLC/526/MS30025/018, 20 April 1847 & 012, 12 February 1839; see also Terry Newman, 'The Light of a Hunter's Moon: A Shallow Grave on St Agnes' in *Scillonian*, Winter 1973.

[205] LMA, Trinity House Archives, CLC/526/MS30025/018, 2 November 1847.

[206] Jennifer Lloyd, 'Women Preachers in the Bible Christian Connexion', *Albion*, Vol. 36, No. 3 (Autumn, 2004), 454-63; David P. Easton, *A History of the Nonconformist Churches on the Isles of Scilly* (Isles of Scilly, 2010), 55.

[207] Edwin's character as remembered in family tradition; Easton, *Nonconformist Churches on Isles of Scilly*, 56-7 & 62.

[208] Glynis Cooper, *The Last Outpost* (Derby, no date), 18; cf 1841 Census & Woodley, *View of Scilly Islands*, 166.

[209] M.D. Costen (ed.), *Wesleyans and Bible Christians in South Somerset, Accounts and Minutes, 1808-1907*, (Somerset Record Office, 1984), xx.

[210] https://cloudfront.net, 'Martha Hutchings' in Joan Mills, 'What Are Our Thoughts on Female Preachers?', unpublished manuscript in Lewis Court Bible Christian Collection, 33-5; William Penrose, Obituary of Martha Davis in *Bible Christian Magazine*, 1885, 170.

[211] Bowley, *Fortunate Isles*, 98-9 & https://www.google.co.uk/books, Report of Rev E. Douglas Tinling, HM Inspector of Schools, 1848, 125.

[212] Penrose, Obituary of Martha Davis, 170.

[213] *Cornishman*, 27 November 1890.

Notes

[214] Census, 1851 and Post Office Directory, 1856.
[215] North, *Week in Scilly*, 71; Zelonie Moyle in *My Cornwall*, 2010 based on memories of John's son, Edwards.
[216] North, *Week in Scilly*, 70, 117 & 143-6; https://archive.org, *Report on Mortality of Cholera* 1848-9, 255.
[217] LMA, Trinity House Archives, CLC/526/MS30025/20, 19 August & 2 September 1851 & 6 December 1852; Digby, *Making a Medical Living*, 98, 135 & 156.
[218] *Cornish Telegraph*, 4 January 1854 & March 1 1855; *Royal Cornwall Gazette*, 10 January, 10 February & 1 December 1854.
[219] See G.C. Boase, 'Moyle, Matthew Paul' in *Dictionary of National Biography* (1885-1900); Denise Crook, 'Matthew Paul Moyle' in *ODNB* (Oxford, 2004).
[220] Quoted in Porter, *Blood and Guts*, 42; George Eliot, *Middlemarch* (first published 1871-2, Penguin 1965), 118-9; *Royal Cornwall Gazette*, 18 May 1860 & 23 November 1855. While the bacillae which cause tuberculosis had yet to be discovered, John was right in relating humidity to the spread of the disease.
[221] Collins, 'The Cruise of the Tomtit' (supplementary sketch in 1861 edition of *Rambles Beyond Railways*), 169, 189 & 191.
[222] Tower, Scilly and its Emperor, 29, Smith to Lady Tower, 31 September 1855; Collins, 'Cruise of the Tomtit',192-3.
[223] George Henry Lewes, *Sea-Side Studies at Ilfracombe, Tenby, the Scilly Isles and Jersey* (1858) 180-1 &187.
[224] Kathleen McCormack, *George Eliot's English Travels* (2005), 67; Lewes, *Sea-Side Studies*, 201, 204-5, 245 & Plate VI 'Comatula rosacea'
[225] Margaret Harris & Judith Johnston (eds.), *The Journals of George Eliot* (Cambridge, 1988), 278; Lewes, *SeaSide Studies*, 267; Wellcome Institute, MS 7337/94, Letter of John Grenfell Moyle to Mrs Augusta Roscorla, 21 February 1888. I am grateful to Jak Stringer of Camidge & Stringer Theatre Makers, Penzance, for pointing out that Moyle was mistaken in attributing his introduction to 'Mr and Mrs Lewes' to 'the late Wilkie Collins' as Collins did not die until 1889.
[226] Lewes, *Sea-Side Studies*, 187 &191; *Journals of George Eliot*, 277; Jenny Uglow, *George Eliot* (2008), 77; image reproduced on artuk website and used by kind permission of IoS Museum, Accession: RN1536.
[227] *Journals of George Eliot*, 16, 276 & 278; Letter to Mrs Bray, 5 April 1877 in https://archive.org, John Cross (ed), *George Eliot's Life as related in her Letters and Journals* (1885), vol 1, 317; McCormack, *George Eliot's English Travels*, 70; Lewes, *Sea-Side Studies*, 194 & 267-8.
[228] Letter to her publisher John Blackwood, 1 May 1857 in Cross, *George Eliot's Life*, 319. This story forms part of Eliot's *Scenes of Clerical Life*.
[229] Uglow, *George Eliot*, 77; McCormack, *George Eliot's English Travels*, 71; Eliot, *Middlemarch*, 177-8.

230 Lewes, *Sea-Side Studies*, 267; IoS Museum, Minute Book of the Select Vestry of the Parish of St Mary's, 30 May 1874, 23 June 1877, 29 June & 29 July 1882 & 23 December 1880.
231 IoS Museum, Vestry Minute Book, 31 January & 7 February 1880, 26 February 1881, 26 July 1884, 4 June 1887 & 16 May 1888.
232 By kind permission of Penlee House, PEZPH:2009.455.
233 Trevellick Moyle, 'Thoughts on Grandfather' in *Scillonian*, Winter 1962; census records, 1841, 1851 & 1861.
234 Bella Bathurst, *The Wreckers* (2005), 123; Lithograph: *Lighthouse in the course of erection on the Bishop Rock*, Day & Son, c 1848.
235 North, *Week in Scilly*, 48; *Royal Cornwall Gazette*, 8 October 1858; LMA Trinity House Archives, CLC/526/ MS30025/35, 5 January 1869. It is a pity that Captain Chaplin's *Story of the St Agnes Lighthouse* does not cover the period after the building of Bishop Rock.
236 *Royal Cornwall Gazette*, 29 October 1858.
237 https://archive.org, Tom Peete Cross, 'Alfred Tennyson as a Celticist' in *Modern Philology*, (University of Chicago Press), January, 1921, 485-492.
238 Letter from Moyle to Augusta Roscorla, 21 February, 1888. Tennyson was clearly rather accident-prone. Ten days earlier his Arthurian quest had taken him to Bude's Falcon Hotel, where, in his eagerness to catch sight of the 'glorious grass-green monsters of waves', he went out of a side door in the dark, fell down and injured his knee.
239 Hallam Lord Tennyson, *Alfred Lord Tennyson* (1897), vol 1, 463; photograph of Tregarthen's Hotel, c 1880, IoS Museum.
240 'Enoch Arden' in *The Works of Alfred Lord Tennyson* (1892), 125-39.
241 Robert Stephen Hawker quoted in Piers Brendon, *Hawker of Morwenstow* (1975), 121; Charles Dickens, 'The Shipwreck' in Daniel Tyler (ed), *The Uncommercial Traveller* (Oxford, 2015) and *Dombey and Son* (first published 1848, Penguin, 2002), 746; Jenny Uglow, *Elizabeth Gaskell* (1999 edn.), 54.
242 *Royal Cornwall Gazette*, 20 October 1854; Lord Byron, *Childe Harold's Pilgrimage*, Canto IV.

Chapter 6
243 *Report of Royal Commissioners on Lights*, vol 1, 13.
244 The 1861 Census shows that the Leggs shared their house at 66 Hugh Street St Mary's not only with the two teenage dressmakers but also with their 9-year-old son Edmund, Elizabeth's 83-year-old father William Davis and a lodger who worked as a laundress. It sounds like a busy and crowded household.

Notes

[245] The 1851 census returns from St Agnes church and Bible Christian chapel show 40-50 children attending morning and afternoon Sunday school sessions when the total number of children on the island was about 55.

[246] Arlott, Island Camera, Plate 69, John Gibson, 'May Day in Hugh Town', c 1876.

[247] Tower, *Scilly and its Emperor*, 20 April 1857 & 15 March 1863.

[248] LoS Museum, Logbook of St Agnes School, 1875-1913.

[249] J. C. Trewin, *Up from the Lizard* (1982 edn), 145 & 36.

[250] Matthews, Isles of Scilly, 229; Tower, *Scilly and its Emperor*, Smith to Lady Tower, 3 September 1857; Waldo Hilary Dunn, *James Anthony Froude, A Biography* (Oxford, 1963), vol 2, 443; J. A. Froude, 'On the Uses of a Landed Gentry' in '*Short Studies on Great Subjects*' (first published 1877, 1894 edn.), vol 3, 395-6.

[251] *Royal Cornwall Gazette* & *West Briton*, 27 February 1863.

[252] Ibid; Olive Anderson, *Suicide in Victorian and Edwardian England* (Oxford, 1987), 162 & 220-5.

[253] IoS Museum, Record Book of the Council House St Mary's Scilly, March 1835-March 1917, 7 March 1863.

[254] https://www.findagrave.com/memorial/257113790; LMA Trinity House Archives, CLC/526/ MS30025/32, 31 March 1863.

[255] Ibid, 6 June 1863 & Census 1871.

[256] 'Retrospect of Shipping Disasters at the Scilly Islands', *Cornishman*, 2 February 1888.

[257] *Royal Cornwall Gazette*, 29 January 1864 & 15 August 1874; *Cornishman*, 16 March 1882.

[258] James Daniel's letter to his wife quoted in Todd Stevens & Edward Cumming, *Ghosts of Rosevear* (Glasgow, 2008), 14-5; letter by Pendarves Vivian quoted in *Royal Cornwall Gazette*, 29 May 1875.

[259] Quotations from *Times*, 15 May 1875 (a newspaper cutting in Dr Moyle's scrapbook) and from *Royal Cornwall Gazette* of same date. A stained-glass window designed for St Agnes Church by Oriel Hicks in 2015 depicts just such a rescue.

[260] 'A Sad Case of Suicide' in *Cornishman*, 27 November 1884; IoS Museum, Record Book of Council House, 22 November 1884. The friend to whom White wrote was W. T. Douglass, supervisor of the renovation of Bishop Rock lighthouse.

[261] Inglis-Jones, *Augustus Smith*, 189; *Royal Cornwall Gazette*, 15 May 1875 & 29 April 1876; https://www.lookandlearn.com *Illustrated London News*, 22 & 29 May 1875.

[262] Apprenticeship and promotion documents from family collection and information courtesy of Roger Banfield; Inglis-Jones, *Augustus Smith*, 77. The Mercantile Marine Act of 1850 made examinations compulsory for advancement to master or mate in the merchant navy.

263 Letter courtesy of Roger Banfield; Obituary of Martha Davis.
264 Information from family history research by my aunt, the late Aline Davis.
265 *Melbourne Argus*, 5 October 1878; death certificate for Charles Davis; Basil Lubbock, *The Colonial Clippers* (Glasgow, 1921), 131; G.F. Gregory, *Clipper Ship Macduff entering Port Phillip Heads*, 1st. Dec. 1865, National Library of Australia. PIC Drawer 6841 #R3645
266 Telegram from Captain George Sherris of Scilly quoted in *Gibson's Guide* c1926, courtesy of Roger Banfield.
267 I have not been able to visit my great-grandfather's grave but my brother- and sister-in-law, Rupert and Chris Brendon, went there in 2019 and kindly took this photograph for me. I have told the story of Charles's death and that of three sailor brothers in 'Scillonian Ancestors', *The Marine Quarterly*, Winter 2022, 94-100.
268 Census records 1871 & 1881; death certificate for John Grenfell Moyle junior, 1878.
269 Information kindly supplied by Peter Malec, great-grandson of Edwards Moyle; obituary in *Scillonian*, September 1935.
270 Trollope, *Doctor Thorne*, 28; https://etheses.whiterose.ac.uk, Nicola Shutt, 'Nobody's Child: The Theme of Illegitimacy in the Novels of Charles Dickens, George Eliot and Wilkie Collins', 40, 17 & 183; Wilkie Collins, *The Woman in White* (first published 1860, 2011 edn.), 624.
271 Census returns for 1851, 1861, 1871, 1891, 1901 & 1911 & Probate records 1914 & 1916; Richard & Bridget Larn, *Augustus John Smith, Emperor and King of Scilly* (St Mary's, 2013), 40-49.
272 Sam Llewellyn, Emperor Smith: *The Man Who Built Scilly* (Wimborne Minster, 2005), 45 & 49; Froude, *Short Studies*, 397; Richard and Bridget Larn, *Augustus John Smith*, 35 & 41.
273 *Cornishman*, 3 March & 5 May 1887; IoS Museum, Record Book of Council House, 26 & 28 February 1887; https://www.midlands-historicalreview.com, Paige Mathieson, 'Bad or Mad? Infanticide: Insanity and Morality in Nineteenth-Century Britain', 13 May 2020, 24.
274 See, for example, *Royal Cornwall Gazette*, 12 March, 13 August 1870 & 7 September 1872.
275 Eg *Daily News* and *Western Daily Press*, 31 December 1872, *North Devon Herald*, 2 January 1873 & *Royal Cornwall Gazette*, 29 March 1873.
276 *Cornishman*, 1 June & 12 April 1882.
277 *Royal Cornwall Gazette*, 22 November 1878; *Cornishman*, 22 November 1978, 9 January 1879 & 18 February 1886.
278 *Royal Cornwall Gazette*, November 1875; *Cornishman*, 17 October 1878; Bella Bathurst, *Wreckers* (2005), 133.

Notes

²⁷⁹ Arlott, *Island Camera*, Plate 29, Alexander Gibson, *The Earl of Lonsdale*, 10-11 & 34-5.

Chapter 7

²⁸⁰ Arlott, *Island Camera*, Plate 23, Alexander Gibson, *The Gleaner*; 'Reminiscences of Scilly's Shipping' in *Cornishman*, 6 April 1882; Bowley, *Fortunate Islands*, 89.

²⁸¹ Tower, S*cilly and its Emperor*, Smith to Lady Tower, 17 November 1853, 29 September 1859 & 5 November 1870.

²⁸² *Cornishman*, 24 January 1884 & (pasted into Moyle's scrapbook) 29 September, 11 & 18 October 1888. Forrester Matthews, 217 wrongly names the pioneer as Trevellick Moyle, who had not been born at this time. The link between the Moyle and Trevellick families is that Edwards Moyle married William Trevellick's niece, Eva Nance, in 1887.

²⁸³ Bowley, *Fortunate Islands*, 108-110; IoS Museum, St Mary's Boys School Logbook, October 1883 & Inspectors' Report 1885.

²⁸⁴ Illustrations from Mothersole, *Isles of Scilly*, 162 & Arlott, Island Camera, Plate 52, Alexander Gibson, 'William Trevellick'.

²⁸⁵ Trewin, *Up from the Lizard*, 253 & 258.

²⁸⁶ Census 1881; https://archive.org, G. P. Dymond, *Thomas Ruddle of Shebbear: A North Devon Arnold. His Life and Selections from his Letters*, 87.

²⁸⁷ William Shortridge quoted by Penrose in his obituary of Martha Davis for *Bible Christian Magazine*.

²⁸⁸ https://guides.sl.nsw.gov.au._ Unassisted Immigrant Passenger Lists 1826-1922. I owe this interpretation of the handwritten passenger list to the expertise of Katharine Thompson of the Churchill Archives Centre, Cambridge.

²⁸⁹ *New South Wales Police Gazette*, 21 July 1886; Penrith Death Register, 1887; Burial Record, St Stephen's, Penrith 23 February 1887.

²⁹⁰ Henry Moule's description of his invention of the earth closet in a letter to the *Hertfordshire Express* in 1870; LMA, Trinity House Archives, CLC/526/MS30025/044, 27 April 1877, 050, 1 May 1882, 052, 8 September, 29 October & 27 November 1885 & 053, 8 October 1886.

²⁹¹ Arlott, *Island Camera*, Plate 125, Alexander Gibson, 'Round Island Light', 1890s; 'Starboard Tack' in *Cornishman*, 13 September 1888.

²⁹² *Cornishman*, 14 April 1880, 19 October 1882, 5 August 1886 & 20 February 1890.

²⁹³ *Scillonian*, 152, Winter 1962, 263ff; obituary in *Cornishman*, 20 April 1893.

[294] Forrester Matthews, *Isles of Scilly*, 214; G.H. Sims, 'Rowdyism at Scilly Checked and Punished' in *Cornishman*, 23 September 1886; 'Nocturnal Adventures at the Scilly Isles' in *Cornishman*, 5 April 1883.
[295] 'A Ball at Scilly' in *Cornishman*, 19 September 1889.
[296] Letter to Augusta Roscorla, 21 February 1888.
[297] https://archive.org, Samuel Cox, *Salvator Mundi or Is Christ the Saviour of all Men?* (1877), 167 & 170-1, copied in John Grenfell Moyle, 'My Book' in 1888.
[298] James Ross, *On Evolution: Address delivered at the opening of Owen College Medical School* (Manchester, 1888), 7, 16 & 22, copied into Moyle, 'My Book'.
[299] Ross, *On Evolution*, 5-6 & 25.
[300] Forrester Matthews, *Isles of Scilly*, 205 & 227.
[301] Owen Chadwick, *The Victorian Church* (1970), vol 2, 113.
[302] *Times*, 8 February 1889.
[303] https://www.findagrave.com/memorial/206053086; Elizabeth's husband Tobias Legg had survived his risky marine career and outlived her by five years, dying in his own bed in 1891. Their joint grave in old St Mary's churchyard bears the epitaph: 'In Heaven above, /Where all is love.'
[304] Digby, *Making a Medical Living*, 15; *Cornishman*, 27 November 1890.
[305] Maud Pember Reeves, *Round About a Pound a Week* (first published 1909-13, 1979), 222.
[306] Extracts from speeches in *Cornishman*, 27 November 1890.
[307] *Cornishman*, 4 December 1890.
[308] *Cornishman*, 27 November 1890.
[309] https://kuscholarworks.ku.edu, David Lynn Adams, 'Putting Pandemics in Perspective: England and the Flu, 1889-1919, 2008.
[310] Mrs Dorrien Smith was thus described in *Illustrated Police News*, 30 January 1892; *Royal Cornwall Gazette*, 31 December 1891 reported that Mr T. Thornton Macklin, the newly appointed Medical Officer of Health, was 'a victim of the malady' and that he was the only 'medical man' on the islands. It is not clear what had happened to Dr Francis Turnly Gage.
[311] Quoted in https://www.whodoyouthinkyouaremagazine.com, James Hoare, 'Before the Coronavirus, there was Russian Flu'.
[312] IoS Museum RN1536 on https://artuk.org; item sold at Bonhams in 2013.
[313] LMA, Trinity House Archives, CLC/526/MS30025/058, 21 January & 20 May 1890.
[314] https://www.bbc.co.uk, Photograph by permission of Cllr John Peacock of St Agnes.
[315] Forrester Matthews, *Isles of Scilly*, 215; Isles of Scilly Historic Environment, 228; *Royal Cornwall Gazette*, 13 August 1891. The Isles of Scilly Council was created as a rural district council outside the administrative county of Cornwall, a separate status which it retains today.

Notes

316 Photograph and painting of sailing vessels, courtesy of Edwards Moyle's great-grandson Peter Malec; Forrester Matthews, *Isles of Scilly*, 237; https://leicester.contentdm.oclc.org, Kelly's Directory 1914; *The Isles of Scilly: The Visitor's Companion in Sunny Lyonesse* (Gibson & Sons, Scilly Isles, no date), 50.
317 *The Scillonian* September 1935, 87-90.
318 Sadly, Francis died shortly before the publication of this book, to which he made a valuable contribution. Images by kind permission of Oriel Hicks.

Chapter 8

319 The photograph taken by J. Moody of Penzance shows Edwin Lewis in retirement with his keeper sons in uniform, Samuel (left) and William (right). Edwin, along with his brother-in-law Tobias Legg and his sailor sons, were commemorated in a list published by the *Cornishman*, 25 June 1931 of 'seagoing captains' from 'the great days of Scilly shipping'.
320 Tony Parker, *Lighthouse* (first published 1975, 2006 edn.), 25.
321 *Report of Royal Commissioners on Lights*, vol 1, 13; Instructions for Lighthouse Keepers, 1839.
322 Parker, *Lighthouse*, 54.
323 Ibid, 59 & 33; Northern Lighthouse Board Commissioners quoted in Bella Bathurst, *The Lighthouse Stevensons* (1999), 237.
324 https://screenrant.com, Katy Rath & Tom Russell, 'The Lighthouse: The True Story That Inspired Eggers' Movie', 2024.
325 *Cardiff Times*, 21 January 1860.
326 Engraving by Souchal. 1870, Public domain, via Wikimedia Commons.
327 LMA Trinity House Archives, CLC/526/50026/044, 24 August 1877, 045, 23 & 29 November 1877 & /047, 23 May 1879.
328 Charles Dickens, *Great Expectations* (first published 1861, Penguin, 1985), 449.
329 https://www.stanford-le-hope.org/galleries.
330 https://www.trinityhouse.co.uk, Aurelie Trezise, 'The Lighthouse Keeper's Wife', 1961.
331 Patricia Gumbrell, *Last of the Line* (Caithness, 2005), 103-5.
332 Ibid, 107.
333 LMA, Trinity House Archives, CC/526/0025, 070, 21 March & 22 & 25 April 1902. Old photograph on uniqhotels.com.
334 Rev W. T. Jones quoted in https://www.bardsey.org.
335 Trezise, 'Lighthouse Keeper's Wife'; https://www.trinityhouse.co.uk, Elder Brother Captain Edward Chapman Bradford quoted by Neil Jones, 'A Decent, Beneficial Objective: 200 Years of Bardsey Island Lighthouse'.

336 LMA, Trinity House Archives, CLC/526/MS30025/060, 1 January & 5 February 1892.
337 The 1901 Census for Holyhead registered Samuel at the Lighthouse and Mary at 57 Newry Street with her three children (Alberta 13, Thomas 11 and Samuel 1) and her widowed sister Julia Jenkins.
338 LMA, Trinity House Archives, MS30025/062, 17 April, 31 July, 7 August & 13 November 1894.
339 Tony Parker, *Lighthouse*, 34.
340 https://hakaimagazine.com, Amorina Kingdon, 'Mouthfuls of molten lead, wild weather, and insanity: the occupational hazards of an early lighthouse keeper' (Coastal Science and Societies, 18 November 2016).
341 The 1931 census was destroyed in a fire. A Register was compiled in 1939 just after the outbreak of war so that the government could produce identity cards and ration books.
342 Rudyard Kipling, 'The Coastwise Lights' in *A Song of the English* (1909).
343 England & Wales, National Probate Calendar (Index of Wills and Administrations).
344 Bathurst, *Lighthouse Stevensons*, 236 & Trinity House Commissioners original mission quoted, 246.

Chapter 9

345 The words of William O'Bryan, founder of the Bible Christian Movement, quoted in Lloyd, *Women Preachers*, 457 & 463.
346 *Primitive Methodist Magazine,* 1844 quoted in Jennifer Lloyd, *Women in the Shaping of British Methodism 1807-1907* (Manchester, 2009), 118.
347 Letter from Martha's granddaughter Alberta quoted in Mills, 'Female Preachers' 7; Penrose, Obituary of Martha Davis.
348 https://www.google.co.uk, Report by Joseph Wood in the *Bible Christian Magazine*, January 1852, 41; Moyle quoted in *Cornishman*, 27 November 1890.
349 Penrose, Obituary of Martha Davis; *West Briton & Cornish Advertiser*, 6 August 1874.
350 Studio photograph posted on Ancestry by Eva's great-great granddaughter Sabrina Bettridge.
351 Penrose, Obituary of Martha Davis; Mills, *Female Preachers'*; Steinbach, *Women in England*, 1-2.
352 https://victorianweb.org, Beth Harris, 'Slaves of the Needle'; Elizabeth Gaskell, Cranford, 197-8; Jose Harris, *Private Lives, Public Spirit*: Britain *1870-1914* (1993), 27.

Notes

[353] Harris, *Private Lives, Public Spirit*, 61.
[354] Elizabeth Gaskell, *Ruth*, (first published 1853, Oxford, 1985), 3. Other examples are Henry Mayhew in the *Morning Chronicle*, November 1849 and Charles Kingsley, *Alton Locke*, (1850).
[355] Royal Albert Memorial Museum, Exeter, Frank Holl, *The Song of the Shirt*, 1875.
[356] The Trade Boards Act of 1909 set up boards to negotiate a minimum wage in the box-, lace-, chain-making and tailoring trades
[357] John Tuffee is so described in the census of 1911. The couple had no children.
[358] IoS Museum, Logbook of St Agnes School 1875-1913, 3 May & 25 June 1875, Inspector's Report 1876.
[359] Kelly's Directory for Cornwall, 1856 & 1883.
[360] Marriage and birth records and electoral rolls of Melbourne and Sydney; *Sands Directory*, 1884; *Sydney Sunday Times*, 17 May 1908; *Sydney Daily Telegraph*, 11 May 1925. https://www.ancientmariner.co.au
[361] https://www.genuki.org.uk, Michael Wickes, *The West Country Preachers: A New History of the Bible Christian Church* (Hartland, 2007), 35; *Port Adelaide News*, 27 February 1895; *Kapunda Herald*, 26 April 1894; *Adelaide Observer*, 10 June 1905.
[362] *Australian Christian Commonwealth*, 2 May 1902; *Adelaide Register*, 14 January 1905; *Adelaide Advertiser*, 19 December 1908; undated letter from Marjorie Telfer. Photograph courtesy of Sabrina Bettridge.
[363] *Express & Telegraph* & *Evening Journal*, 12 October 1903.
[364] None of the Davis widows is described as 'annuitant' (pensioner) in the census returns.
[365] See Cynthia Curran, *When I First Began My Life Anew: Middle-Class Widows in Nineteenth-Century Britain* (Bristol, 2000), 31 & https://www.researchgate.net, Michael Quinlan, 'Precarious and hazardous work: the health and safety of merchant seamen 1815-1935', *Social History*, 38:3, 2013, 300.
[366] Curran, *Middle-Class Widows*, 115.
[367] Ibid, 146.
[368] https://www.hackneysociety.org, Michael Hunter, *The Victorian Villas of Hackney* (Hackney History Society), 25. See also census records for the area which confirm this picture.
[369] Scillonian.com, This photograph was taken in 1919 after the building of an extension to the right which housed girls: 'Pupils outside Carn Thomas School, St Mary's Isles of Scilly 1919.'
[370] IoS Museum, St Mary's Boys' School Logbook 1864-1890 & Carn Thomas Logbook 1891-1910; letter from Harold Davis, 14 January 1964.
[371] *Hackney & Kingsland Gazette*. 17 July 1869.

[372] http://www.british-history.ac.uk/vch/essex, 'Leyton: Introduction', in *A History of the County of Essex: Volume 6*, ed. W R Powell (London, 1973), 174-184.

[373] Census 1901.

[374] Undated letter from his son (my father), John Grenfell Davis, to Michael and Aline Davis.

[375] Memoir written for his sons by Anthony Davis.

[376] Death Notice for Janie Kirkpatrick Davis in Scillonian, 1930, courtesy of the late Colin Mumford. J.C. Trewin also visited his sea-captain father's vessel, where he saw 'what a kingdom a ship could be with its Old Man as absolute monarch', *Up From the Lizard*, 137.

[377] Review in *Cornishman*, 14 March 1889.

[378] 1901 Census; IoS Museum, Carn Thomas logbook, 1898-1900.

Chapter 10

[379] *Cornishman*, 27 November 1890.

[380] Elizabeth Gaskell, *Wives and Daughters* (first published 1864-6, Penguin, 1969), 131 & 364; Gillam, *Of Patient Bearing*, 133.

[381] The photograph appears in the Moyle Heritage website compiled by Sophie May Lewis.

[382] Steinbach, *Women in England*, 13.

[383] Definition given in https://archive.org, Edmund Burke Huey, *Backward and Feeble-Minded Children* (1912).

[384] IoS Museum, St Mary's Infant School Logbook, 1865-1893, 17 April; Newcastle Commission report of 1861 quoted in R.W. Rich, *The Training of Teachers in England and Wales during the Nineteenth Century* (Bath, 1972), 142-3; M. Graham Brown, *Training in Truro 1813-1938* (1938), 18.

[385] IoS Museum, St Mary's Infant School Logbook, 22 June, 10 & 16 October & 20 November, 1871; 15 January, 4 March, 22 August & 12 November, 1872.

[386] Rich, *Training of Teachers*, 121.

[387] IoS Museum, St Mary's Girls' School Logbook, 1864-1891, 29 September, 1 November 1876 & 19 January 1877.

[388] *Royal Cornwall Gazette*, 6 December 1878.

[389] Coventry Patmore's popular poem of the 1860s, 'The Angel in the House', portrayed women as paragons of domesticity, virtue and humility.

[390] Brown, *Training in Truro*, 22; Kresen Kernow, STR46/1/1. The logbooks of St Paul's School make regular mention of unnamed students giving 'criticism lessons' and observing those given by one of the college staff.

[391] Brown, *Training in Truro*, 36, 21-2 & 30-1.

Notes

³⁹² Ibid, 21 & 27-8; Kresen Kernow, STR46/1/1, Logbook of St Paul's School, 19-23 June 1878 records 'the annual visit of Canon Tinling to see the students give their prepared lessons' and, in company with Canon Cornish (the Principal), Miss Wilkinson (the Head Governess) and Miss Barter, 'to see the ordinary work of the students there'.

³⁹³ *Royal Cornwall Gazette*, 6 December 1878; Crispin Gill, *The Isles of Scilly* (Newton Abbot, 1975), 180; Census 1881.

³⁹⁴ *Cornishman*, 13 January 1883 & Kresen Kernow, SKEN 1-3, Logbook of Chacewater School, 3 June 1883. I owe this discovery to Kim Piper of Kresen Kernow, who spotted both the advertisement and the logbook.

³⁹⁵ Ibid, 20 August 1884, 2 January, 19 March & passim. *Poems by Lord Byron* (1866), Preface & contents list; photograph of book inscription by kind permission of Terry Lewis; https://freeclassicebooks.com/Thomas Hardy/ Short Stories, 'A Mere Interlude', 4.

³⁹⁶ *Surrey Mirror*, 8 September 1888 & Surrey History Centre, CC269/2 Logbook of St Matthew's Girls' School, 24 September 1888.

³⁹⁷ John Lawson & Harold Silver, *A Social History of Education* (1973), 292 & 330.

³⁹⁸ Surrey History Centre, CC269/2 Logbook, entries for 3 December 1888, 11 April, 3, 4 & 23 & July 1889 and pages 235 & 254. My sympathy with Emma Moyle springs from my own experience with Ofsted while I was chair of the trustees of a local nursery school. In February 2020 the inspector found all the school's educational practices remained 'outstanding' but relegated it to the overall category of 'requiring improvement' because of an administrative error in the registration of trustees. Even though I took the blame for this and rectified the error immediately the bureaucratic verdict remained in place until the next inspection, which restored the school's 'outstanding' status. For a period of nearly two years, therefore, the Ofsted inspectors jeopardised the future of the school.

³⁹⁹ Eg *Surrey Mirror*, 2 April 1892, 10 March & 16 June 1894.

⁴⁰⁰ https://docslib.org, Chacewater Conservation Area Character Appraisal, Appendix 1, 50.

⁴⁰¹ Eg Surrey History Centre, CC269/2, Reports for 1905 & 1910. I attended St Matthew's Girls' School myself in 1951-2 after moving to Redhill from Devon. I remember a very large room containing many children at their desks and suspect that different classes were still mixed together.

⁴⁰² Ibid, 22 February 22 1894, 18 June 1902 & 23 February 1904.

⁴⁰³ *Surrey Mirror*, 30 June 1903 & 20 January 1914.

⁴⁰⁴ Surrey History Centre, 3155/4/2 Admissions Book for 'Redhill Girls' Secondary School and Pupil Teachers' Centre', September 1905.

405 Surrey History Centre, 3155/7/3, Reigate County School for Girls' Magazine, Report by Headmistress, Miss A.B. Anderton. I attended the same school myself fifty years later and compared our experiences in Reigate County School Old Girls' Magazine, March 2024, '"A Merry Schoolgirl": My Pioneering Granny at RCS'.
406 *Surrey Mirror*, 23 & 24 June 1911; reference by Hilda Oakley from King's College for Women, London, 9 June 1912 in family archive.
407 *Epsom Journal*, 1 January 1896.
408 Surrey History Centre, 7338/1/42 Register of Female Patients 1909-48.
409 https://archive.org, *Report of the Royal Commission on the Care of the Feeble-Minded* (1908), sections 547, 559, 551 & 553; Martin Gilbert, 'Churchill and Eugenics' in *Finest Hour* (Churchill Society, 2009).
410 Mary Dendy, *The Importance of Permanence in the Care of the Feeble-Minded*, a pamphlet published in 1899 in the *Educational Review*, quoted by Mark Jackson, 'Institutional Provision for the Feeble-Minded in Edwardian England' in Anne Digby & David Wright (eds), *Historical Perspectives on People with Learning Disabilities* (1996), 161 & 178.
411 Light, *Common People*, 163. Alison Light's own great-grandmother entered Netherne in May 1911 and died there a month later. The website of Surrey History Centre states that most of the patients in such county asylums were 'pauper lunatics' and Light concurs that it was 'necessary to be registered by the local relieving officer as a pauper' before entering. This was clearly not true of Margaretta Moyle as she lived with her headmistress aunt, Emma Moyle, who earned an adequate (though not generous) salary of around £100 a year. Emma may even have had to contribute towards the cost of Margaretta's maintenance.
412 Surrey History Centre, 7338/1/4/2 Register of Female Patients 1909-48, 7338/1/5 Female Medical Journal passim, CC767/15/1/12 Visiting Committee Minute Books 1912-30, 22 July 1913.
413 1911 Census for Penzance. See also article by his descendant, Sophie May Lewis, about John's time at Trengwainton in Barbara Santi (ed), *Home of Springs: Trengwainton* (2018), 131.
414 Elizabeth Gaskell, *North and South* (first published 1854, 1975 edn.), 54.
415 Surrey History Centre, CC269/3 Logbook, 9 November 1914, 18 January, 24 February & 10 September 1915, 13 September & 10 July 1916, March 20 & 1 October 1918.
416 https://www.surreyinthegreatwar.org.uk.
417 Surrey History Centre, 7338/1/3 (1) Reports of Medical Superintendent, 1917-23; John Welch & George Frogley, *A Pictorial History of Netherne Hospital* (Redhill, 1993), no page numbers; death certificate of Margaretta Moyle.
418 This and other details of the Halls' participation in the war comes from Paul Shevlin's research in https://chacewater.net/whats-on, May 2020.

Notes

[419] Photographs of John Grenfell Hall and Thomas Gerald Hall from interview with Sophie May Lewis in *My Cornwall*, April/May 2015.
[420] *Leeds Mercury*, 21 July 1919 quoted in https://bradfordmuseums.org, 'Dimmed by personal grief'.
[421] Photograph courtesy of Peter Malec; Richard Larn, *The Isles of Scilly in the Great War* (Barnsley, 2017), 113-4.
[422] National Archives, ASM 337/2/10 & WO 339/100176.
[423] The poems are quoted courtesy of Terry and Sophie May Lewis.
[424] Rovena's daughter Georgina was the only one of her children to settle in the Moyle homeland after meeting and marrying Scillonian Alfred Trenear while on a visit to the islands. In 1936 Georgina and Alfred's son, also named Alfred, was born while they were visiting Rovena in Bradford. Alfie, as he is known, regrets his non-Scillonian birth but lives in St Mary's to this day, working as the islands' only funeral director.
[425] 1939 Register, electoral roll for 1929 and memoir of Anthony Davis. The lack of records means that it is not clear how long Rovena and George Edmonds had lived in Bradford before 1939 or when Mary moved back to Cornwall. The success of the Edmonds' business is suggested by the fact that Rovena left an estate of £362 9 3 when she died in 1960.
[426] Surrey History Centre, CC269/ 3, Logbook of St Matthew's School, 2 June, 30 January, 7 March, 19 December 1919; https://files.eric.ed.gov, Raymond W. Sies, *Teachers' Pension Systems in Great Britain* (Washington, 1913), 34; *Surrey Mirror*, 26 December 1919.
[427] Sies, *Teachers' Pension Systems*, 75.
[428] Electoral Register, 1928, 1929 & 1930; incoming passenger list 1924; 1939 register.

Epilogue

[429] H.G. Wells, *The War That Will End War* (1914).
[430] Phrases from Mary Hall's 'Mother's Lament for her son killed 'Somewhere in France'.
[431] The wedding was reported at some length in *Western Times*, 28 April 1939. Gren's Scillonian uncle, Charles Royer Davis was editor of the *Western Times* and it could well have been this connection with 'a well-known West Country journalist' which drew Gren to enter his chosen profession in Devon. See Charles's obituary in *Torquay Herald Express*, 20 April 1957.
[432] Bernard Edwards, *Convoy Will Scatter: The Full Story of* Jervis Bay *and Convoy HX84* (Barnsley, 2013), 41, 45, 56 & 59.

433 *Express & Echo*, 18 November, 1940; *Western Morning News*, 29 November 1940.

434 Edwards, *Convoy Will Scatter*, 157.

435 National Archives, ADM 199/721, Report 27 November 1942; Richard Woodman, *The Arctic Convoys 1941-1945* (1994), 32, 445-6, 52 & 182.

436 Ibid 182; National Archives, ADM 237/176, Report from Archangel, 8 July 1942.

437 Many of the women's stories are told in Olga Golubtsova, *Love on Land-Lease* (Arkhangelsk, 2016). In 'A letter to my Russian half-brother', *Guardian*, 12 November 2011, Jean Glasberg told the story of her father, a radio controller on a minesweeper accompanying convoy PQ17, who fell in love with a Russian librarian in Archangel and had a son. Jean has now been able to meet and befriend the deceased son's daughter and granddaughters.

438 Woodman, *Arctic Convoys*, 446; 'Shipwreck Story' in *Western Morning News*, 28 March 1948.

439 *News Chronicle*, 5 & 12 January 1952.

440 Eric Williams, *The Tunnel* (Barnsley, 2007), 93 & 108.

441 These details and many more are to be found in *Stalag Luft III: An Official History of the 'Great Escape' PoW Camp*, ed. Howard Tuck (Barnsley, 2016). This is based on records held by National Archives, WO208/3283.

442 Williams, Tunnel, 90 & Tuck, *Stalag Luft III*, 157.

443 Ibid, 11 & 36.

444 John Nichol & Tony Rennell, *The Last Escape: The Untold Story of Allied Prisoners of War in Germany 1944-45* (2002), 75.

445 Ibid, 250.

446 Quoted in Ibid, 370.

447 Lines from Wilfred Owen, 'Strange Meeting', 1918.

448 Barrie Davies and Tony Brooker quoted at Tony's funeral service in 2008.